The Remarkable

WISDOM *of*
SOLOMON

The Remarkable

WISDOM *of* SOLOMON

Ancient

insights from

the Song of Solomon,

Proverbs, and Ecclesiastes

HENRY M. MORRIS

Master
Books

A Division of New Leaf Publishing Group

First printing: July 2001
Fifth printing: October 2016

ISBN-13: 978-0-89051-356-9
Library of Congress Number: 01-090935

Cover design by Farewell Communications

Please consider requesting that a copy of this volume be purchased by your local library system.

Printed in the United States of America

Please visit our website for other great titles:
www.masterbooks.com

For information regarding author interviews, please contact the publicity department at (870) 438-5288.

Master
Books®
A Division of New Leaf Publishing Group
www.masterbooks.com

Acknowledgments

My grateful thanks go to Dr. Art Peters for reviewing the manuscript for this book and writing the Foreword. He and his talented and gracious wife, Shirley, have been good friends of mine ever since he, Dr. Tim LaHaye, and I served together as co-founders of Christian Heritage College back in 1970. Art and Shirley had actually taught a successful course on the Book of Proverbs at the college (and other places as well) and were thus already actively interested in the writings of Solomon, so I was especially pleased when they agreed to review this book.

My two sons, Dr. Henry Morris III and Dr. John Morris, also reviewed the manuscript, and my daughter Mary Smith typed it, so sincere thanks go to them as well.

Contents

Contents

Foreword

Dr. Henry Morris, whom it has been my privilege to be a friend and colleague of for over 30 years, has written not a mere textbook but a fascinating biography of a singular man in history. *The Remarkable Wisdom of Solomon* traces the life of a man who spoke more wisely than he lived. Dr. Morris brings to this commentary on King Solomon and his three Bible books — Song of Solomon, Proverbs, and Ecclesiastes — his unashamed adherence to the plain, literal translation and teaching of the Word of God. His dedicated exploration and interpretation of the books of the Bible written by Solomon convey details of Solomon's heritage and personal story on which other authors have only lightly touched.

In all three commentaries Dr. Morris emphasizes the place of Solomon's one and only love, Naamah. He ably defends his suggestion that the other women were in Solomon's harem for purposes of politics and prestige. Could this be the reason, he questions, that no names of the other women or of any children born of these other women are recorded? At least, Dr. Morris attributes the candid view of romantic love as described in the Song of Solomon to Solomon's wife Naamah. He sets forth clearly and beautifully the physical delights of married love and, not surprisingly, extends his exploration of the relationship to a discussion of Christ and His church.

Dr. Morris uncovers vivid details tucked away in the proverbs of Solomon that add context to the relevant, often stand-alone instructions for living well. He weaves the warnings and blessings to his son Rehoboam, revealed in the first nine chapters of Proverbs in the form of 17 sermons. He reveals the organization of Proverbs, clarifying where formal outlines and divisions work and where it's better to treat a verse as complete in itself. Among other things, his exposition of the Book removes what has often been a stumbling block to Bible students by demonstrating that the Proverbs are cast in the form of generalizations. They were not meant to be read as inflexible rules that allow no exceptions.

The commentary on Ecclesiastes further develops the fact that, like any other person, Solomon had his share of mistakes — which he calls "vanities." Yet the theme of married love returns with Solomon's exhortation to live "joyfully with the wife of one's youth" (Eccles. 9:9). Dr. Morris shows that Solomon is referring to Naamah, the true love of his life. There is good marriage counseling in his commentary on this passage. His meticulous scholarship is revealed in the exposition of the word "joyfully" which occurs only this one time in the Old Testament. It refers to keeping one's marriage happily alive, and not allowing it to become routine.

There are rich gems of the truth to be mined in his commentary of the wisdom literature of the Bible. Wisdom's crown jewel — the gospel of Jesus Christ is appealingly laid out at the conclusion of the book. Characteristically, Dr. Morris ends by inviting readers to trust Christ as their personal Lord and Savior.

Among the founders of Christian Heritage College, Dr. Morris brought to the school a commitment to academic excellence and to creation, which continues to characterize the college. *The Remarkable Wisdom of Solomon*, along with Dr. Morris's many other books, grows out of this same scholarship and faithful interpretation of the truth of God's word. It is an important book for earnest Christians, lay and clergy.

Dr. Art Peters

Introduction

The life and writings of King Solomon, who reigned over Israel during the 40-year period of her greatest glory, have always been an intriguing mystery to me. How could a man who was said to be the man of greatest wisdom in the world of his day ever think he needed seven hundred wives and three hundred concubines, as we read in 1 Kings 4:31; 11:3? Most of these were acquired when he was old, and one wonders whether he could even remember all their names.

And why did none of these seven hundred wives, all of whom were "princesses," ever give him any children? If they did, why are none of them ever mentioned in the records? How, too, would a man of such God-given wisdom and blessing, a man who truly loved the Lord, have his heart partially turned away from God by these pagan wives?

Perhaps the most pressing question of all is why God would use Solomon to write three of the most fascinating books of the Bible — Proverbs, Ecclesiastes, and Song of Solomon. These three books all have many marks of divine inspiration, and each can bring great blessing and deeper understanding of God and His ways to its readers. So far as we know, none of the other writers of the books of the Bible ever later wavered in their commitment to God as Solomon did. Yet even the Lord Jesus spoke of the wisdom of Solomon and the glory of Solomon, with no hint that these had been compromised by his later failures.

I have tried to explore some of these and other questions in this book. Although I am an engineer and scientist by training and experience, I have also studied the Bible daily for 60 years, so I hope it is not too presumptuous for me to attempt a commentary on Solomon's three unique books and a summary analysis of his life. Very few older commentaries on these books are still in print, and very few of our modern Bible scholars have written on them for some reason, so perhaps this book will help meet a need felt by many pastors and Sunday school teachers today.

There are just seven chapters in this book. The first deals with the enigma of Solomon himself. Then there is a chapter containing a verse-by-verse commentary on Song of Solomon, four chapters of commentary on Proverbs, and one on Ecclesiastes. Each of these books is vastly different from the others, and commenting on them verse by verse is a daunting task, to say the least. Many, no doubt, will disagree with my expositions of some of these verses, but I hope the net impact of the book as a whole will be helpful. In any case, I have approached the task prayerfully and in full confidence in the inerrancy and authority of every verse in every book of the Bible.

I should mention that the apocryphal book known as "The Wisdom of Solomon" is not included, because Solomon almost certainly did not write it. Like the other books of the Apocrypha, it was composed one or two centuries before Christ and written as though it came with Solomonic authority. Despite many worthwhile components, practically all authorities — liberal and conservative, Catholic, Jewish, and Protestant — agree it was not really written by Solomon, so it is not discussed in this book.

However, there is much wonderful material in Solomon's three canonical books that I *have* tried to study and expound, and I do hope and am praying that many readers will find the analyses and comments helpful.

1

The Enigmatic Life
and Times of King Solomon

One of the most fascinating careers in all history was that of the great King Solomon, who reigned 40 years over Israel during its period of greatest influence, approximately from 971 to 931 B.C. This included a brief period when God's ancient promise to Abraham (Gen. 15:18) concerning the geographical extent of his promised land was precursively fulfilled (1 Kings 8:65), going all the way from "the river of Egypt" to the Euphrates in northern Syria.

The influence of Solomon, however, extended far beyond the boundaries of his kingdom. According to the biblical record, Solomon was "wiser than all men . . . and his fame was in all nations round about" (1 Kings 4:31). "And there came of all people to hear the wisdom of Solomon, from all kings of the earth, which had heard of his wisdom" (1 Kings 4:34).

Furthermore, his reign was uniquely prosperous. "King Solomon passed all the kings of the earth in riches and wisdom" (2 Chron. 9:22). And finally his reign was one of peace. Whereas his father, King David, had to fight many wars — even the civil war led by his son Absalom — Solomon "had peace on all sides round about him" (1 Kings 4:24), at least during most of his reign. He built the great temple in Jerusalem, as well as many other large construction projects.

All of these blessings had come from God, and Solomon was aware of this. For a long time, "Solomon loved the Lord, walking in the statutes of David his father" (1 Kings 3:3).

Yet Solomon, blessed beyond measure in every way by his God, later "loved many strange [that is 'foreign'] women," eventually acquiring "seven hundred wives, princesses, and three hundred concubines: and his wives

13

turned away his heart" (1 Kings 11:1–3). He even built shrines for all their pagan gods, thus introducing many false religions into the very center of Israel, flagrantly disobeying the specific commandments of the Lord who had blessed him so much.

But amazingly, in spite of all this, God used him to write three wonderful books of His inspired Scriptures — that is, Proverbs, Ecclesiastes, and Song of Solomon. These books are very different from any other books of the Bible, and quite different from each other, yet still are undoubtedly part of the divine canon of Scripture. Each is unique, with a uniquely vital message and with great blessing to the thoughtful reader.

All other Bible books were written by holy men of God, true to the Lord throughout their lives — men like Moses, Paul, John, the prophets and apostles. So we wonder how God could use an apparently apostate king like Solomon to write three of His inspired books — at least one of which (Ecclesiastes) was certainly written near the end of his life.

Did Solomon repent and return to the Lord? If so, why does the biblical record not say so? This is the enigma of Solomon. We need to look carefully at the records, reading both the lines and between the lines, as well as we are able.

We must do this with full confidence in the absolute inerrancy and perspicuity of these divinely inspired records and writings of Solomon, for that is certainly the way in which Christ and the apostles viewed all the Old Testament Scriptures, including these three books written or compiled by Solomon. And we shall find, as many before us have found, that there is rich blessing for us in each of them.

Solomon's Background and Early Life

First of all, we need to look as closely as the evidence allows at the circumstances of Solomon's birth and early life, before he became king of Israel. In doing this, we are limited almost entirely to the records in the Bible, since there are no extra-biblical writings of the time available, or any archaeological artifacts that even mention his name.

However, the Lord Jesus referred to him on two occasions, both of which speak of him in a positive light, not mentioning his apostate years at all. One was in a passing reference to him in relation to our anxieties about suitable clothing. "And why take ye thought for raiment? Consider the lilies of the field, how they grow; they toil not, neither do they spin: And yet I say unto you, That even Solomon in all his glory was not arrayed like one of these" (Matt. 6:28–29).

The other was in the context of a rebuke to the scribes and Pharisees for rejecting His teachings. "The queen of the south shall rise up in the judgment with this generation, and shall condemn it: for she came from the uttermost part of the earth to hear the wisdom of Solomon; and, behold, a greater than Solomon is here" (Matt. 12:42).

Solomon's mother was a beautiful woman named Bathsheba, whom David had loved so much that he had committed adultery with her, then arranged for her Hittite husband to be in lethal danger in battle so that he could take her for his own wife. Presumably, Bathsheba also loved David, although it might have been almost impossible to refuse the great king's invitation even if she had wanted to.

The story of David and Bathsheba is one of the most familiar narratives in the Old Testament, so it need not be repeated here. After Uriah was slain in battle and Bathsheba spent the necessary time in mourning, "David sent and fetched her to his house, and she became his wife, and bare him a son" (2 Sam. 11:27).

David already had at least six wives (Ahinoam, Abigail, Maachah, Haggith, Abital, and Eglah — 1 Chron. 3:1–3) in addition to Saul's daughter Michal (1 Sam. 18:27), and probably others as well. Nevertheless, David desired Bathsheba so much that he was willing to disobey at least three of God's basic ten commandments (those against covetousness, adultery, and murder) in order to have her.

And, of course, "the thing that David had done displeased the LORD" (2 Sam. 11:27), and the prophet Nathan was sent by the Lord to rebuke him, saying he had "despised the commandment of the LORD." David had always been very committed to the Lord and His Word, despite this and other sins of the flesh into which he had fallen, as evidenced in so many of his psalms.

Nathan's rebuke, therefore, brought him under deep conviction and then to repentance and eventual restoration. Psalms 32 and 51 memorialize this traumatic event in his life, and God continued to bless and use him. Nevertheless, despite David's fasting and intensive prayer, God allowed his illegitimate son to die.

The timeless lesson from this tragic event is that sin does have consequences, even when it is confessed and forgiven. Another valuable insight from the death of this child, however, is that infants who die before they have become conscious sinners are safe in heaven. "I shall go to him," David said, after the child's death, "but he shall not return to me" (2 Sam. 12:23).

But what has all this to do with Solomon? In God's inscrutable providence, Solomon was the next son of David and Bathsheba, and God chose him to be David's successor as king of Israel. Bathsheba, of course, had also grieved over the loss of her child, but "David comforted Bathsheba his wife, and went in unto her, and lay with her: and she bare a son, and he called his name Solomon: and the LORD loved him" (2 Sam. 12:24).

David already had many sons and would yet have others (19 are named in 1 Chron. 3:1–9), and it may seem strange that God would choose the son of Bathsheba, who had committed adultery with David, to be the king. Under the law, an adulterous wife was supposed to be executed by stoning (John 8:4–5; see Lev. 20:10), and so was the man involved. But David had been forgiven, and it had been he who initiated the liaison; in fact, in all probability, Bathsheba felt she had no choice but to submit to the great king. She almost certainly was also repentant, especially after she learned of David's sorrow and then the death of her son.

Whatever the reason, God chose to bless her then with a son who would be the next king. The fact that this was God's choice and not David's only was later clearly confirmed by David: "And of all my sons, (for the LORD hath given me many sons,) he hath chosen Solomon my son to sit upon the throne of the kingdom of the LORD over Israel" (1 Chron. 28:5).

David spoke these words to all the leaders of Israel at the time he told them also of his plans to build a temple in Jerusalem for the worship of God. He had previously given the same testimony to Solomon: "And David said to Solomon, My son . . . the word of the LORD came to me, saying . . . Behold, a son shall be born to thee, who shall be a man of rest from all his enemies round about: for his name shall be Solomon, and I will give peace and quietness unto Israel in his days. He shall build an house for my name; and he shall be my son, and I will be his father; and I will establish the throne of his kingdom over Israel for ever" (1 Chron. 22:7–10).

God had, therefore, even chosen Solomon's name before he was born, a name which means "peaceful." Actually, when Solomon was born, God also gave him another name as well. "And He sent by the hand of Nathan the prophet; and he called his name Jedidiah, because of the LORD" (2 Sam. 12:25). Jedidiah means "beloved of the LORD." Both names were highly appropriate, at least at the time, indicating clearly God's love of Solomon and His great purpose for him.

Considering Bathsheba's background, this was surely an act of loving grace on God's part. An adulterous wife was chosen to be the mother of the great King Solomon!

But there were other factors involved as well — Bathsheba's first husband, Uriah, was a Hittite, from one of the pagan tribes that had been in the land of Canaan since before the days of Abraham. Possibly so was Bathsheba, but both had been somehow won to faith in the true God, and Uriah was even in David's army, as one of his 37 special "mighty men" (2 Sam. 23:8, 39).

Bathsheba was a beautiful woman — evidently beautiful in heart as well as appearance, and she had undoubtedly come to love David dearly, as well as her first son, now with the Lord, and then Solomon. David must certainly have told her of the Lord's great plans for Solomon, assuring her that he would sit on the throne as David's successor when the time came for him to die. The time eventually did come when she would have to remind David of that promise (1 Kings 1:11–17).

But first we should learn what we can about Solomon's childhood and youth, and how his parents (and the Lord) had prepared him to assume that high calling. The narrative itself does not tell us much, but we can read between the lines, as it were, and also study Solomon's own reminiscences in his own later writings.

One of these notable writings, of course, is the Book of Proverbs. It is uncertain whether Solomon wrote the first nine chapters or David wrote them for Solomon's instruction. Assuming Solomon was the author (as most conservative scholars believe), then one passage is especially significant in this connection. "For I was my father's son," wrote Solomon, "tender and only beloved in the sight of my mother. He taught me also, and said unto me, Let thine heart retain my words: keep my commandments, and live. Get wisdom, get understanding: forget it not; neither decline from the words of my mouth. Forsake her not, and she shall preserve thee: love her, and she shall keep thee. Wisdom is the principal thing; therefore get wisdom: and with all thy getting get understanding" (Prov. 4:3–7).

Evidently both David and Bathsheba were diligent in teaching young Solomon, and David especially emphasized the importance of seeking true wisdom in his understanding of the world and its people. Much of Solomon's own writings in the Book of Proverbs no doubt reflected his father's teaching, as well as the divinely inspired wisdom in his father's many psalms. This influence surely was behind Solomon's reply to God when he was asked what he desired from God most of all. His reply to God was this: "Give therefore thy servant an understanding heart to judge thy people, that I may discern between good and bad: for who is able to judge this thy so great a people" (1 Kings 3:9). This choice pleased the Lord, and He not only gave Solomon his request but much more besides.

David's instruction of his son must have included, in addition to his counsel about dealing with women and people in general, much also about the world of nature. David himself had spent his youth as a shepherd, out in the fields and forests of his country, and also had written much about God's creation and about history in his psalms. He loved the streams and meadows, the sky and stars, the birds and beasts, the sea and the mountains, and wrote often about these in his psalms.

Although the record never mentions it directly, it is reasonable to believe that Solomon was also encouraged to spend much time in studying nature. He probably was provided the best teachers available as pedagogues to help him in these studies. He also must have spent time in traveling around his father's kingdom, learning to know the land and its people as well as its plants and animals. It could well be that he even spent some time tending his father's flocks and herds, in order to experience the life of a shepherd, as his father had done with his grandfather's (i.e., Jesse's) animals. All this is at least suggested as one reads between the lines in Proverbs, Ecclesiastes, and Song of Solomon.

One might also infer (as we shall see later in studying the Song of Solomon) that it was during this portion of his life that he met his first — and only true — love. Although he eventually "loved" and married many other women, he did counsel his own son, and his readers in general, to stay and be content with "the wife of your youth" (Prov. 5:18–20; note also Eccles. 9:9). He (as well as his father, who also had several wives) had to learn the hard way that God's way of lifelong monogamous marriage was the best way after all.

Solomon was still a young man when all the responsibilities of being king suddenly were placed on his shoulders. As noted, David had several sons older than Solomon. Six sons had been born during the seven years David had reigned just over Judah from Hebron, each with a different mother. Possibly, other sons were also born later in Jerusalem before Solomon was born.

The oldest son, Amnon, the son of David's first wife, Ahinoam, very likely thought he would be David's successor, but he was slain by another son, Absalom, in revenge for Amnon's rape and subsequent abandonment of Absalom's sister Tamar (see 2 Sam. 13 for this unsavory story). Then Absalom, who was David's third son, later rebelled against his father and thought to usurp the crown for himself, but this ill-advised rebellion resulted only in his own death.

Still another son, Adonijah, the fourth son, then thought he should be king. As David was aging rapidly, Adonijah actually had himself proclaimed king by Abiathar the high priest (1 Kings 1:25), and was all set to take over the kingdom.

But at this juncture Bathsheba and Nathan interceded with David for Solomon, reminding him of God's choice of Solomon and David's promise to Bathsheba. Bathsheba said, "My lord, thou swarest by the LORD thy God unto thine handmaid, saying, Assuredly Solomon thy son shall reign after me, and he shall sit upon thy throne" (1 Kings 1:17).

Nathan the prophet then also confirmed Bathsheba's statement and told him about Adonijah's attempted coup. David, unaware until then of Adonijah's action, immediately reaffirmed his promise and set about to carry it out. Solomon was immediately proclaimed king with appropriate pomp, ritual, and public celebration. Adonijah then quickly realized his own self-coronation had failed.

Although the account does not give Solomon's exact age at the time when he became king, he was definitely quite young, probably no more than 20 years old. David had spent many years under Saul's reign, then seven years reigning himself in Hebron, and then an unknown but substantial number of years in Jerusalem before Solomon's birth. So, when David formally presented Solomon to the congregation of Israel's leaders at the time of his coronation ceremony, he noted that "Solomon my son, whom alone God hath chosen, is yet young and tender, and the work is great" (1 Chron. 29:1).

Nevertheless, David knew that God had chosen Solomon and had been preparing him throughout his young life for this position, so he was confident the time was right when Adonijah in effect forced his hand by trying to usurp the throne for himself.

By this time, David "was old and stricken in years" and had taken still another wife, Abishag, strictly to care for him in his old age and to keep him warm. She "was very fair, and cherished the king, and ministered to him: but the king knew her not" (1 Kings 1:4). Thus, Abishag was still a virgin when David finally died at age 70 (note 2 Sam. 5:4) even though she was nominally married to him.

In the meantime, however, during the years when Solomon was growing up, David had been making preparations to build a great temple in Jerusalem to take the place of the old tabernacle still standing in Gibeon (six miles away), and the temporary tent which David had prepared in Jerusalem to house the ark of the covenant after it had been recovered from the Philistines and eventually returned to Jerusalem. He had purchased a site on Mount Moriah (2 Chron. 3:1), the place where Abraham long before had gone to offer up his son Isaac (Gen. 22:2), and where David himself had seen "the angel of the LORD . . . by the threshingplace of Araunah the Jebusite" and where he had then built "an altar unto the LORD, and offered burnt-offerings and peace-offerings" (2 Sam. 24:16–25). There he had "called upon the LORD; and He answered him from heaven by fire upon the altar of burnt-offering" (1 Chron. 21:26).

As a result of this experience, David prepared materials and workmen "to build the house of God" on the site (1 Chron. 22:2). David had been wanting to build such a "house" for God ever since the ark had been restored to Jerusalem, but God had said no (1 Chron. 17:1–4), that his son should do it. He "prepared abundantly before his death" (1 Chron. 22:5), however, and had given Solomon clear instructions concerning his responsibility to build the temple (1 Chron. 22:6–18), concluding with the following exhortation. "Now set your heart and your soul to seek the LORD your God; arise therefore, and build ye the sanctuary of the LORD God, to bring the ark of the covenant of the LORD, and the holy vessels of God, into the house that is to be built to the name of the LORD" (1 Chron. 22:19).

Furthermore, David not only gave abundantly of his own wealth in preparing for the temple, but he also encouraged the people to do likewise. "Then the people rejoiced, for that they offered willingly, because with perfect heart they offered willingly to the LORD: and David the king also rejoiced with great joy" (1 Chron. 29:9).

Thus David and Solomon and the people in general were all anticipating with joy the coming accession of Solomon to the throne and then the building of the holy temple. It is not completely clear whether the abortive attempt of Adonijah to take the throne occurred before or after David's counsel to Solomon about the temple took place. The account in Chronicles does not mention this attempted coup at all. It seems most likely that most of the preparations must have been made before this, since these would have taken considerable time, and therefore have been largely complete before this sudden emergency arose, necessitating an immediate action by David to make Solomon the king.

It is significant that Adonijah had invited all of David's sons to his own coronation, except Solomon (1 Kings 1:19). He was evidently well aware of David's intentions and hoped by this sudden move to thwart them. He apparently had reason to believe that the other living sons of David would support him. He would most likely have executed Solomon if he were successful in gaining the crown. Bathsheba implied that she feared this very thing would happen. When she told David about it, she was sure that "I and my son Solomon should be counted offenders," if Adonijah should prevail (1 Kings 1:21).

Then it was natural that, when he failed in his attempt, Adonijah felt that he should beg Solomon to spare *his* life. This Solomon was willing to do at first. After David died, however, Adonijah became so presumptuous as to ask Bathsheba to ask Solomon to let him marry David's beautiful young widow, Abishag. Such a request was not only a gratuitous insult to Solomon (practically assuming the right of the king) but also an incestuous violation of the divine law, subject to capital punishment (Lev. 18:6–8, 29), and Solomon immediately ordered Adonijah executed.

Also, Solomon decided to honor his father David's final request to have Joab and Shimei put to death as well. Joab had been David's commander-in-chief but, unknown to David, had slain Abner, captain of the host of Israel under Saul, and Amasa, captain of the host of Judah, and had done so by trickery (see 2 Sam. 3:27; 20:9, 10). Shimei was a prominent relative of Saul, and he had cursed David bitterly, casting stones at him as David was fleeing from Absalom (2 Sam. 16:5–13).

Therefore, Solomon told his own chief captain, Benaiah, to carry out all these executions. Solomon's reign, promised by God to be one of peace, thus began with bloodshed. Although all three executions were evidently warranted, at least in terms of the standards of the day, they surely were a source of grief to Solomon, just as they would have been to David.

These events were soon followed by a political marriage of Solomon to the daughter of Egypt's pharaoh. This also was contrary to God's will, and Solomon must have been exercised deeply in his conscience before doing it (Exod. 34:12–16). It may be that these matters were weighing heavily on his mind and heart, as he decided to offer a thousand burnt offerings at the altar at the tabernacle in Gibeon, perhaps seeking cleansing from whatever sinful actions he felt guilty about. And it was then that God appeared in a very special dream to Solomon — a dream that would profoundly affect the rest of his life.

Among David's final words to his son Solomon had been a fervent exhortation not only to build the temple but also to remain true to the Lord. "I go the way of all the earth," he said to his son. "Be thou strong therefore, and shew thyself a man; And keep the charge of the LORD thy God, to walk in his ways, to keep His statutes, and His commandments, and His judgments, and His testimonies, as it is written in the law of Moses, that thou mayest prosper in all that thou doest, and whithersoever thou turnest thyself: That the LORD may continue His word which He spake concerning me, saying, If thy children take heed to their way, to walk before me in truth with all their heart and with all their soul, there shall not fail thee (said He) a man on the throne of Israel" (1 Kings 2:2–4).

With such a charge weighing on his mind, plus the trauma of having to order several executions and then somehow being persuaded to marry a pagan princess from the great nation of Egypt (while possibly, as we shall see later, already married to his true love), there was much to think about and, perhaps, to pray about, without his father there to counsel him. But then, after the sacrificial offerings, God appeared to him in a dream.

Solomon and His Great Kingdom

The great God of creation has occasionally in the past condescended to speak directly to men, although now that His written word is complete and inscripturated, He speaks to us almost always strictly through the Scriptures. He sometimes appeared directly to men — as to Abraham (Gen. 18:1; etc.), to Paul (Acts 9:3–7), and others in a theophany, or Christophany. Often, He spoke through prophets, as He had to David (2 Sam. 7:4–17; etc.), and even by direct inspiration (2 Sam. 23:1–2).

To Solomon, however, He appeared and spoke in a dream, saying, "Ask what I shall give thee" (1 Kings 3:5). Very likely concerned deeply about the difficult decisions already thrust on him, Solomon answered him in the dream, saying, "O Lord my God, thou hast made thy servant king instead of David my father: and I am but a little child: I know not how to go out or come in. And thy servant is in the midst of thy people which thou hast chosen, a great people, that cannot be numbered or counted for multitude. Give therefore thy servant an understanding heart to judge thy people, that I may discern between good and bad: for who is able to judge this thy so great a people?" (1 Kings 3:7–9).

This request of Solomon's greatly pleased the Lord, so He promised not only to grant his request for wisdom, but also to give him great riches and honor, so great as to be absolutely unique among all the great men of the world. "I have given thee a wise and an understanding heart," God said, "so that there was none like thee before thee, neither after thee shall any arise like unto thee" (1 Kings 3:12–14). He also promised to "lengthen thy days," if he would keep His ways, His statutes and commandments.

This was a dream, of course, but Solomon realized it was not an ordinary dream but a real revelation of God. Furthermore, God fulfilled all He had promised in the dream. "God gave Solomon wisdom and understanding exceeding much, and largeness of heart. . . . For he was wiser than all men . . . and his fame was in all nations round about. . . . And there came of all people to hear the wisdom of Solomon, from all kings of the earth, which had heard of his wisdom" (1 Kings 4:29–34).

The account gives us only one example of Solomonic wisdom and only one of a royal visit to his palace to hear his wisdom, but these are evidently included as typical of many others.

The oft-cited incident of the two harlots arguing over the surviving son of one woman after the son of the other had died, both of them claiming the live son was hers, illustrates how to solve a dispute when all one has to go on are the words of the two disputants. The Solomonic method was to propose a solution so drastic as to cause the person in the right to yield to the other rather than to accept the solution. In this case, Solomon proposed to give half the baby to each, and the real mother quickly offered to give her child to the other rather than to see its life forfeited. This account is found in 1 Kings 3:16–28, and it resulted in the real mother receiving back her child.

Although it is implied that many "kings of the earth" came to visit Solomon, it was only the visit of the queen of Sheba that was actually described, and it is included in both 1 Kings 10:1–13 and in 2 Chronicles 9:1–12. Sheba was a rich nation some 1,200 miles south of Jerusalem in the area generally around modern Yemen. It was the homeland of the Sabaeans.

Thus, the queen of Sheba and her "very great company" of servants had to travel a great distance by camel caravan to meet Solomon. They were probably on a trade mission also, but the biblical account stresses only the interest of the rich queen in Solomon's wisdom. "And Solomon told her all her questions: and there was nothing hid from Solomon which he told her not" (2 Chron. 9:2). She paid him great compliments and also large amounts of gold and valuable spices. Solomon also "gave to the queen of Sheba all her desire, whatsoever she asked" (2 Chron. 9:12).

Some writers have thought that Sheba may have been the same as Ethiopia, and that Ethiopia's "black Jews" were descendants of Solomon and the queen of Sheba. There is no basis for this idea, however. Ethiopia and the Ethiopians are mentioned frequently, both before and after the time of Solomon, including a reference during the reign of Rehoboam, Solomon's son (2 Chron. 12:3), and there would have been no reason at all for the same writer not to call her the queen of Ethiopia, if Sheba was really Ethiopia.

In any case, not only the queen of Sheba but also Hiram, king of Tyre, the various kings of Arabia, Tarshish, Syria, Egypt, the Hittites, and other nations and city-states came to meet Solomon and to give him gifts. "So king Solomon exceeded all the kings of the earth for riches and for wisdom. And all the earth sought to Solomon, to hear his wisdom, which God had put in his heart. And they brought every man his present, vessels of silver, and vessels of gold, and garments, and armour, and spices, horses, and mules, a rate year by year" (1 Kings 10:23–25).

The most notable accomplishment of King Solomon, however, was undoubtedly the construction of the great temple. Certainly the greatest amount of space (seven chapters) in the biblical record (1 Kings 5–7 and 2 Chronicles 2–5) deals with the construction and furnishing of the temple, and then three more chapters (1 Kings 8 and 2 Chron. 6–7) with its dedication.

The work began on the 480th year after the Children of Israel left Egypt (in the 4th year of Solomon's reign) and was completed seven years later (1 Kings 6:1, 38). These dates, incidentally, are key data points in any attempt to construct a complete Old Testament chronology.

To accomplish the work, Solomon conscripted an almost incredible number of workmen to do the work of cutting timber in the mountains of Lebanon (by arrangement with Hiram, king of Tyre), to hew stones in the quarry, and to carry the burdens to the temple site on Mount Moriah. He had 150,000 "strangers" to do all this work, probably from the conquered Canaanite tribes still in the land, all supervised by 3,600 Israelites, in addition to 30,000 Israelites, working in Lebanon in three-month shifts, 10,000 at a time (see 1 Kings 5:13–16 and 2 Chron. 2:17–18).

Of special interest is the fact that he had the stonecutters not only cut the stones for the temple from the limestone quarries beneath the city, but also to pre-shape them there for their respective places in the temple, "so that there was neither hammer nor axe nor any tool of iron heard in the house, while it was in building" (1 Kings 6:7). This unusual construction practice could be regarded as a type of the manner in which the Holy Spirit quietly is adding "living stones" to the spiritual house of God today, "built upon the foundation of the apostles and prophets, Jesus Christ himself being the chief corner stone; In whom all the building fitly framed together groweth unto an holy temple in the Lord" (Eph. 2:20–21; note also 1 Pet. 2:4–5).

The temple, of course, was much larger and more ornate than the wilderness tabernacle which it was replacing, but its main features were similar and its basic purpose the same. Just as God had given Moses detailed instructions concerning the design of the tabernacle (Exod. 25–27), so the temple layout was apparently given by God to David for the planning and to Solomon for the construction. When giving Solomon the plans, David had told him as much. "All this, said David, the LORD made me understand in writing by his hand upon me, even all the works of this pattern" (1 Chron. 28:19). Later, when Solomon began to build, the account precedes the description of the temple construction by saying, "Now these are things wherein Solomon was instructed for the building of the house of God" (2 Chron. 3:3).

Thus, the temple, like the tabernacle before it, became the earthly dwelling place of the glory of God. When the tabernacle was completed and dedicated, "the glory of the LORD filled the tabernacle" (Exod. 40:34). Likewise, when the temple was dedicated and Solomon had finished his prayer, "the fire came down from heaven, and consumed the burnt-offering and the sacrifices; and the glory of the LORD filled the house. And the priests could not enter into the house of the LORD, because the glory of the LORD had filled the LORD's house" (2 Chron. 7:1–2).

Solomon had spent 7 years building the temple and then spent 13 more years building his own palace, as well as a number of the major buildings in the palace complex (1 Kings 7:1–8). These 20 years, in addition to the first 4 years before he began work on the temple, were apparently all years of spiritual faithfulness to the Lord and His commandments, even though he had erred in taking the daughter of Pharaoh as his wife early in his reign. It was after all this that the Scriptures still note that "Solomon loved the Lord, walking in the statutes of David his father" (1 Kings 3:1–3).

Certainly his prayer at the temple's dedication (1 Kings 8:22–53; 2 Chron. 6:12–42) had demonstrated a deep love for God and desire to do His will. He clearly recognized the Lord as the God of creation, not in any way comparable to the many pagan deities whom the many wives he later would acquire worshiped. "O Lord God of Israel," he prayed, "there is no God like thee in the heaven, nor in the earth . . . behold, heaven and the heaven of heavens cannot contain thee" (2 Chron. 6:4–18). He also recognized the very real danger of sin on the part of his people (though he never seemed to mention the possibility that he himself might sin), and prayed repeatedly that God would forgive their sin when they would repent and pray.

And it was, of course, in God's response to Solomon's prayer that God made the familiar promise that has since become the text for a thousand sermons across Christian lands, whether or not the children of Israel ever paid heed to it. "If my people, which are called by my name, shall humble themselves, and pray, and seek my face, and turn from their wicked ways; then will I hear from heaven, and will forgive their sin, and will heal their land" (2 Chron. 7:14).

Then, however, God repeated to Solomon His conditional promise of blessing, not only to Solomon but also to his posterity. "If thou wilt walk before me, as thy father David walked, in integrity of heart, and in uprightness, to do according to all that I have commanded thee, and wilt keep my statutes and my judgments: Then I will establish the throne of thy kingdom upon Israel for ever, as I promised to David thy father, saying, There shall not fail thee a man upon the throne of Israel. But if ye shall at all turn from following me, ye or your children, and will not keep my commandments and my statutes which I have set before you, but go and serve other gods, and worship them: Then will I cut off Israel out of the land which I have given them; and this house, which I have hallowed for my name, will I cast out of my sight; and Israel shall be a proverb and a byword among all people" (1 Kings 9:4–7).

Subsequent history has demonstrated the fulfillment of God's prophetic warning to Solomon and his people. Despite all his unique wisdom and riches, as well as his great heritage and the teaching of his parents, Solomon eventually let himself forget God's commandments and fell into gross disobedience. This sad development will be discussed in the next session.

During his own lifetime, however, Solomon and his kingdom continued to enjoy great material blessings. He built a large "navy of ships" birthed at "Ezion-geber . . . on the shore of the Red sea, in the land of Edom" (1 Kings 9:26), the trade of which brought in much of his wealth, especially gold from the mysterious land of Ophir. "And Solomon gathered together chariots and horsemen: and he had a thousand and four hundred chariots, and twelve thousand horsemen" (1 Kings 10:26). For use by the horsemen, "Solomon had horses brought out of Egypt" (1 Kings 10:28), and built "four thousand stalls for horses and chariots" (2 Chron. 9:25).

This in itself was an act of rebellion, for God had clearly commanded that no future king of Israel shall "multiply horses to himself, nor cause the people to return to Egypt, to the end that he should multiply horses" (Deut. 17:16). Interestingly, remains of some of these stables have been found at Megiddo, which was one of the "cities for chariots" (1 Kings 10:25–26). The University of Chicago archaeologists who excavated these stables estimated that one of them could have accommodated as many as five hundred horses.

To finance his extensive construction works, as well as his naval and cavalry establishments, Solomon made semi-slaves out of the many conquered (but still living) Canaanites still in the land. "And all the people that were left of the Amorites, Hittites, Perizzites, Hivites and Jebusites, which were not of the children of Israel, Their children that were left after them in the land, whom the children of Israel also were not able utterly to destroy, upon those did Solomon levy a tribute of service unto this day" (1 Kings 9:20–21).

The nations on the periphery of Canaan (Philistia, Zobah, Moab, Ammon, Syria, Edom, and Amalek) had all been conquered by David (see 1 Chron.18), and these subjugated people also were under tribute to Israel, though still intact as nations.

All in all, the first 20 years or more of Solomon's reign were years of unprecedented blessing. "Judah and Israel were many, as the sand which is by the sea in multitude . . . and Solomon reigned over all kingdoms from the river unto the land of the Philistines, and unto the border of Egypt" (1 Kings 4:20–21).

The knowledge and wisdom of King Solomon were legendary. "He spake three thousand proverbs: and his songs were a thousand and five. And he spoke of trees, from the cedar tree that is in Lebanon even unto the hyssop that springeth out of the wall: he spake also of the beasts, and of fowl, and of creeping things, and of fishes. And there came of all people to hear the wisdom of Solomon, from all kings of the earth; which had heard of his wisdom" (1 Kings 4:32–34).

Thus he was an authority on literature and psychology, botany and zoology, ornithology and herpetology, entomology and ichthyology, and many other things. He probably wrote many books (later he commented on how many books there were, with many of these surely being his own books — note Eccles. 12:12), of which only a fraction have come down to us, as part of God's inspired Word.

Possibly he even conducted seminars or had some other means of sharing his knowledge and wisdom with all the many people who came to learn from him. Much of this, no doubt, he had learned from his youthful training and experimental observations, as well as reading from the works of previous writers, but the unique wisdom to assimilate and apply all this knowledge in practical living and teaching was the special gift of God. We shall explore and comment on much of this knowledge and wisdom (that is, the portions that have been preserved for us in his Books of Proverbs, Ecclesiastes, and Song of Solomon) in later chapters of this present book.

And, of course, he was almost incredibly rich, as we have already noted. He even "made two hundred targets of beaten gold. . . . And three hundred shields made he of beaten gold. . . . Moreover the king made a great throne of ivory, and overlaid it with pure gold. . . . And all the drinking vessels of Solomon were of gold" (2 Chron. 9:15–20).

In fact, as the account summarizes, "King Solomon passed all the kings of the earth in riches and wisdom" (2 Chron. 9:22). God blessed him in the material things of this world probably more than any man who ever lived.

Somehow, however, such prosperity and intellectual superiority seemed eventually to become more than he could handle spiritually. The admonition of the Lord through the prophet Jeremiah, written over half a millennium later, would have been appropriate for him to know and follow. "Let not the wise man glory in his wisdom, neither let the mighty man glory in his might, let not the rich man glory in his riches: But let him that glorieth glory in this, that he understandeth and knoweth me, that I am the LORD which exercise lovingkindness, judgment, and righteousness, in the earth: for in these things I delight, saith the LORD" (Jer. 9:23–24).

The Unfaithful Later Years of Solomon

Surrounded by opulence and wielding almost absolute power, as well as suffused by universal admiration of his knowledge and wisdom, Solomon gradually became more and more self-centered and less and less God-centered in his thinking and doing. Though he never completely forgot God and His commandments, he eventually became almost apostate with reference to worship of the true God of creation.

Probably the first step in his decline was his political marriage to the daughter of Egypt's pharaoh. This treaty (for that's what it was) was a mark of special recognition by the great nation of Egypt, acknowledging that Israel and Solomon were very important even to such a nation as Egypt.

Even though Solomon may already have had a wife whom he truly loved (see the analysis of the Song of Solomon in chapter 2 of this book), he recognized the worldly prestige that such an alliance would bring to him and his nation this early in his reign, and he must have justified it on that basis. After all, he also had the polygamous example of his father

David and his several wives, as well as that of other kings of that day and age, and so went ahead with it.

Nevertheless, he must have known, from the Genesis record of the creation of Adam and Eve, that polygamy was not God's primeval plan for marriage. He must also have known that God did not want the Children of Israel to marry "strange" (that is "foreign") wives who worshiped some god other than the true God who had created heaven and earth. Moses had written, "[The king] shall not . . . multiply wives to himself, that his heart turn not away" (Deut. 17:17).

Lest we judge Solomon too sharply, however, we must remember that similar mixed marriages (that is, believers with non-believers) have become all too common even among well-instructed Christians today. There are many ways to rationalize disobedience to God's law, and Solomon probably assumed that it was just a political marriage and so was not a real marriage anyway. It would not affect his own faith, he assured himself, and it would be of significant economic benefit to his nation. Probably he could win this wife to the Lord, and possibly even Pharaoh, so he may have thought.

But he did *not* win her to the Lord, and Solomon eventually "brought up the daughter of Pharaoh out of the city of David unto the house that he had built for her: for he said, My wife shall not dwell in the house of David king of Israel, because the places are holy, whereunto the ark of the LORD hath come" (2 Chron. 8:11).

Once the ice was broken, however, he eventually decided to take another wife, and then another, and on and on, until finally "he had seven hundred wives, princesses, and three hundred concubines: and his wives turned away his heart" (1 Kings 11:3). This sounds almost incredible, but it is known that ancient kings of the east did often have large harems, and it was considered a mark of prestige to do so. Solomon had more riches and more knowledge than any of them, and apparently he decided that it would also be fitting for him to have the most wives.

Many of these marriages, perhaps all, were also at least quasi-political marriages, for the account says these wives were "princesses." There were a great many small city-states in the surrounding regions, each with their own "king," as well as the larger nations themselves, and somehow all these unions were arranged by Solomon and the various kings and chieftains. How he could deal with seven hundred wives (how he could even know all their names!) is a mystery, in spite of all his wisdom.

The account does say he "loved" them all, though even this may be ambiguous. The Hebrew word for "loved" (*ahab*) can refer to various meanings of "love" in addition to romantic love or marital love. For example, 2 Chronicles 26:10 says that King Uzziah "loved husbandry" and Psalm 109:17 speaks of an enemy of God as one who "loved cursing."

Perhaps Solomon "loved many strange women" (1 Kings 11:1) mainly in the sense that he loved the idea of having numerous foreign princesses in his harem as a matter of national prestige.

Whatever may have been his rationalization, he surely must have known his actions were wrong in the sight of God. It was not only the gross polygamy that this involved, of course, but even more the fact that many of his wives brought their own idolatrous nature religions with them. One would assume that Solomon originally felt confident that, while he would allow these women freedom to worship their own "gods," he himself would not be influenced by them.

But the fact is that one compromise almost inevitably leads to another, and then another, and so on. The road of compromise eventually ends in a precipice. Somehow Solomon was gradually drawn, not only into tolerating their religions, but then also into approving of them and eventually participating in them. These were all just "different ways of approaching God," he might gradually have come to believe, as so many people do today. As long as they were sincere in what they believed, then a gracious Heavenly Father would accept them, so he must have decided. Then, to show his broadmindedness, he would even occasionally join in their own forms of worship with them. After all, they were his wives, and he must be considerate of their feelings.

But if these or similar sophistries were what he was thinking, he was dead wrong! Wisdom is supposed to increase with age, but it didn't work that way with Solomon. "For it came to pass, when Solomon was old, that his wives turned away his heart after other gods: and his heart was not perfect with the LORD his God, as was the heart of David his father" (1 Kings 11:4).

Although he had built a palace for his first foreign wife, the daughter of Pharaoh, he erected altars and worship centers for his other wives — from Zidon, Ammon, Moab, and other nations. "Likewise did he for all his strange wives, which burnt incense and sacrificed unto their gods" (1 Kings 11:8).

This, of course, was exactly what God had warned him about — as, in fact, He had been warning all the Children of Israel about ever since He had led them out of Egypt. After Solomon's earnest prayer at the temple dedication, and God's response, "the LORD appeared to Solomon the second time, as He had appeared unto him at Gibeon, and the LORD said unto him. . . . But if ye shall at all turn from following me, and...go and serve other gods, and worship them: Then will I cut off Israel out of the land which I have given them" (1 Kings 9:2–7).

When Solomon finally did exactly that, then "the LORD was angry with Solomon" (1 Kings 11:9), and proceeded to fulfill His prophetic warning, saying, "I will surely rend the kingdom from thee, and will give it to thy servant. Notwithstanding in thy days I will not do it for David thy father's sake: but I will rend it out of the hands of thy son. Howbeit I will not rend away all the kingdom; but will give one tribe to thy son for David my servant's sake, and for Jerusalem's sake, which I have chosen" (1 Kings 11:11–13).

Up until this time, Solomon's reign had been peaceful, as God had promised, but now things began to change. An Edomite named Hadad and a man of Zobah in Syria both stirred up rebellions (1 Kings 11:21, 23).

Even more serious was the rebellion that was being organized by Jeroboam, a "mighty man" of the tribe of Ephraim, whom Solomon had made "ruler over all the charge of the house of Joseph" (1 Kings 11:28). God had sent the prophet Ahijah to Jeroboam, to tell him that He would take ten tribes from Solomon and give them to Jeroboam (1 Kings 11:29–31). When Solomon learned of this, Jeroboam had to flee to Egypt for his life, to wait for his opportunity after Solomon's death.

In the meantime, unrest had been brewing quietly in Israel because of the heavy burden of taxation and conscription he had placed on them with all his construction activity and commercial ventures. This came out openly once Solomon died and his son Rehoboam became king. At that time Jeroboam and other tribal leaders petitioned Rehoboam to make their burdens lighter. They said, "Thy father made our yoke grievous: now therefore ease somewhat the grievous servitude of thy father, and his heavy yoke that he put upon us, and we will serve thee" (2 Chron. 10:4).

When Rehoboam rebuffed these leaders and told them his reign would be more despotic than his father's, then "Israel rebelled against the house of David unto this day" (2 Chronicles 10:19), and Jeroboam became king of the ten-tribe northern kingdom of Israel, just as God had warned Solomon and then promised Jeroboam.

Possible Repentance and Forgiveness

But we must at least raise the question as to whether Solomon ever repented of his gross disobedience and received God's forgiveness before he died. When God severely rebuked him and told him that his sin would result in the loss of ten tribes, one could reasonably assume that this would bring Solomon under deep conviction and remorse, even though the Bible never mentions it.

This, however, is an argument from silence: the account does not say that he did *not* repent. It is altogether silent about Solomon's reaction. His later attempt to slay Jeroboam and thereby to prevent him from succeeding in his rebellion would suggest that Solomon's repentance, if any, was only partial at this time. On the other hand, Jeroboam's success in eluding him could well have persuaded Solomon that God was protecting his adversary so that he would, indeed, eventually become ruler over ten tribes as God had said. Perhaps *this* would have brought Solomon under conviction by showing him again that God could and would do what He said.

It is worth considering the possibility, at least, that Solomon may, in his last years, have turned back to the Lord in true repentance and faith. There are several indications that this could really have happened, even though the biblical accounts of his life and death never say so specifically.

For example, it seems significant that the Lord himself, in His human incarnation as Jesus the Christ, referred to Solomon's glory and his wisdom, but never to his apparent apostasy. It is also interesting to note that the account of Solomon's career as recorded in the two Books of Chronicles, covering some 13 chapters in the two books, never refers to Solomon's foreign wives at all, except for the one verse (2 Chron. 8:11) that mentions Pharaoh's daughter, the first and most important of these wives. And *that* is the verse that tells us how Solomon took her out of Jerusalem, building a special house for her. The reason he did this was because of the holy places in Jerusalem and the presence of the ark of God's covenant there, the implication being that her presence as a pagan religionist in Jerusalem was incompatible with these sacred items in the city.

Neither does the Chronicles account refer at all to Solomon's apostasy as caused by these foreign wives or God's rebuke to him because of them and their idols. Furthermore, the Chronicler never mentions Bathsheba and the rather unsavory background of her affair with David that eventually led to Solomon's own birth. Neither does it mention the rebellion of Adonijah and the subsequent executions of Adonijah, Joab, and Shimei that were ordered by Solomon. All this is found only in 2 Samuel and 1 Kings.

It seems very much as though Ezra (who is believed by most scholars to have written 1 and 2 Chronicles) deliberately omitted all the "negative" aspects of Solomon's birth, life, and career, recording only the "positive" items, as far as possible. Yet he surely had access to the books of 1 and 2 Samuel and 1 and 2 Kings when he compiled the Books of Chronicles. A number of passages in these earlier books are quoted almost verbatim in Chronicles (for example, compare 2 Chronicles 10:1–19, describing the initial acts of Rehoboam, who succeeded Solomon as king, with 1 Kings 12:1–19). Thus, Ezra certainly knew about Solomon's problems, so why did he omit them in his own account?

It seems most likely that Ezra wanted the exiles returning from Babylon, for whom he was first writing, to dwell only on the positive things in the life of Solomon. Yet he did not hesitate to write about the sins and weaknesses of Rehoboam, Jehoram, Ahaziah, Uzziah, Ahaz, and the other later kings of Judah. So why did he spare Solomon? After all, it was through his initial disobedience that the idolatrous practices that later led to the Babylonian exile had been introduced into Jerusalem.

One reasonable answer might be that he knew somehow — or at least had reason to believe — that Solomon had indeed repented and received forgiveness in his later years.

A later evil king of Judah, Manasseh, had been worse than any of the kings before him, according to 2 Kings 21:9, causing God to pronounce the certainty of Jerusalem's coming destruction. No offsetting goodness was ever found in King Manasseh, at least according to the record in 2 Kings (21:1–18).

Yet Manasseh *did* later repent and turn back to God, and Ezra the scribe recorded *this* in his account (2 Chron. 33:12–17), happy to be able to show his people that even such a wicked king as Manasseh could and did repent and return to the God of his fathers.

Now, even though he did not have positive evidence of Solomon's repentance (as he did for Manasseh, who had lived much nearer his own lifetime), he evidently felt that he had enough reason to believe that Solomon had returned to the Lord to warrant omitting the unsavory items and only "accentuating the positive" in his life.

It may also be significant that, although the account in 1 Kings notes that Solomon had seven hundred wives and three hundred concubines, neither Kings nor Chronicles mentions any sons or daughters, with the exception of Rehoboam and two daughters, Taphath and Basmath, each of whom married one of Solomon's 12 regional governors (1 Kings 4:11, 15).

If Solomon ever really had marital relations with his seven hundred wives — not to mention the three hundred concubines — there must have been literally hundreds of Solomon's children in Jerusalem! Why is this never mentioned? The account in 1 Chronicles 3:1–9 has no hesitation in listing 19 sons of David, not including his daughters (except for Tamar) or the sons of his concubines. Why was nothing said about any of Solomon's sons other than Rehoboam?

Could it possibly be that all of Solomon's wives were there merely for show and prestige, rather than connubial relations? Did he reserve *that* for his first and one true love, who bore him one son and two daughters? This obviously is pure speculation, and rather unreasonable speculation at that, but these are the only children we know about, and it does seem strange that no others are even hinted at anywhere in the Bible. This is not the usual practice in the Scriptures.

Remember also that Solomon had a great deal to say about children, especially in his Book of Proverbs, as well as the importance of being true to the "wife of thy youth." Was all of this nothing but hypocrisy on his part? The mother of his son Rehoboam was Naamah, an Ammonitess (2 Chron. 12:13). Although she was from another country, Ammon, she could not have been one of the foreign wives he married later in life, for Rehoboam was 41 years old when he began to reign (2 Chron. 12:13), and thus had been born a year before Solomon began his reign of 40 years (2 Chron. 9:30).

Now, as already noted, Solomon was no more than 20 years old when he became king, which means that he was in his late teens when he wed Naamah. Thus she must have been his first love, the "wife of his youth." Most likely, she was the beautiful young woman praised by him so highly in his "Song of Songs." This will be discussed more fully in chapter 2 of this book, as we try to look in greater depth at this beautiful love song of the young King Solomon.

But if the Song of Solomon was written early in his life, his Book of Ecclesiastes was surely written very late in his life. In this book, he is clearly looking back at the "vanity" of his former dedication to wisdom, riches, and fame with apparent deep regret. He finally concluded his book (and probably his last written words) with the admonition to young people to "fear God and keep His commandments: for this is the whole duty of man. For God shall bring every work into judgment, with every secret thing, whether it be good, or whether it will be evil" (Eccles. 12:13–14).

This will conclude our general study of the life of Solomon, as a background for understanding the marvelous wisdom revealed by God through Solomon in his three canonical books. We shall consider these books chronologically, the Song of Solomon in the next chapter, then the wonderful Book of Proverbs, and finally the unique Book of Ecclesiastes. Perhaps the best evidence of Solomon's eventual repentance and return to God is that God elected to write these three key books of the Bible using Solomon's pen and God-given wisdom.

2

Solomon's Song of Songs

We have now looked in summary fashion at the fascinating and somewhat enigmatic life of the remarkable son of David named Solomon. Among other achievements, it is said that "he spake three thousand proverbs and his songs were a thousand and five" (1 Kings 4:32). Many of these proverbs and at least one of his songs were apparently written under the inspiration of God's Holy Spirit, for they have been preserved (undoubtedly by divine guidance) here in the Old Testament of the Bible.

These are surely among the most remarkable books of the Bible, and it is now our purpose to explore each of them in some detail, for in them is recorded much of the unique wisdom which God gave to Solomon. The first of these, chronologically, must be the book known as the Song of Solomon, written while he was a young man, in contrast to Ecclesiastes, written in his old age. The Book of Proverbs was evidently accumulated and written during his middle years.

They will be discussed, each in turn, in this chronological order, and each in light of what we have learned about Solomon's life in chapter 1. We begin, therefore, with the Song of Solomon, which must have been written in Solomon's younger years, or at least as reflecting those younger years.

The Song of Solomon is unique among the Bible's 66 books, for it is written somewhat like a play, with different actors speaking (or singing) as the theme unfolds. Those speaking are: (1) Solomon himself; (2) Solomon's bride, the Shulamite; (3) the daughters of Jerusalem; and (4) the brothers of the bride. Explanatory comments will then follow each of the successive sections of dialogue between these participants.

The Bridegroom and His Bride

Song of Solomon 1:1

1. *The song of songs, which is Solomon's.*

Solomon introduces this book with what seems to be his conviction that, out of all the thousand-and-five songs he had written, this was the one he thought was the most important. It was his *"song of songs,"* a beautiful poem of love, which God himself, in some mysterious way, inspired and incorporated in His written Word.

Because it is so different from other books of the Bible, and perhaps because God's name is never mentioned in the book, and because it is never quoted in the New Testament, some writers have questioned whether it *should* be part of the Bible. Nevertheless, the ancient Jewish authorities, as well as all the church fathers, accepted it unanimously as part of the canon of Scripture. Many who question its romantic, even erotic, aspects have treated it as an allegory, either of Jehovah's love for Israel or of Christ for the church, not wanting to take it literally.

There is no doubt, however, that Solomon himself wrote it as a song of love, speaking of the romantic and marital love between himself and his very first wife, called simply the Shulamite. As such, God has shown thereby His approval of such love, on the physical level as well as the spiritual. God made Adam and Eve for each other, declaring them *"one flesh"* (Gen. 2:24) and the Lord Jesus Christ endorsed lifelong monogamous marriage founded on premarital chastity and marital fidelity as God's primary plan for men and women (Matt. 19:3–9). "Marriage is honorable in all, and the bed undefiled" (Heb. 13:4), the Scripture says.

Yet the Song can, in addition, perhaps be viewed in part as also a type (not an allegory) of Christ and His church. The apostle Paul did treat the relation between husbands and wives as such a type, of course (see Eph. 5:22–33; 2 Cor. 11:2; etc.). One should be tentative in any such typological interpretations, however, remembering that none of the New Testament writers use it as a type, or even quote from it.

The exposition of the Song of Solomon in this book, therefore, will be based on its literal intent as a love song between a man and woman illustrating God's intended pattern for honorable and fruitful marriage. Secondarily, however, typological parallels can be quoted whenever appropriate to show also the love between Christ and His redeemed followers in the church.

Song of Solomon 1:2–7

2. *Let him kiss me with the kisses of his mouth: for thy love is better than wine.*

3. *Because of the savour of thy good ointments thy name is as ointment poured forth, therefore do the virgins love thee.*

4. *Draw me, we will run after thee: the king hath brought me into his chambers: we will be glad and rejoice in thee, we will remember thy love more than wine: the upright love thee.*

5. *I am black, but comely, O ye daughters of Jerusalem, as the tents of Kedar, as the curtains of Solomon.*

6. *Look not upon me because I am black, because the sun hath looked upon me: my mother's children were angry with me; they made me the keeper of the vineyards; but mine own vineyard have I not kept.*

7. *Tell me, O thou whom my soul loveth, where thou feedest, where thou makest thy flock to rest at noon: for why should I be as one that turneth aside by the flocks of thy companions?*

The Song begins with a six-verse testimony sung mainly by the young bride, in the hearing of "the daughters of Jerusalem," who respond intermittently and briefly as they listen. It is appropriate that she begins by speaking first of the universal physical expression of love, "the kisses of his mouth," evidently as sealing the espousal or perhaps even their wedding — God thus immediately indicating approval of this aspect of true marriage by including her song in the inspired record.

The bridegroom, young King Solomon, is undoubtedly very handsome, as he is loved from afar, as it were, even by the virgin attendants at the wedding, the "daughters of Jerusalem." They follow the happy couple at a discreet distance, as the bride and groom depart for "his chambers."

As they go, the bride speaks to them again, seemingly somewhat apologetically. "Although my skin is very dark," she seems to be saying to them, "my features are quite beautiful." The Hebrew word for "black" can also mean "dusky," and she goes on to say that she is dark in skin because of much time in the sun, not by heredity. She compares her dark skin to those who live in Kedar, a region in sunny Arabia inhabited by descendants of Ishmael (note Gen. 25:13), and similar to her own rural home.

But we need to digress a moment to try to discern more closely her identity — evidently Solomon's first love and first bride. The song itself merely calls her "the Shulamite" (Song of Sol. 6:13), but there is no such place as Shulam mentioned in Scripture or known to secular history, so that is of little help. Presumably it was a small village known at the time, but later forgotten.

A significant clue may be found in the record of Solomon's death, in relation to the birth of his son Rehoboam. "And Solomon reigned in Jerusalem over all Israel forty years" (2 Chron. 9:30). "For Rehoboam was one and forty years old when he began to reign. . . . And his mother's name was Naamah an Ammonitess" (2 Chron. 12:13). When these verses are compared, we encounter the surprising fact that Rehoboam was born a year before Solomon was made king of Israel. As already noted in chapter 1, Solomon was quite young when he became king, probably no more than 20 years old, yet he already had a son, and therefore a wife!

That wife was Naamah, of the Ammonite kingdom. Although we cannot be definite about this, it certainly seems that Naamah must have been Solomon's first love, and only true love, bearing him a son shortly before he became king; she was thus the Shulamite beauty of Solomon's Song of Songs.

Now the Ammonites were idol worshipers, but they had been conquered by David, so that Ammon had been incorporated in the Davidic kingdom. Evidently many Ammonites had been converted to the true God. One of them, Zelek, was even one of David's "mighty men" (2 Sam. 23:8, 37), and it is intriguing to wonder whether Naamah was his daughter. That might explain how Solomon met her. That is, perhaps Zelek lived in a small rural village in Ammon named Shulam, where he had flocks and vineyards, sons and daughters. He had been somehow chosen by David, and so almost certainly was acquainted with Solomon. The latter, deeply interested in nature anyway, could well have visited Zelek's rural home, where he met and fell in love with Naamah.

That is speculation, of course, but it does at least make sense. The name Naamah means "pleasantness," and she evidently was aptly named. She undoubtedly, like her father, was a believer in Jehovah, rather than the Ammonite god Milcom, or else Solomon would never have married her, as young and faithful to God as he was at that time.

As we proceed with our discussion, therefore, we shall call her Naamah, rather than the Shulamite, or the bride. As she continues to reminisce, in her testimony to the daughters of Jerusalem, she recalls how she first met Solomon (see Song of Sol. 8:11–12). Solomon had vineyards of his own, and had leased them out to her older brothers. Naamah even mentions the vineyards of En-gedi (Song of Sol. 1:14), just across the Dead Sea from the southern boundary of Ammon. Naamah had been assigned to care for all the family vineyards, but had neglected to care for her own, once she was engaged to Solomon.

Naamah then turned to her beloved young Solomon, inquiring about his own flocks. In the event she should need to find him some day, it would not be well for her to be searching among the flocks of other shepherds.

Verses 1:8–10

In these verses, Solomon answers Naamah, calling her the "fairest among women," assuring her that she could feed her own flocks safely regardless, implying that it would be well known among other shepherds that she was Solomon's bride, and they would not dare harm her or misjudge her intentions.

8. *If thou know not, O thou fairest among women, go thy way forth by the footsteps of the flock, and feed thy kids beside the shepherds' tents.*
9. *I have compared thee, O my love, to a company of horses in Pharaoh's chariots.*
10. *Thy cheeks are comely with rows of jewels, thy neck with chains of gold.*

Solomon then compares her grace and strength to a company of the finest horses in Egypt, and the beauty of her cheeks and neck to rows of jewels and golden chains. These are imaginative similes, to be sure, but highly appropriate and complimentary in the culture of that time and place.

Song of Solomon 1:11–17

As Solomon and Naamah are departing for the king's chambers, somewhere out in the forest, the daughters of Jerusalem promise to present her a gift appropriate for her beauty and position.

11. *We will make thee borders of gold with studs of silver.*
12. *While the king sitteth at his table, my spikenard sendeth forth the smell thereof.*
13. *A bundle of myrrh is my well-beloved unto me; he shall lie all night betwixt my breasts.*
14. *My beloved is unto me as a cluster of camphire in the vineyards of En-gedi.*
15. *Behold, thou art fair, my love; behold, thou art fair, thou hast doves' eyes.*
16. *Behold, thou art fair, my beloved, yea, pleasant: also our bed is green.*
17. *The beams of our house are cedar, and our rafters of fir.*

Then the young bride and groom go off to dine together and to anticipate their coming night together. Naamah's perfume is appropriate for the occasion, which is probably the wedding supper. She anticipates happily their imminent marital union in Solomon's forest home. She calls *him* "my beloved" in verse 14, and he calls *her* "my beloved" in verse 16. Two different Hebrews words are used, but the meanings are both flexible and interchangeable. Actually, there are three different Hebrew words translated "love," "beloved," etc., in the Song of Solomon, used altogether some 60 times in this short book. Truly, Solomon's "Song of Songs" is a love song!

This, of course, is why it seems so natural to many to think of the Song as almost an allegory — or at least a type — of the love of Christ and His bride, the church.

In the next-to-last verse of chapter 1, there is an interesting word used by Solomon as he speaks to his beloved. "Behold, thou art fair, my beloved, yea pleasant." It seems unusual that Solomon never speaks of, or to, his bride by name, merely calling her "the Shulamite," and *that* only twice in Song of Solomon 6:13. We have deduced, however, that she must have been Naamah, who became the mother of Rehoboam, Solomon's only named son. Now Naamah means "pleasantness" in the Hebrew, and in this last verse of the first chapter, he calls her "pleasant," the Hebrew word actually used by him being *naim*, derived in effect from the word *naamah*. One can at least speculate that Solomon was actually calling her by an affectionate diminutive form of her name here, when he called her *Naim*. She was not just "pleasantness" to the world in general but "pleasant" in a special individual way to him, as his own beloved, well-pleasing bride.

The Song of Naamah

Except for verse 2 and possibly verse 15, chapter 2 of Song of Solomon is spoken (or sung) entirely by Naamah.

Song of Solomon 2:1–2

1. *I am the rose of Sharon and the lily of the valleys.*
2. *As the lily among thorns, so is my love among the daughters.*

Although it is commonly assumed that Christ is symbolized by the rose of Sharon and the lily of the valleys, it is actually the bride who is speaking in this first verse of chapter 2, and she is depreciating herself by using these comparisons. The rose of Sharon and the lily of the valleys were two relatively insignificant wildflowers growing in the land, and thus unworthy to grow in the royal gardens.

Solomon, however, thinks otherwise. Compared to the other maidens in attendance, the daughters of Jerusalem, all of whom were undoubtedly very fair, Solomon declared that if Naamah was a lily, the other virgins were thorns. To him, she was absolutely the fairest among women.

Song of Solomon 2:3–7

The next several verses constitute a further testimony by Naamah to the daughters of Jerusalem, perhaps later, after the wedding, while Solomon is away.

3.   *As the apple tree among the trees of the wood, so is my beloved among the sons. I sat down under his shadow with great delight, and his fruit was sweet to my taste.*

4.   *He brought me to the banqueting house, and his banner over me was love.*

5.   *Stay me with flagons, comfort me with apples: for I am sick of love.*

6.   *His left hand is under my head, and his right hand doth embrace me.*

7.   *I charge you, O ye daughters of Jerusalem, by the roes, and by the hinds of the field, that ye stir not up, nor awake my love, till he please.*

She speaks of her beloved in glowingly romantic, even erotic, figures of speech. Again we note the implied divine approval on the intimate aspects of true marital love.

She likens her beloved Solomon to the most beautiful and nourishing tree of all the trees, mentioning the other "sons" of David (perhaps also all the sons of the tribe of Judah) as ordinary trees. The apple tree provides restful shade as well as delicious fruit. Sitting under Solomon's "shadow" was like a banqueting room, and his fruit was sweet, with his love stretching over her like a great banner (perhaps a flag denoting ownership) over the banquet table.

Typological inferences can easily be drawn from these figures. The Scriptures speak of abiding "under the shadow of the Almighty" (Ps. 91:1), of the Lord's guiding presence as being like "the shadow of a great rock in a weary land" (Isa. 32:2) and of being "under the shadow of thy wings" (Ps. 17:8; 36:7; 57:1). The wedding banquet can be considered rather naturally as being in effect a type of the great future "marriage supper of the Lamb" (Rev. 19:9).

Then, lest her rapturous description of the delights of their love-making stir the emotions of the virgin attendants to seek such experiences for themselves prior to marriage, she raises an important caution, charging them to "stir not up nor awake love [the word "my" is not in the original] till [it] please." That is, she charges them to maintain their virginity and sexual purity until true loves comes, as it has to the bride, in marriage. The word for "please" here can mean "is proper." This charge is repeated in verses 3:5 and 8:4. In view of the numerous Biblical injunctions against pre-marital sex, we can be sure that nothing in the Song of Solomon would encourage it.

Song of Solomon 2:8–14

8. *The voice of my beloved! behold, he cometh leaping upon the mountains, skipping upon the hills.*
9. *My beloved is like a roe or a young hart: behold, he standeth behind our wall, he looketh forth at the windows, shewing himself through the lattice.*
10. *My beloved spake, and said unto me, Rise up, my love, my fair one, and come away.*
11. *For, lo, the winter is past, the rain is over and gone;*
12. *The flowers appear on the earth; the time of the singing of birds is come, and the voice of the turtle is heard in our land;*
13. *The fig tree putteth forth her green figs, and the vines with the tender grapes give a good smell. Arise, my love, my fair one, and come away.*
14. *O my dove, that art in the clefts of the rock, in the secret places of the stairs, let me see thy countenance, let me hear thy voice; for sweet is thy voice, and thy countenance is comely.*

In this next section (Song of Sol. 2:8–14), Naamah turns away from the daughters of Jerusalem, as she hears the voice of Solomon calling as he is bounding down the mountain slope and skipping along the low foothills leading to the forest home where his bride is waiting. He reaches the wall, then the windows of the house, then the lattice at the door.

He speaks, with the beautiful and exciting invitation: "Arise, my love, my fair one, and come away." The winter is over and both bridegroom and bride love the outdoors in the springtime. There are flowers and tender grapes and early figs. There are birds singing, especially the turtledove. A pleasant aroma fills the air, and he wants to hear her sweet voice and see her beautiful face, calling her to come out and go with him to the fields and hills.

Song of Solomon 2:15–17

Verse 15 briefly interrupts her idyllic recital of Solomon's invitation, as she realizes that little words and deeds, if not anticipated and controlled, might spoil their love, and they must guard against them.

15. *Take us the foxes, the little foxes, that spoil the vines: for our vines have tender grapes.*
16. *My beloved is mine, and I am his: he feedeth among the lilies.*
17. *Until the day break, and the shadows flee away, turn, my beloved, and be thou like a roe or a young hart upon the mountains of Bether.*

Naamah is probably here recalling experiences in her own vineyard and those of her brothers, when the young foxes in the fields and woods had to be caught and kept from the vineyards before they could ruin the vine roots. Possibly she was merely recalling the admonitions of her brothers back home, as their vineyards were important to their livelihood. She was anxious that nothing interfere with the love she and Solomon shared with each other.

This lovely passage, especially verses 10–14, has served many commentators as a beautiful type of the return of Christ for His church at the end of the present age. The passage seems to parallel Luke 21:28–31, where Christ says, "When these things begin to come to pass, then look up, and lift up your heads; for your redemption draweth nigh. And He spake to them a parable; Behold the fig tree [possibly symbolizing Israel] and all the trees [possibly the other nations of the Bible]; When they now shoot forth, ye see and know of your own selves that summer is now nigh at hand. So likewise ye, when ye see these things come to pass [referring to the signs of His coming, as given in his message to the disciples on the Mount of Olives]; know ye that the kingdom of God is nigh at hand."

At that great day, Christ will say to His beloved ones in the true church, in effect using the same invitation as that of Solomon to his own bride, beautiful Naamah: "Arise my love, my fair one, and come away."

Naamah's Dream

Song of Solomon 3:1–5

The first five verses of this chapter seem to reflect a dream experienced by Naamah, possibly before her marriage, and possibly as she recalled the dream and was telling it to the "daughters of Jerusalem."

1. *By night on my bed, I sought him whom my soul loveth; I sought him, but I found him not.*
2. *I will rise now, and go about the city in the streets, and in the broad ways I will seek him whom my soul loveth: I sought him, but I found him not.*
3. *The watchmen that go about the city found me: to whom I said, Saw ye him whom my soul loveth?*
4. *It was but a little that I passed from them, but I found him whom my soul loveth: I held him, and would not let him go, until I had brought him into my mother's house, and unto the chamber of her that conceived me.*
5. *I charge you, O ye daughters of Jerusalem, by the roes, and by the hinds of the field, that ye stir not up, nor awake my love, till he please.*

In her dream Naamah realized her beloved had gone, and so began desperately seeking him. In type, this could suggest a believer's troubled conscience, aware that he had somehow displeased the Lord, and is now anxious to have the joy of his salvation restored.

In the dream, she was no longer in the forest home of her beloved nor out with the flocks and vineyards, but in the city, possibly in the palace. But, then she dreamed that she rushed out in the streets searching, but could find at first no one except the city's watchmen.

Finally, however, she did find him, and then would not let him go, insisting that he go with her to meet her mother, sure that her mother would approve their marriage, once she herself knew Solomon. Still dreaming, Naamah realized again the importance of maintaining her own sexual purity, as well as urging the same on the daughters of Jerusalem, until after marriage, as approved by their parents. See comment on chapter 2, verse 7.

Song of Solomon 3:6–11

The remaining section of this chapter describes the actual wedding procession itself, not part of Naamah's dream, but the actual fulfillment of what she was seeking in her dream. We need to remember that Solomon's Song is a love poem, with a degree of poetic license, skipping around between subjects and speakers but nevertheless describing real thoughts and real events. It is the inspired record of the first love marriage of the great King Solomon, son of David and heir to his throne.

6. *Who is this that cometh out of the wilderness like pillars of smoke, perfumed with myrrh and frankincense, with all powders of the merchant?*

7. *Behold his bed, which is Solomon's; threescore valiant men are about it, of the valiant of Israel.*

8. *They all hold swords, being expert in war: every man hath his sword upon his thigh because of fear in the night.*

9. *King Solomon made himself a chariot of the wood of Lebanon.*

10. *He made the pillars thereof of silver, the bottom thereof of gold, the covering of it of purple, the midst thereof being paved with love, for the daughters of Jerusalem.*

11. *Go forth, O ye daughters of Zion, and behold king Solomon with the crown wherewith his mother crowned him in the day of his espousals, and in the day of the gladness of his heart.*

This surely was a majestic wedding ceremony, beginning with a great procession ascending to Jerusalem from the desert below. Solomon was already king, though he had probably first met and courted Naamah before he became king. We have noted, however, that his son Rehoboam had been born a year before Solomon was crowned king, so the wedding must have taken place still earlier.

Any problem is resolved by recalling the unusual circumstances in which Solomon became king. David was still living at the time, though bed-ridden, when Adonijah attempted his own presumptuous self-coronation. David, however, had promised Bathsheba (and God had ordained) that Solomon should be king, so David had Solomon declared king, even though he himself could not participate directly in the ceremony.

Yet David himself also continued as king, so that he and Solomon were co-regents for an unspecified period of time. It was apparently during their co-regency that Solomon's wedding, as well as the subsequent birth of his son Rehoboam, must have taken place. Thus Solomon could be recognized as King Solomon in the Song of Solomon even though it would be another two years or more before he would become the sole King of Israel.

This would also explain why David was not present at the wedding and why Solomon's mother (Bathsheba) placed the marriage crown on his head (verse 11). David no doubt would have presided there if he could.

The wedding procession itself was magnificent, with Solomon riding in a unique "chariot." The Hebrew word here is used nowhere else in the Bible, but seems to refer to something like a palanquin, or sedan chair. It had been specially built of valuable wood from Lebanon, with silver posts and gold support beams, and with its interior lovingly covered with purple cloth by the daughters of Zion. In fact, it may be these "daughters of Jerusalem" who are actually set forth in the Song as those singing the words of verses 6–11. They note also there that Solomon's royal bed is being carried in the procession, protected by an elite armed guard of 60 warriors. It must have been quite a day!

The Beautiful Naamah

Song of Solomon 4:1-5

The fourth chapter of the Song of Solomon consists solely of the praises of Solomon for the beauties of his new bride, the fair Naamah.

1. *Behold, thou art fair, my love; behold thou art fair; thou hast doves' eyes within thy locks: thy hair is as a flock of goats, that appear from mount Gilead.*
2. *Thy teeth are like a flock of sheep that are even shorn, which came up from the washing: whereof every one bear twins, and none is barren among them.*

3. *Thy lips are like a thread of scarlet, and thy speech is comely; thy temples are like a piece of a pomegranate within thy locks.*
4. *Thy neck is like the tower of David builded for an armoury, whereon these hang a thousand bucklers, all shields of mighty men.*
5. *Thy two breasts are like two young roes that are twins, which feed among the lilies.*

Solomon praises his bride in words of deep-felt admiration for her physical beauty, but he uses analogies which seem strange to our western ears. We can understand comparing her eyes to those of a gentle dove, with her locks of hair serving almost as a veil. But then these flowing locks are also reminding him of a flock of goats descending the mountain, and her teeth seem to him like a flock of freshly shorn and washed sheep. Naamah, familiar with nature, could understand and appreciate such robust rural similes better than someone raised in a city.

Solomon speaks of her beautiful lips and gracious speech. The word for "speech" here seems to include both the mouth and the gracious words flowing from it. Her cheeks, though dark from the sun, are also beautifully colored like a slice from a pomegranate.

Her neck shows such strength of form and character as to remind him of his father's great armory, storing the shields of a thousand warriors. Her breasts somehow speak of two young fawns of a gazelle, feeding among lilies. Lovely of form and face is Naamah, and Solomon is not content with ordinary clichés used by lovers. And Naamah will shortly respond in kind (chapter 5).

In like fashion, the Lord Jesus Christ will some day be able to speak of His own dear Bride, once she has been cleansed by "the washing of water by the word" as "not having spot, or wrinkle, or any such thing; but that it should be holy and without blemish" (Eph. 5:26–27).

Song of Solomon 4:6–9

Having spoken such words of praise to his beloved, Solomon continues speaking of his loving desire to possess her in intimate marital union.

6. *Until the day break, and the shadows flee away, I will get me to the mountain of myrrh, and to the hill of frankincense.*
7. *Thou art all fair, my love; there is no spot in thee.*
8. *Come with me from Lebanon, my spouse, with me from Lebanon: look from the top of Amana, from the top of Shenir and Hernon, from the lions' dens, from the mountains of the leopards.*
9. *Thou hast ravished my heart, my sister, my spouse; Thou hast ravished my heart with one of thine eyes, with one chain of thy neck.*

He longs to spend the entire night after the wedding in sharing his love with Naamah, comparing her beautiful form to a mountain of sweet-smelling myrrh and frankincense, which he will "climb" as it were, to claim her fully. Now that she is fully one with him, he can say she is "*all* fair;" before he had called her the "fairest among women" (Song of Sol. 1:8), as well as "fair" (Song of Sol. 1:15, 16; 4:1) and "my fair one" (Song of Sol. 2:10, 13). But now he can see that she is "all fair," there is "no spot" in her (Song of Sol. 4:7).

It is as though they were ascending together the great plateau of Lebanon or the hill of Amana in Syria, or even the highest peak in Mount Hermon (same as Senir), some 9,200 feet in elevation, in Israel's far north, where the lions and leopards had their lairs. He tells her she has "ravished" — that is, "completed, enclosed" — his heart, with one of her beautiful necklaces, as it were, or even just with one of her eyes.

Note the unique appellation with which he endows her here — "my sister, my spouse." This is the second time she is actually called his spouse (the first is in the previous verse). There can be no doubt that they are properly married when they are thus making love, and that these passionate expressions of love in both word and deed are therefore worthy of divine approval. But to call her also his sister would indicate that they are united spiritually as well as physically. They are becoming "one flesh," as intended for Adam and Eve (Gen. 2:24) and also "one spirit" (1 Cor. 6:17), as intended for all who belong to Christ.

Song of Solomon 4:10–16

Most of the rest of the chapter records the even more lovingly intimate thoughts and words of Solomon to his bride.

10. *How fair is thy love, my sister, my spouse! how much better is thy love than wine! and the smell of thine ointments than all spices!*
11. *Thy lips, O my spouse, drop as the honeycomb: honey and milk are under thy tongue; and the smell of thy garments is like the smell of Lebanon.*
12. *A garden inclosed is my sister, my spouse; a spring shut up, a fountain sealed.*
13. *Thy plants are an orchard of pomegranates, with pleasant fruits; camphire, with spikenard.*
14. *Spikenard and saffron; calamus and cinnamon, with all trees of frankincense; myrrh and aloes, with all the chief spices:*
15. *A fountain of gardens, a well of living waters, and streams from Lebanon.*

*16. Awake, O north wind: and come, thou south; blow upon my
garden, that the spices may flow out. Let my beloved come into
his garden, and eat his pleasant fruits.*

Again he calls her "my sister, my spouse" (verses 10, 12), as he does
in Song of Solomon 5:1. The Hebrew word translated "spouse" in Song
of Solomon is translated "bride" when used elsewhere, and could just as
well be so applied here.

Her pre-marital chastity is referred to several times by the bridegroom,
a history which he deeply appreciates. He calls her "a garden inclosed, a
spring shut up, a fountain sealed," but a garden which he is about to enter,
a spring he will open, a fountain soon to become a well of living waters,
now that she has become his bride.

His prospect naturally constrains us to compare it to the promise of
the Lord Jesus Christ to the woman at the well in Samaria. "The water
that I shall give him shall be in him a well of water springing up into everlasting life" (John 4:14). Then, later he said to the people in Jerusalem,
"He that believeth on me, as the scripture hath said, out of his belly shall
flow rivers of living water" (John 7:38).

Solomon's loving appeal to Naamah is answered quickly, as she re-
sponds, "Let my beloved come into his garden [note that it is no longer her
garden!] and eat his pleasant fruits." As already seen in earlier chapters,
she loves and desires him as much as he does her. Although the text itself
never directly mentions God or His holy plan for marriage and family, it
does seem very clear that this love of Solomon and Naamah, so beautifully
memorialized in his Song of Songs, was ordained by their Creator.

God had called Solomon to be king of His chosen nation even before
he was born, and the future establishment of his everlasting kingdom, as
promised to David, obviously must include a properly prepared wife for
Solomon. The deep love passionately expressed for each other by both
Solomon and Naamah, by all reason, must surely have had its source in
the One who *is* love. This inference is confirmed by the fact that, by the
leading of God, both the ancient Jewish teachers and the early church
fathers of Christianity unanimously agreed that Song of Solomon was
part of the canon of Scriptures.

Naamah's Dream and Testimony

Song of Solomon 5:1–7

Naamah's invitation was quickly accepted, and Solomon entered his
garden.

*1. I am come into my garden, my sister, my spouse: I have gath-
ered my myrrh with my spice; I have eaten my honeycomb with*

my honey; I have drunk my wine with my milk: eat, O friends; drink, yea: drink abundantly, O beloved.

2. *I sleep, but my heart waketh: it is the voice of my beloved that knocketh, saying, Open to me, my sister, my love, my dove, my undefiled: for my hand is filled with dew, and my locks with the drops of the night.*

3. *I have put off my coat; how shall I put it on? I have washed my feet: how shall I defile them?*

4. *My beloved put in his hand by the hole of the door, and my bowels were moved for him.*

5. *I rose up to open to my beloved; and my hands dropped with myrrh, and my fingers with sweet smelling myrrh, upon the handles of the lock.*

6. *I opened to my beloved; but my beloved had withdrawn himself, and was gone: my soul failed when he spake: I sought him, but I could not find him; I called him, but he gave me no answer.*

7. *The watchmen that went about the city found me, they smote me, they wounded me; the keepers of the walls took away my veil from me.*

Just after the bridegroom describes the love of their wedding night, using the lovely analogies of the garden, the honeycomb and the wine, it seems that someone — perhaps God himself — offers His encouragement and approval. "Eat, O friends," he is saying, "drink, yea drink abundantly, O beloved" (verse 1). We are reminded again of God's creation of man and woman, and Christ's acknowledgement that in the act of marriage they become "one flesh" (Matt. 19:5). God has assured us that "marriage is honorable in all, and the bed undefiled" (Heb. 13:4).

After they finish for the night, they drift off to sleep. But then Naamah has a strange dream. "I sleep," she says, speaking of her body, "but my heart waketh." She dreams that her new husband has gone somewhere and returned, seeking entrance again to her chamber. She hesitates, having settled in for the night. She quickly changes her mind, however, when she sees his hand reaching inside searching for the door latch. Her desire for his love overpowers her hesitation and she hurries to open the door, only to find him gone — apparently discouraged by her seeming coolness toward his call.

She then — still in her dream — hurriedly dons her coat and veil and sets out in the night to find him and call him back to her wedding chamber. But she cannot find him; instead the city's night watchmen find *her*, and rebuke and wound her, snatching off her veil, evidently thinking she is a harlot.

This particular scene, incidentally, proves this is all a dream. No watchman would dare treat Solomon's new bride, whom they undoubtedly would recognize, in such a fashion as this.

Song of Solomon 5:8–9

Suddenly, the dream scene changes. Instead of the rude watchmen, Naamah sees her new friends, the "daughters of Jerusalem."

8. *I charge you, O daughters of Jerusalem, if ye find my beloved, that ye tell him that I am sick of love.*
9. *What is thy beloved more than another beloved, O thou fairest among women? what is thy beloved more than another beloved; that thou dost so charge us?*

The daughters of Jerusalem were, presumably, regular maiden attendants at the royal courts, so Naamah assumes they might know where to find him.

Instead of expressing interest or sympathy, however, these young women respond in petulance. "Why should we seek *your* loved one?" they seem to be saying. "What is so special about *him*?" In real life, they would know very well what was special about Solomon — they were probably envious of Naamah, in fact — but, remember, this is a dream!

Song of Solomon 5:10–16

In any case, their question gives Naamah an opportunity to respond in what is surely one of the most beautiful passages in the Song of Solomon.

10. *My beloved is white and ruddy, the chiefest among ten thousand.*
11. *His head is as the most fine gold, his locks are bushy, and black as a raven.*
12. *His eyes are as the eyes of doves by the rivers of waters, washed with milk, and fitly set.*
13. *His cheeks are as a bed of spices, as sweet flowers: his lips like lilies, dropping sweet smelling myrrh.*
14. *His hands are as gold rings set with the beryl: his belly is as bright ivory overlaid with sapphires.*
15. *His legs are as pillars of marble, set upon sockets of fine gold: his countenance is as Lebanon, excellent as the cedars.*
16. *His mouth is most sweet: yea, he is altogether lovely. This is my beloved, and this is my friend, O daughters of Jerusalem.*

Whether Solomon really looked like this might be a question, but Naamah viewed him thus in her dream (presumably she later told about her dream search to Solomon, who eventually incorporated it in his "Song of Songs").

In any case, it may not be too far-fetched to see this wonderful dream as a divinely revealed spiritual vision of the greater Son of Solomon, as He would someday be seen spiritually by His own dear bride, the assembled church of all the redeemed. For example, "white and ruddy" is literally "dazzling white and red," speaking of both His perfect righteousness and His sacrificial blood offered up for our sins. He is the spotless Lamb of God, "slain from the foundation of the world" (Rev. 13:8).

The descriptor "chiefest among ten thousand" was a common expression in Israel meaning, simply, "greatest of all." Solomon was, indeed, the greatest earthly king for a brief moment in history, but Christ will be King of kings forever.

The Gospels reveal nothing of the physical appearance of the human Jesus, but perhaps the fine gold speaks of a kingly crown on His head, and the bushy black locks of youthful vigor. In His human incarnation, He lived and died as a young man, but as our Creator, He is the "Ancient of days" (Dan. 7:9). When He later appeared to John in His glorified human body, "His head and His hairs were white like wool, as white as snow" (Rev. 1:14).

His eyes, appearing as the eyes of doves by rivers of waters would remind us that Jesus' eyes were often wet with tears because of sin and unbelief on the part of those whom He had created. One day, however, "His eyes [will be] as a flame of fire" (Rev. 1:14, 19:12).

In the vision, Naamah sees her beloved as having a beautiful countenance, like spices and flowers, with scent of myrrh. In Christ's humiliation, however, "His visage was so marred more than any man" (Isa. 52:14), and "when we shall see him, there is no beauty that we should desire him" (Isa. 53:2). But when He comes in glory, we shall see "His face as the appearance of lightning" (Dan. 10:6).

His lips were "like lilies, dripping sweet smelling myrrh." Even His enemies recognized that "never man spake like this man" (John 7:46), even as Solomon was recognized far and wide for his wisdom of speech. But when Christ comes again, men will hear "His voice as the sound of many waters" (Rev. 1:15), and "like the voice of a multitude" (Dan. 10:6).

His hands, "as gold rings" once blessed little children and healed the sick, but then they were nailed to a cross with cruel spikes. Yet He holds the whole wide world in His hand, "upholding all things" (Heb. 1:3).

His belly (or better, "body") was so bruised by the beatings after His mock trial that "his form" no longer even looked like a man, disfigured "more than the sons of men" (Isa. 52:14). But He "bare our sins in his own body on the tree" (1 Pet. 2:24) and He now has a "glorious body" (Phil. 3:21), alive forevermore.

His legs, seen by Naamah as "pillars of marble, set upon sockets of fine gold" will one day soon be set astride both land and sea (Rev. 10:2). His countenance, excellent as the mighty cedars of Lebanon, in that coming day will be "as the sun shineth in his strength" (Rev. 1:16). His mouth, "most sweet," with grace poured into His lips (Ps. 45:2), will soon breathe out "a sharp sword, that with it he should smite the nations" (Rev. 19:15).

Finally, the bride describes her bridegroom as "altogether lovely," and no doubt she sincerely thought of Solomon, her loved one, in this way. But her words (as reported by Solomon) could really be literally true of no one but the Lord Jesus Christ, perfect in His humanity and perfect throughout all eternity as our Lord of lords and King of kings.

In Praise of Naamah's Beauty

Song of Solomon 6:1-3

Naamah's high praise of her beloved changes the attitude of the daughters of Jerusalem from one of petulant indifference to one of excited concern.

1. *Whither is thy beloved gone, O thou fairest among women? whither is thy beloved turned aside? that we may seek him with thee.*
2. *My beloved is gone down into his garden, to the beds of spices, to feed in the gardens, and to gather lilies.*
3. *I am my beloved's, and my beloved is mine: he feedeth among the lilies.*

When we speak sincerely of the love of Christ and our love for Him, as Naamah did of Solomon, then (like the daughters of Jerusalem) others will want to know Him, too.

Although the poetic language of the Song tends to make transitions from one "scene" to another somewhat ambiguous, it seems most likely that this sudden interest in finding Solomon on the part of the maidens was enough of a surprise to cause Naamah to waken out of her dream.

She realizes her loved one has not really forsaken her, nor is he lost somewhere. It is just that he is temporarily away on other important duties. After all, he is a king. He has gone off to work in another "garden" for a time. This "garden" is not, however, another wife, but rather some duty of state which Naamah may not know. To reassure herself and others, however, she insists again that he and she belong to each other, without any question. At this time, at least, she is his first and only true love. He is young and the wedding ceremony is only a short time past. She knows he will return shortly, for he wants to be with her as much as she wants to be with him.

Song of Solomon 6:4–10

As if to answer her unspoken plea, Solomon does quickly arrive again at the palace where his bride is waiting, and there is no lessening of his love and admiration for the beautiful young Naamah.

4. *Thou art beautiful, O my love, as Tirzah, comely as Jerusalem, terrible as an army with banners.*

5. *Turn away thine eyes from me, for they have overcome me: thy hair is as a flock of goats that appear from Gilead.*

6. *Thy teeth are as a flock of sheep which go up from the washing, whereof every one beareth twins, and there is not one barren among them.*

7. *As a piece of a pomegranate are thy temples within thy locks.*

8. *There are threescore queens and fourscore concubines and virgins without number.*

9. *My dove, my undefiled is but one; she is the only one of her mother, she is the choice one of her that bare her. The daughters saw her, and blessed her; yea, the queens and the concubines, and they praised her.*

10. *Who is she that looketh forth as the morning, fair as the moon, clear as the sun, and terrible as an army with banners?*

As he returns, Solomon again is effusive in his praise of his wife's beauty. As before, his analogies are strange to our western ears, but evidently very meaningful and expressive in the context of their time and place. He compares her beauty to that of two cities, Tirzah and Jerusalem. Tirzah was a lovely city on a high hill in the territory of Manasseh, later chosen by Jeroboam as the capital of the northern kingdom of Israel. Jerusalem, of course, was the capital of all Israel until the kingdom was divided under Rehoboam, and has continued as the capital of Judah — and of modern Israel — until this present day. The Psalmist has said that Jerusalem was "beautiful for situation, the joy of the whole earth" (Ps. 48:2).

Not only beautiful like a great city was Naamah, but also "terrible as an army with banners" — a simile used twice, in fact, in verses 4 and 10. She was so beautiful as almost to cause awe in the eyes of a beholder, like a great army with unfurled battle flags. Her very eyes were almost too lovely and penetrating to gaze into.

Then, strangely, in verses 5b, 6, and 7, Solomon repeats the complimentary comparisons he had used just before the wedding night (see Song of Sol. 4:1–3). Remarkable indeed are the sights his bride makes him think about! She is like a great city, like a conquering army, like a flock of goats descending a mountain, like a flock of shorn and fruitful sheep, like an armory tower — but also like a slice of pomegranate, a thread of scarlet, and two young roes feeding among the lilies! Solomon had called her a mountain of myrrh and a hill of frankincense, as well as a fountain of gardens, a well of living waters, and streams from the mountains of Lebanon (Song of Sol. 4:4–6, 15). Her royal mien and her queenly beauty must have been something to see!

He also deemed her superior to 60 queens, 80 royal concubines and innumerable virgins who might have been candidates for a king's court. These were not in Solomon's harem — at least not yet — for he was still young and Naamah was his first bride and only true love. Quite possibly, they had been guests at the wedding, and all of them — perhaps in spite of themselves — could not help but bless and praise lovely Naamah.

Solomon had also met and been approved by Naamah's mother (see Song of Sol. 3:4), and he was appreciative of her influence in raising Naamah, evidently her only daughter.

He concluded this song of praise of his beloved bride with a striking rhetorical question, Just who *was* this remarkable young woman he had married, "fair as the moon, clear as the sun, and terrible as an army with banners?" Even the great King Solomon, son of David, was in awe of her, even as she was of him. They were, quite probably, intended by the Holy Spirit (who was, behind the scenes, so to speak, guiding Solomon in his writing) to serve as types of Christ and the Church, and thus both seem larger than life.

Solomon, however, later proved very humanly fallible, and probably so did Naamah. Solomon almost certainly continued to love her most of all, as intimated in a number of passages in Proverbs and Ecclesiastes, but he eventually acquired many other wives and concubines, at least in name. Naamah bore his son Rehoboam, but (for whatever reason) Rehoboam himself was so flawed in character that he eventually saw most of his father's kingdom taken away from him by Jeroboam.

Despite such later failures, however, these first years of the marriage of Solomon and Naamah were almost idyllic, and so could well serve at least as a type, if not a full allegory, of the relation of Christ and His bride, the true Church, consisting of all true believers/followers of Christ, redeemed by grace through faith in His saving gospel.

Song of Solomon 6:11–13

At this point, the scene and emphasis suddenly change. Naamah is speaking and telling one of her own experiences some time later.

11. *I went down into the garden of nuts to see the fruits of the valley, and to see whether the vine flourished and the pomegranates budded.*

12. *Or ever I was aware, my soul made me like the chariots of Ammi-nadib.*

13. *Return, return, O Shulamite: return, return, that we may look upon thee. What will ye see in the Shulamite? As it were the company of two armies.*

Before Solomon had met her and won her for his bride, Naamah had had possessions of her own, evidently including an orchard garden and vineyard, as well as flocks of animals. Since her involvement with Solomon, however, she had paid little attention to them (Song of Sol. 1:6), assuming her brothers would care for them. Now, however, while Solomon was away for a while, she went back home to see how her trees and vines were doing.

Before she knew it, however, her thoughts carried her back again to the palace and her beloved Solomon, as though she were being transported back in a swift chariot belonging to Amminadib, evidently a friend with a stable of fine horses. Alternatively, since this man is mentioned nowhere else, this word could be translated as something like "the prince's people" (*ammi* is "people," *nadib* is most often translated "prince"), so it possibly could refer to Prince Solomon's charioteers.

In any case, Naamah wanted to hurry back to Solomon. She could seem to hear (in her mind's ear, so to speak) the daughters of Jerusalem calling her to return. It is here in this call that Naamah is called, for the first and only time, "the Shulamite," and there has been much speculation about what this might mean.

Although no town called Shulam is mentioned in the Bible, it is just possible that there may once have been such a town in the country of Ammon, which was Naamah's native land. However, the name "Shulamite" is said to mean "peaceful," the same as "Solomon." In calling her, at least in Naamah's day-dreaming about it, it may seem that they were recognizing her as so like Solomon in temperament and mutual love that they had indeed become "one flesh."

One wonders why Solomon never used the actual name of his loved one in his Song of Songs. He does use his own name no less than seven times, so why not his bride's? Her name means "pleasantness" and it is perhaps hinted at twice (Song of Sol. 1:16; 7:6), but never used directly. As discussed before, there does seem to be good reason to believe that she was Naamah, the mother of Rehoboam, but (whoever she was) Solomon evidently wanted just to use intimate terms of love when speaking to or about her in his Song. This is not so unusual, after all, for it is rather typical even today for husbands who truly love their wives (or songwriters who write love songs about their wives or sweethearts) to do this very thing.

There is another intriguing question raised in verse 13. Why did these daughters of Jerusalem want to "look upon" the Shulamite when she returned? The answer given is "as it were the company of two armies." But what is that?

The interesting fact is that the Hebrew word for "company" is translated in its every other occurrence as "dance" or "dances." Furthermore, "two armies" is the Hebrew *Mahanaim*, the name of a town later built at the site where Jacob had met an angelic host (Gen. 32:2). This name, meaning literally "two hosts," was given to the place by Jacob in recognition that, in facing Esau, he was accompanied not only by his own family and small body of servants but also by the great army of God.

Thus it seems that an intimate wedding dance had been developed commemorating this ancient encounter with God's host, somehow reflected in the marital encounter of bride and bridegroom, and it was customary for a bride to perform the dance for her new husband. Naamah had evidently not yet done this for Solomon, and the daughters of Jerusalem wanted her to return and do it. The dance, of course, would be intended only for the eyes of her husband, but the other maidens, impressed with the unique beauty of Naamah, could at least picture it in their minds' eyes, and were anxious for Solomon himself to enjoy it.

The Wedding Dance

Song of Solomon 7:1–9

The mention of the traditional "dance of the two hosts" serves to introduce the actual dance. Solomon now is the enraptured speaker as he observes his beautiful bride perform her dance of love. They are all alone, so it is natural for her to dance free of clothing, thereby enabling her beloved to rapturously enjoy her total beauty.

1. *How beautiful are thy feet with shoes, O prince's daughter! The joints of thy thighs are like jewels, the work of the hands of a cunning workman.*
2. *Thy navel is like a round goblet, which wanteth not liquor: thy belly is like an heap of wheat set round about with lilies.*
3. *Thy two breasts are like two young roes that are twins.*
4. *Thy neck is as a tower of ivory; thine eyes like the fishpools in Heshbon, by the gate of Bath-rabbim: thy nose is as the tower of Lebanon which looketh toward Damascus.*
5. *Thine head upon thee is like Carmel, and the hair of thine head like purple; the king is held in the galleries.*
6. *How fair and how pleasant art thou, O love, for delights!*
7. *This thy stature is like to a palm tree, and thy breasts to clusters of grapes.*

8. *I said, I will go up to the palm tree, I will take hold of the boughs thereof: now also thy breasts shall be as clusters of the vine, and the smell of thy nose like apples;*

9. *And the roof of thy mouth like the best wine for my beloved, that goeth down sweetly, causing the lips of those that are asleep to speak.*

As Solomon watches Naamah perform her graceful dance of submissive love, he describes in elegant metaphors her physical beauty, beginning with her sandal-shod feet (evidently her only article of clothing) then proceeding upward to her thighs and joints, her navel and belly, her breasts and neck, her eyes and nose, and finally her head and hair. The similes he employs in each case are — as in his previous poems of praise — strikingly picturesque, no doubt more full of meaning to her (and to his contemporary readers in Israel) than to us today, but still enchantingly beautiful. The place-names which he mentions refer to a high hill in Israel (Carmel), an ancient city in Syria (Damascus), a Moabite city just east of the Jordan (Heshbon), and a gate in that city opening toward the city of Rabbah in Ammon (Bath-rabbim). One assumes that Naamah, with her background in Ammon, would be familiar with the beautiful fishbowls by the gate of Bath-Rabbim, and would be pleased when Solomon compared them to her eyes.

The word "galleries" in verse 4 is elsewhere always translated as "gutters" or "troughs," and probably refers in context to the flowing "tresses" of Naamah's hair, to which Solomon was referring as he completed his survey of her beautiful form. As his eyes had moved up from toe to head, his gaze was there "held captive," as it were, by her hair "like purple threads" flowing down across her shoulders. She had compared his head to a kingly crown of gold (Song of Sol. 5:11); now he likens *her* head to a queenly crown of royal purple.

Next, in verse 6, he summarizes his survey by exclaiming that her "delights" are "fair" and "pleasant." The word for "pleasant" (Hebrew *naam*) just might be a play on her own name (recall that Naamah means "pleasantness"). "How delightful is my loved one, beautiful Naamah!" he could be saying, though using a shortened, more intimate, form of her name.

He also summarizes his survey of her features by likening her whole figure to a stately palm tree, with its "clusters" (presumably of dates, the words "of grapes" are not in the Hebrew text) compared to his wife's breasts.

Solomon can restrain his ardor no longer. He must go up to his beautiful palm tree and take hold of its boughs. The word for "boughs" is used only this one time in the Bible, and may possibly refer to the trees' fruit stalks. He delicately refers now to his initiation of intimate lovemaking with his beloved bride.

The phrase "roof of thy mouth" in verse 9 is only one word in the original (*chels*), and is also translated simply as "*mouth*" (e.g., Prov. 8:7) or "*taste*" (e.g., Ps. 119:103). It is even so translated here in Solomon's Song, when Naamah says that "his fruit was sweet to my taste" (Song of Sol. 2:3). It is rendered by the phrase "roof of the mouth" four other times (Job 29:10; Ps. 137:6; Lam. 4:4; Ezek. 3:26). The word can assume these three slightly different connotations, with the context governing which is appropriate in a given case.

The final part of verse 9 is problematic in meaning. The word for "lips" can have a very wide variety of meanings, and the word for "causing to speak" occurs only this one time. The words "those that are" are not in the original. Possibly in the context, the intent of Solomon was to stress that the beauty of Naamah and her dance would elicit praise and excitement even while sleeping.

Song of Solomon 7:10–13

Solomon's ardent expressions of admiration and desire had culminated in his claiming Naamah in total physical union, and she had willingly and joyfully submitted, making only one happy comment as she yields.

10. *I am my beloved's, and his desire is toward me.*
11. *Come, my beloved, let us go forth into the field; let us lodge in the villages.*
12. *Let us get up early to the vineyards; let us see if the vine flourish, whether the tender grape appear, and the pomegranates bud forth: there will I give thee my loves.*
13. *The mandrakes give a smell, and at our gates are all manner of pleasant fruits, new and old, which I have laid up for thee, O my beloved.*

When Naamah says, "I am my beloved's," we are to understand that her submission to her beloved bridegroom is total. "His desire" refers to sexual desire, and it is directed fully toward his bride. The same rare Hebrew word was used by God in His statement to Eve (after she had led Adam to disobey God's command) as follows: ". . . and thy desire shall be to thy husband" (Gen. 3:16).

The last three verses of the chapter evidently refer either to the next morning or, perhaps, to a later time altogether. Naamah is speaking, and suggesting that they go together (instead of going alone, as she had done before) to see how their mutual vineyards and orchards are doing. But this will not detract from their lovemaking. They can stay overnight in the outlying villages, or even in the fields — "*there* will I give thee my loves," she promises.

She mentions the availability of ripe mandrakes, which were believed in the ancient world to be aphrodisiacs (note Gen. 30:14–16). This leads her on to promise her beloved, not just grapes and pomegranates, but "all manner of pleasant fruits, new and old" — obviously referring to the erotic fruits of their love which they would enjoy away from the palace and the vicarious joys of the daughters of Jerusalem.

This particular chapter of the Song of Solomon, even more than the rest of the book, is obviously erotic in tone, but it is what might be called sanctified eroticism, rather than prurient. God created man and woman, with the instruction to be fruitful and multiply, and He was gracious to make the process enjoyable as well as purposeful. It is true that sin had introduced a significant element of suffering and sorrow into the bearing of children. Nevertheless, the marvelous phenomena of sexual love and reproduction, with the amazing complex of mechanisms involved, could never have originated by some random evolutionary process. God created it all, and He has, in effect, reminded us of its grandeur by including this beautiful Song of Solomon in His divinely inspired Scriptures.

We remember again that God has said that "marriage is honourable in all, and the bed undefiled" (Heb. 13:4). At the same time, the very same verse warns that "whoremongers and adulterers God will judge." Marital love, with all the delights available to husbands and their wives therewith (as to Solomon and Naamah) is pleasing in God's sight, but sexual commerce in any other form (note that the Greek word translated "whoremongers" in Hebrews 13:4 can also apply to any type of fornication) is very displeasing to Him, though He is also a forgiving God. As Solomon said in one of his later writings, "God hath made man upright; but they have sought out many inventions" (Eccles. 7:29).

You Can't Go Home Again

Song of Solomon 8:1–4

Naamah had persuaded Solomon to go back to her home for a visit, to see how the vineyards and flocks were faring, and also to visit her family. She had said — and no doubt believed — that their time together on what could be considered a honeymoon trip would be even better than back in the palace. But it would not work out quite as hoped.

1. *O that thou wert as my brother, that sucked the breasts of my mother! when I should find thee without, I would kiss thee; yea, I should not be despised.*

2. *I would lead thee, and bring thee into my mother's house, who would instruct me: I would cause thee to drink of spiced wine of the juice of my pomegranate.*
3. *His left hand should be under my head, and his right hand should embrace me.*
4. *I charge you, O daughters of Jerusalem, that ye stir not up, nor awake my love, until he please.*

Apparently, Naamah's brothers were not as pleased to see Solomon with their sister as she had thought they would be. Even though Solomon was a king, and Naamah was supremely happy as his bride, they were both made to feel uncomfortable with any open display of affection. Perhaps because her people were of a conquered nation (the Ammonites) and also because Solomon was an absentee landlord and of much higher social status than they, or for some more subtle complex of reasons, it was not easy for the royal couple.

Naamah had looked forward to talking again with her mother, who had once been so close to her, and she wanted to share some of the pomegranate wine from her own trees with Solomon. She also would like to have Solomon make love to her there, as she may once have dreamed about in the early days of their acquaintance.

But it could never work out that way. Her brothers had long protected her and her mother had counseled her, and now things were different. All of them tried, no doubt, to be gracious and considerate to each other, but it was strained.

The mention of wine in verse 2 of this chapter, incidentally, is the sixth and last reference to wine in the Song (1:2, 4; 4:10; 5:1; 7:9; 8:2), and it is significant that none of these hint of any drunkenness involved. Solomon himself frequently rebuked the use of the fruit of the vine or the pomegranate or any other source to induce drunkenness (note Prov. 20:1; 23:20–21; 23:29–35; 31:4–5; etc.). The same Hebrew word is used to indicate both unfermented wine and fermented wine, and it can usually be assumed that the wine mentioned in the Bible is non-intoxicating fruit juice whenever it is not associated with drunkenness.

In verse 4 of this chapter, Naamah repeats her warning of Song 2:7, urging her maiden friends not to stir up their desire for sexual love until marriage (see comments on Song 2:7). She remembers the concern of her older brothers that she keep herself sexually pure until marriage, and it had resulted eventually in her being chosen by Solomon for his bride. It had been well worth maintaining her virginity, even though the Ammonite society in general was largely an immoral society.

Song of Solomon 8:5–7

The scene suddenly changes again, as an old family friend or relative sees Solomon and Naamah approaching a site that has special memories for them.

5. *Who is this that cometh up from the wilderness, leaning upon her beloved? I raised thee up under the apple tree: there thy mother brought thee forth: there she brought thee forth that bare thee.*

6. *Set me as a seal upon thine heart, as a seal upon thine arm: for love is strong as death; jealousy is cruel as the grave: the coals thereof are coals of fire, which hath a most vehement flame.*

7. *Many waters cannot quench love, neither can the floods drown it: if a man would give all the substance of his house for love, it would utterly be contemned.*

The friend (or relative) who is speaking poses what seems to be a rhetorical question, asking "Who is this?" but realizing that it is Naamah returning home, this time with her bridegroom and clearly showing her love for him. The phrase "raised thee up" actually has the connotation of "awakened thee." It is the same phrase translated "stir up" three times in the Song (2:7; 3:5; 8:4). This friend — or possibly Naamah's aunt or grandmother — reminds her that it was she who taught and counseled Naamah in former days under the familiar apple tree, preparing her for the time when she would meet and marry a husband. It was under that same apple tree that Naamah's mother made a sacred pledge regarding Naamah. The Hebrew word for "brought thee forth" is never so translated anywhere else; it is usually translated "pledged" or "took a pledge." In the context, it seems most likely that Naamah is being reminded how this teaching and her mother's pledge had confirmed her intent to wait for love until the one man for whom she was intended would come to meet and marry her. And now, finally, here they were — coming up from the wilderness together, to the old apple tree!

Then Naamah, having been reminded of her mother's pledge, speaks to her husband, urging him to seal the pledge himself, placing her like a seal on his arm and in his heart. She realizes how desirable her husband may be to the other maidens of the court, or may become to others later, and is fearful of the fires of jealousy that this could kindle in her own heart.

But Solomon, in response, assures her that his love for her is like a fire itself, so strong that no floods could ever quench it. It was, he insisted, worth more to him than everything else he possessed.

Assuming this is what Solomon was writing here in his Song of Songs
— and this seems the most natural way of understanding these verses (although we need to remember that poetic license may make it difficult to
sort everything out with precision), then we must wonder what happened
to these flames in later years, when Solomon began to multiply wives and
concubines in his harem. We can at least hope that his love for Naamah
did remain as strong as he had promised, and that his harem was strictly
for politics and prestige rather than love or lust. There are certain hints
to this effect in Proverbs and Ecclesiastes.

Song of Solomon 8:8–12

At this point, Naamah's older brothers come upon the scene, either at
the apple tree or later at the vineyards. They had been caring for Naamah's
possessions while she was gone, and still felt responsible to look after her
welfare, just as they had while she was growing up. They had been angry with
her to some degree for leaving (Song of Sol. 1:6), and now remind her how
they had protected her, also wanting to let Solomon know their concerns.

8. *We have a little sister, and she hath no breasts: what shall we
   do for our sister in the day when she shall be spoken for?*
9. *If she be a wall, we will build upon her a palace of silver: and if
   she be a door, we will inclose her with bands of cedar.*
10. *I am a wall, and my breasts like towers: then was I in his eyes
    as one that found favour.*
11. *Solomon had a vineyard at Baal-hamon; he let out the vineyard
    unto keepers; every one for the fruit thereof was to bring a
    thousand pieces of silver.*
12. *My vineyard, which is mine, is before me: thou, O Solomon
    must have a thousand, and those that keep the fruit thereof two
    hundred.*

It may not be clear whether Naamah's brothers at this point are just
reminding the young couple how they had cared for her as she was growing up or whether they actually still had a younger sister at home and
were reminding Naamah by way of the example of how they were still
protecting her little sister, as they had cared for her earlier.

In either case they were using the metaphor of the door and the wall.
If she were inclined to be an easily opened door to any young man who
made advances to her, they would enclose her within a house of strong
cedar timbers for protection. If, however, she proved herself to be a strong
wall through which none could pass until the time was right, they would
build around her a lovely silver palace within which to display her beauty
and desirability.

Naamah responded in appreciation, noting that she had indeed been as a wall until full grown as a young woman ready for marriage. As a result, when Solomon finally met her, she did find favor in the eyes of the king himself, and now she had come home as his bride.

Then she mentions that Solomon had leased out a vineyard to "keepers" in return for an annual payment of a thousand pieces of silver. This vineyard was in a place called Baal-Hamon, but the location is not clear, since this is the only reference to it in the Bible. Possibly the keepers were Naamah's brothers, and, if so, this was probably how Solomon met Naamah.

But Naamah also had a vineyard of her own, which she could no longer care for herself. Therefore, she offered to lease it to her brothers on a similar basis. They would pay Solomon a thousand pieces of silver, which would leave them at least the equivalent of two hundred pieces each year for themselves.

Finally, with all the personal and family business taken care of, Naamah is ready to devote her full time and attention to her husband and her responsibilities as his queen and the mother of his future children.

Song of Solomon 8:13–14

For a short time, Naamah had to be with her family and friends, but now she could turn back to Solomon, and to their "gardens" of love for each other.

13. *Thou that dwellest in the gardens, the companions hearken to thy voice: cause me to hear it.*
14. *Make haste, my beloved, and be thou like to a roe or to a young hart upon the mountains of spices.*

These are the concluding verses of Solomon's Song, as he hears the voice of his beloved calling him to come to her, now that she has finished with her necessary personal commitments.

She calls to him, addressing him as "thou that dwellest in the gardens." To her, he is not so much a king in his royal palace as he is a man devoted to caring for the plants and animals of God's creation. She first met him as one dwelling in gardens, so to speak, and their happiest and most joyful times had been spent in such settings. She had mentioned his "companions" and their flocks once before (Song of Sol. 1:7), and while she has been interacting with her family, he has again been out with these companions. He has been conversing with *them*, but now *she wants to hear his voice again!*

"*Make haste*," she calls, urging him *(as she had before — Song of Sol. 2:17) to race like a gazelle or a young stag to her side. She was anxious again to mount with him up on the "hill of frankincense" and "the mountain of myrrh" (Song of Sol. 4:6), there to be with him forever.*

It is noteworthy that the Song of Solomon ends on a very similar note to that with which God has ended His own love song (that is, the Bible) to the men and women He had created for himself. "He which testifieth these things saith, Surely I come quickly. Amen. Even so come, Lord Jesus. The grace of our Lord Jesus Christ be with you all. Amen" (Rev. 22:20–21).

As we have seen, there are a number of passages in the Song of Solomon where the beautiful professions of admiration and love between Solomon and his bride lead one to see therein analogies to the mutual love of Christ and His bride, the Church. In fact, over the centuries, there have been many devout Bible theologians who have treated the entire Song as an allegory of Christ and the Church. It is understandable why they would want to do this, but such an approach necessarily requires very imaginative interpretations in much of the book. It is significant that no New Testament writer ever quotes from the Song or ever refers to it at all, in spite of the fact that marriage itself is often treated as a type of Christ and His church (especially Eph. 5:22–33). Nowhere within the Scriptures themselves is there any intimation whatever that the Song of Solomon is anything but what it seems to be on the surface — that is, a love song in narrative form, and with an interactive dialogue format, composed by Solomon in honor of his first and only true love.

Yet it is also very significant that the Song of Solomon has always been accepted as a part of the canon of divinely inspired Scriptures, by both the devout scribes of the Old Testament (e.g., Ezra) and the fathers of the New Testament church, during both apostolic and later eras. It therefore must have an important instructional purpose for the people of God. It tells us that the God-ordained purpose of marriage is more than merely being fruitful and multiplying, though that indeed was a fundamental part of the Edenic mandate given the human race through Adam and Eve.

True love was to be involved as well; husband and wife were to become "one flesh," in joyful physical love as well as spiritual love. There are many biblical passages assuring us — as does Hebrews 13:4 — that "marriage is honourable" and that the marital "bed [is] undefiled." Furthermore, although God has allowed such distortions of the marriage bond as polygamy and divorce, Christ made it plain that "from the beginning it was not so" (Matt. 19:8). God's will clearly is that there should be just one man for one woman for life. The ability to have children was created not as a mere mechanical process like eating and sleeping, but as one accompanied by physical delights of unique excellence and enjoyment, all in a context involving both body and soul in unity and true love.

This joyful expression of love, of course, was never to be used for mere physiological gratification. Such corruptions of this divinely given process as fornication, adultery, homosexuality, incest, and bestiality have been explicitly forbidden in God's Word, and will certainly be judged. Hebrews 13:4 also reminds us that "whoremongers and adulterers God will judge."

Now, although the institution of marriage is often extolled in the Bible, the Song of Solomon is evidently the only book where the physical delights of love and marriage are set forth so clearly and beautifully. Furthermore, this is done with no reference at all to any reproductive purpose. This surely must mean that — contrary to the opinion of some that procreation is the sole purpose of human sexuality — the physical aspects of marital love are to be enjoyed by husbands and wives regardless of whether or not children are begotten in the process. This is yet another gift of the loving grace of God. In no way does this fact minimize the importance and the blessing of having children in the marriage ("Happy is the man that hath his quiver full of them," according to Ps. 127:5), but this is not its sole purpose.

When Solomon wrote his Song of Songs (under divine inspiration, we must not forget), he was, indeed, writing about true love, courtship and marriage, as God had intended it to be, and as he himself undoubtedly meant his own marriage to be. Unfortunately, many years later, he allowed the desire for political prestige (perhaps lust also, although this is at least doubtful) to come in and undermine his original intention to remain forever true to the wife of his youth and to the God of his father.

He thereby incurred severe divine judgment as a result, and he and his descendants have suffered severely through the years because of it.

But this also yields significant instruction for us who read the Song of Solomon today. May each of us, by the grace of God, determine to do our best to make our own marriage, in all its aspects, conform to God's loving purpose, now and always.

3

Seventeen Sermons for Solomon's Son

Proverbs 1–9

The Book of Proverbs consists of more than just a string of pithy sayings written or collected by Solomon. There are several major divisions, and it was not until the time of Hezekiah, some three hundred years later, that it assumed its present form.

Apart from the seven-verse introduction, the first major segment comprises chapters 1 through 9, apparently written originally by King Solomon to "my son" (e.g., Prov. 1:8). Then, from Proverbs 10:1 through 22:16, there are 375 individual proverbs, each independent of the others.

From Proverbs 22:17 through 24:34 is a short segment attributed to "the wise," containing various wise sayings, each covering several verses. Proverbs 25–29 consists of Solomonic sayings collected by scribes of the time of King Hezekiah. Finally, Proverbs 30 is attributed to "Agur the son of Jakeh" and Proverbs 31 to King Lemuel, both of whom are otherwise unknown.

In any case, Solomon wrote most of the book, and all of it is rich in practical wisdom, undoubtedly reflecting the divine wisdom with which he was endowed by God as he became king (2 Chron. 1:7–12). It was most likely written after the Song of Solomon (written while Solomon was young, just after his marriage to his first and only true love, who was almost certainly Naamah, the mother of Rehoboam (1 Kings 14:21). But it was written *before* Ecclesiastes, when Solomon was an old man, reflecting on the vanity of every pursuit of his life except that of seeking and doing the will of the Creator.

In this present chapter, therefore, we want to explore in some detail his writings in the Book of Proverbs. We can discern therein, between the lines, as it were, further insights into the life of this remarkable man. More importantly, we can learn to apply his divinely inspired words of wisdom to our own lives.

Proverbs 1:1–7

1. *The proverbs of Solomon the son of David, king of Israel;*
2. *To know wisdom and instruction; to perceive the words of understanding;*
3. *To receive the instruction of wisdom, justice, and judgment, and equity;*
4. *To give subtilty to the simple, to the young man knowledge and discretion.*
5. *A wise man will hear, and will increase learning; and a man of understanding shall attain unto wise counsels:*
6. *To understand a proverb, and the interpretation; the words of the wise, and their dark sayings.*
7. *The fear of the LORD is the beginning of knowledge: but fools despise wisdom and instruction.*

In the very first verse, Solomon identifies himself as the author of the Book of Proverbs. According to 1 Kings 4:32, Solomon "spake three thousand proverbs," and there are only about 915 verses in the Book of Proverbs, including the two chapters written by Agur and Lemuel. Less than a third of his proverbs have been included in the book, therefore, but these were the ones appropriated by the Holy Spirit as "given by inspiration of God" (2 Tim. 3:16).

The next six verses outline Solomon's basic purpose in writing (and/or) collecting all these proverbs in one place. Thinking mainly of his own son (presumably Rehoboam) as he was writing, he desired for him to learn the wisdom he himself had been given by the Lord.

There is, however, another possibility that must at least be kept in mind. The second segment of the book, beginning at Proverbs 10:1, is introduced by the words, "The proverbs *of* Solomon." This seems somewhat redundant. It may be, therefore, that Proverbs 1:1 should be read in the sense: "The proverbs *for* Solomon the son of David, king of Israel." The Hebrew preposition could take either meaning, "of" (in the sense of "intended for"), or "of" (in the sense of "written by"), and the context would have to determine which. The context here might slightly favor Davidic authorship (in view of the possible redundancy noted above), but Jewish tradition uniformly attributes it to Solomon.

Thus the exposition here will assume that Solomon is the author, but will keep the other option at least open. In any case, these introductory verses allude to seven different words related to wisdom, all with slightly different emphases. Each of these (wisdom, instruction, understanding, knowledge, discretion, learning, wise counsels) occurs more in Proverbs than in any other book of the Bible. It was Solomon's purpose and desire (possibly David's) that his son be characterized by all these attributes exhibited in full and mature measure.

He also wanted him to be able to understand properly the "proverbs" (or parables — same Hebrew word) and "dark sayings" (often translated as "riddles") of the wise.

But by far the most important truth — both for Solomon and his son, and also for us — is the timeless and vital fact that "the fear of the LORD is the beginning of knowledge." Such a proverb is, if possible, more relevant and urgent in our modern age of science and information — *knowledge*, if you will — than in Solomon's day or any period since. All this vast modern "knowledge," not being founded on the fear of God, is leading rapidly to an atheistic world government, utter amorality, exploding hatreds and violence, and final chaos, if God does not intervene soon with the true knowledge and wisdom and instruction. "Professing themselves to be wise, they became fools" (Rom. 1:22). That was God's verdict on the pantheistic philosophers of the ancient world, and it surely applies even more pungently to the evolutionary atheistic intellectuals of these last days.

Proverbs 1:8–14

8. *My son, hear the instruction of thy father, and forsake not the law of thy mother:*
9. *For they shall be an ornament of grace unto thy head, and chains about thy neck.*
10. *My son, if sinners entice thee, consent thou not.*
11. *If they say, Come with us, let us lay wait for blood, let us lurk privily for the innocent without cause;*
12. *Let us swallow them up alive as the grave, and whole, as those that go down into the pit:*
13. *We shall find all precious substance, we shall fill our houses with spoil:*
14. *Cast in thy lot among us: let us all have one purse.*

Beginning here at Proverbs 1:8 and continuing on through Proverbs 9:18, there are 17 sermons, or lessons, Solomon is seeking to import to Rehoboam and, therefore (since this is all in God's inspired Word), that the Holy Spirit would convey to us. Each of these lessons begins with *"My son"* (Prov. 1:8, 10, 15; 2:1; 3:1, 11, 21; 4:10, 20; 5:1; 6:1, 20; 7:1) or *"Hear, ye children"* (Prov. 4:1; 5:7; 7:24; 8:32). Presumably when he began with "My son," Solomon was thinking particularly of Rehoboam and of young men in general. When he addressed a lesson to "ye children," he was also including his two daughters, Taphath and Basmath (1 Kings 4:11, 15), and all young people in general.

Parenthetically, it is noted again that only three children are listed in Scripture as coming from Solomon. In addition to Rehoboam (whose name means "enlarger"), there were two daughters, Taphath (meaning "ornament") and Basmath (meaning "fragrance"), both of whom married important officers over Solomon's kingdom.

We shall look briefly at each of these 17 sermons, as addressed originally to Solomon's one son and two daughters. The first lesson (verses 8 and 9) consists simply of an introductory exhortation to young Rehoboam (and, indirectly, to all sons of concerned parents) to give obedient heed to the standards and instruction of his parents (in this case, Solomon and Naamah). The exhortation comes with the assurance that such obedience would yield a gracious and attractive character in his life.

It is significant that these lessons are always addressed specifically to "my son," and occasionally to "ye children," but never to "my sons." This fact also supports the inference that Solomon only had one son, and thus probably only one *real* wife out of his hundreds of political wives.

Then follows the second lesson (verses 10–14). At first it seems surprising that it would be necessary to warn any son of Solomon's against taking up with robbers and murderers, especially giving such a warning the first priority in his lessons. How could a scion of wealth ever desire more wealth so desperately as to kill for it?

But teen peer-pressure can be highly intimidating. The very fact that Rehoboam was a child of such privilege would tempt other young men of limited means and conscience themselves to challenge him to commit acts of rebellious disobedience, assuring him that his father would shield him from governmental punishment if they were caught. Solomon, perhaps sensing weaknesses in his son's developing character, evidently felt such a warning, with its shock value, would be necessary right at the beginning.

Proverbs 1:15–19

15. *My son, walk not thou in the way with them; refrain thy foot from their path.*
16. *For their feet run to evil, and make haste to shed blood.*
17. *Surely in vain the net is spread in the sight of any bird.*
18. *And they lay wait for their own blood; they lurk privily for their own lives.*
19. *So are the ways of every one that is greedy of gain; which taketh away the life of the owners thereof.*

The third sermon to "my son" is the sequel to the second. Crime, in the long run, really does *not* pay. Those who "lay wait for blood" (verse 11) really will "lay wait for their own blood" (verse 18). Those who "lurk privily for the innocent" actually "lurk privily for their own lives." Solomon's warning to his own son to be very selective in choosing his companions surely applies at least as strongly today.

Unlike a bird, wise enough to avoid a trap when he sees it being set for him, these evil companions, knowing their course of action will ultimately lead to their own destruction, insist on taking it anyway, and find pleasure in taking others down with them.

Proverbs 1:20–33

20. *Wisdom crieth without: she uttereth her voice in the streets:*
21. *She crieth in the chief place of concourse, in the openings of the gates: in the city she uttereth her words, saying,*
22. *How long, ye simple ones, will ye love simplicity? and the scorners delight in their scorning, and fools hate knowledge?*
23. *Turn you at my reproof: behold, I will pour out my spirit unto you, I will make known my words unto you.*
24. *Because I have called, and ye refused; I have stretched out my hand, and no man regarded;*
25. *But ye have set at nought all my counsel, and would none of my reproof:*
26. *I also will laugh at your calamity; I will mock when your fear cometh;*
27. *When your fear cometh as desolation, and your destruction cometh as a whirlwind; when distress and anguish cometh upon you.*
28. *Then shall they call upon me, but I will not answer: they shall seek me early, but they shall not find me:*
29. *For that they hated knowledge, and did not choose the fear of the LORD:*
30. *They would none of my counsel: they despised all my reproof.*
31. *Therefore shall they eat of the fruit of their own way, and be filled with their own devices.*
32. *For the turning away of the simple shall slay them, and the prosperity of fools shall destroy them.*
33. *But whoso hearkeneth unto me shall dwell safely, and shall be quiet from fear of evil.*

The remaining portion of Solomon's third lesson to his son introduces the conflict between Wisdom and Folly which is repeatedly stressed throughout the Book of Proverbs. Wisdom is first introduced here as personified by a virtuous woman, whereas Folly, or Foolishness, is personified by a strange woman — that is a foreign woman — so named at least ten times in Proverbs. This strange woman is introduced first in the fourth lesson, in Proverbs 2:16. There are both literal and figurative applications of these two "women" and their influence on God's people, as we shall see along the way.

First of all, Wisdom is seen on the lips of the virtuous woman as though she were crying out her counsel in every place of influence. In actuality, of course, such counsel would be coming literally from God's prophets and teachers — and especially from the Holy Scriptures. By any of these or other agencies, the true wisdom rebukes those who scoff or who ignore this counsel (which really comes from God himself) and promises blessing to those who believe and obey.

Wisdom first rebukes those who are scornful of true knowledge, in effect calling them simpletons and fools, but then graciously offers forgiveness and blessing to those who will "turn at my reproof."

And now note a remarkable transition in these words and what follows! Solomon here is no longer offering words of divine wisdom and reproof in terms of his own experience, but rather becomes a spokesman for God himself, evidently under direct inspiration of the Holy Spirit.

Neither he nor the godly woman personifying Wisdom could make the statements that Solomon has written in the remaining words of this third lesson. "Behold, I will pour out my Spirit unto you," we read, and such a promise could come only from God. "I will make known my words unto you" obviously is an assertion made by God — no one else!

Then, however, God issues a strong rebuke: "I have called, and ye refused." Therefore, He issues a terrible word of judgment: "I also will laugh . . . I will mock when your fear cometh. . . . Then shall they call upon me, but I will not answer."

There are very few instances mentioned in Scripture when God laughs — and these few times of divine laughter are never exercised in joy or merriment, but only in derision. Another is in Psalm 2:4. When men seek to dethrone God and ignore His will, the result is merely that "He that sitteth in the heaven shall laugh: the Lord shall have them in derision." Note also Psalm 37:13 and Psalm 59:8.

God often urges men to pray, of course, but there are times when He refuses to answer their prayers, and this is certainly one. The reason in this case is "that they hated knowledge, and did not choose the fear of the LORD." Solomon had noted in the beginning of his counsel that "the fear of the LORD is the beginning of knowledge" (verse 7). The so-called "knowledge" (or "science") of ungodly men is structured around their attempt to ignore God in its development, and it is not surprising that, when calamity comes on them and they call for God's help, He ignores them!

On the other hand, God promises that those who "hearken" unto Him (and this is done essentially by reading, believing, and obeying what He has written in His Word) "shall dwell safely, and shall be quiet from fear of evil."

This assurance marks the end of Solomon's third sermon. Then, in the next lesson, he follows up this discussion by telling how to receive God's guidance and protection, through His Word.

Proverbs 2:1–5

1. *My son, if thou wilt receive my words, and hide my command-ments with thee;*

2. *So that thou incline thine ear unto wisdom, and apply thine heart to understanding;*

3. *Yea, if thou criest after knowledge, and liftest up thy voice for understanding;*

4. *If thou seekest her as silver, and searchest for her as for hid treasures;*

5. *Then shalt thou understand the fear of the LORD, and find the knowledge of God.*

The fourth sermon of Solomon for his son begins with a classic presentation of how to attain a true and in-depth understanding of God's Word and, therefore, of His great plan for His creation and His will for each of us as we prepare to fill our intended place in His creation.

Such knowledge is more than a general and superficial understanding of Scripture and His will, though this must come first. One must first "incline thine ear unto wisdom." But that is not enough. There must develop a deep and intense desire to know the Word of God.

"If thou criest after knowledge, and . . . seekest her as silver, and searchest for her as hid treasures" (note again the personification of Wisdom as a pure and virtuous woman, now, however, to be found in the revealed words of God himself, through the Holy Scriptures), then she can be found. "Then shalt thou understand the fear of the LORD, and find the knowledge of God." Only then, after intense desire, earnest prayer, and diligent study, together with willingness to believe what God has said and obey what He has commanded, only *then* does one find the true knowledge of God.

Proverbs 2:6–9

6. *For the LORD giveth wisdom: out of His mouth cometh knowl-edge and understanding.*

7. *He layeth up sound wisdom for the righteous: He is a buckler to them that walk uprightly.*
8. *He keepeth the paths of judgment, and preserveth the way of His saints.*
9. *Then shalt thou understand righteousness, and judgment, and equity; yea, every good path.*

Thus true wisdom can come only from God, and this was the promised wisdom given to Solomon at the beginning of his reign. Solomon, here in his proverbs, is undoubtedly hoping that his son Rehoboam will diligently seek that wisdom when he inherits the kingdom. Unfortunately, however, when that time eventually came, Rehoboam sought and took counsel from his young contemporaries rather than from his father and his father's God (see 2 Chron. 10:8–15), and the sad result was the loss of much of his kingdom.

But that gives us even greater incentive to search the Scriptures, if we would follow "the good path," the "narrow . . . way which leadeth unto life" (Matt. 6:14), for "out of His mouth cometh knowledge and understanding."

Proverbs 2:10–15

10. *When wisdom entereth into thine heart, and knowledge is pleasant unto thy soul;*
11. *Discretion shall preserve thee, understanding shall keep thee:*
12. *To deliver thee from the way of the evil man, from the man that speaketh froward things;*
13. *Who leave the paths of uprightness, to walk in the ways of darkness;*
14. *Who rejoice to do evil, and delight in the frowardness of the wicked;*
15. *Whose ways are crooked, and they froward in their paths.*

True discretion and understanding are promised, therefore, to those who diligently seek and follow the true wisdom and knowledge. They will prevent one from falling into the traps laid by the evil companions described back in Proverbs 1:10-19, in Solomon's previous lessons for his son.

The old English word "froward," which sadly has fallen out of usage in our modern jargon, is used three times in verses 12, 14, and 15. It expresses the idea of not traveling *toward* God, as we ought, but froward, away from Him. Instead of "toward," it is "untoward," perverse, obstinate. There are four or more Hebrew words that have been translated by "froward," and all mean essentially "perverse." Clearly such an attitude is intensely displeasing to God.

Proverbs 2:16–22

16. *To deliver thee from the strange woman, even from the stranger which flattereth with her words;*
17. *Which forsaketh the guide of her youth, and forgetteth the covenant of her God.*
18. *For her house inclineth unto death, and her paths unto the dead.*
19. *None that go unto her return again, neither take they hold of the paths of life.*
20. *That thou mayest walk in the way of good men, and keep the paths of the righteous.*
21. *For the upright shall dwell in the land, and the perfect shall remain in it.*
22. *But the wicked shall be cut off from the earth, and the transgressors shall be rooted out of it.*

At this point, Solomon introduces his metaphor of "the strange woman" — that is, the foreign woman, the woman from some alien land where the true God (Jehovah, the LORD) was not worshiped. Just as the woman of Proverbs 1:20 personified Wisdom, so now this alien woman personifies Folly. Later, both are discussed as literal women, but here they are being used metaphorically.

All the alien nations, of course, were originally one nation, under the true God, having come from the ark with father Noah after the Flood. At Babel, however, they chose to follow Nimrod, Noah's great-grandson, in rebelling against God. This was wicked foolishness, of course, and God had to scatter them and confuse their languages, causing them to establish some 70 different nations (see Gen. 10). These eventually proliferated into still other nations, all of which (with the exception of a few individuals such as Job) had "forgotten the covenant of their God," as made with father Noah (see Gen. 9:9–17), and had gone after various pagan "gods," representing the fallen "host of heaven," Lucifer and his angels, who were likewise in rebellion against God.

God, therefore, had chosen Abraham to establish an elect nation to maintain the true Wisdom and true worship as over against the alien Wisdom introduced by Nimrod (no doubt as "inspired" by Lucifer, or Satan) and pagan worship carried by the other nations dispersed from Babel. God's true Wisdom is thus represented by the godly Woman of Israel and the false wisdom by the strange woman of the pagan nations.

There are always many attractive features to these false religions (actually variants of the one religion which denies Jehovah as the true Creator).

In effect, the strange woman "flattereth with her words," drawing many into "her house" which eventually "inclineth unto death."

However, as Solomon was seeking to assure Rehoboam, he would be safe from such danger if he would only adhere to the revealed words of true Wisdom, as found only in the Holy Scriptures, which had proceeded from the mouth of the true Creator of all things.

How urgently our modern generation needs this message today! Not only in the many pagan nations, but even in our own, multitudes are following the false wisdom of man-made systems and rejecting the true Wisdom of God the Creator, as recorded in the Bible. One day, "the wicked shall be cut off from the earth," but "the upright shall dwell in the land" forever.

This, of course, is what Solomon desired for his son (and we today for our children, of course), and so the next lesson, or sermon, focuses on practical ways to keep active in serving the true God.

Proverbs 3:1–6

1. *My son, forget not my law; but let thine heart keep my commandments:*
2. *For length of days, and long life, and peace, shall they add to thee.*
3. *Let not mercy and truth forsake thee: bind them about thy neck; write them upon the table of thine heart.*
4. *So shalt thou find favour and good understanding in the sight of God and man.*
5. *Trust in the LORD with all thine heart; and lean not unto thine own understanding.*
6. *In all thy ways, acknowledge Him, and He shall direct thy paths.*

Solomon's fifth sermon is again addressed to "My son," but it surely provides inspired counsel to believers of every age. First of all, the promise of a long and peaceful life is given to Rehoboam, and perhaps implied also to others, who "forget not my law" and "keep my commandments." It is sad to note, however, that Rehoboam failed significantly in this, and therefore died at age 58 (1 Kings 14:21), after having a large part of his kingdom taken away from him. Even Solomon failed to keep God's commands in his later years, so he also died relatively young, after reigning 40 years (1 Kings 11:42). He was quite young when he became king, probably less than 20 years old. God had promised to "lengthen his days" if he kept God's commandments (1 Kings 3:14), but he failed to do so, and the Lord finally *shortened* his days, not even allowing him to attain the

70 years listed by Moses as man's allotted normal life span (Ps. 90:10). We note also that although many godly people die young, *eternal* life is theirs, as well as eternal rest and peace.

Mercy and truth (like two sides of a coin) are also stressed as conditions for finding favor in the sight of both God and man. Verses 5 and 6 have, of course, been favorite verses to multitudes of Christian believers (not even to mention the godly men and women of Old Testament times), all through the centuries. To place complete trust in God for guidance and to acknowledge Him in everything we do, however, are much easier said than done, but we surely ought to try! What could be better than to know that God is directing our paths! "The steps of a good man are ordered by the LORD: and He delighteth in his way" (Ps. 37:23).

Proverbs 3:7–10

7. *Be not wise in thine own eyes, fear the LORD, and depart from evil.*
8. *It shall be health to thy navel, and marrow to thy bones.*
9. *Honour the LORD with thy substance, and with the firstfruits of all thine increase.*
10. *So shall thy barns be filled with plenty, and thy presses shall burst out with new wine.*

Solomon continues his lesson with more practical instructions for successful living. A boastful and arrogant attitude is not appropriate for a man who trusts God. As Paul who perhaps could have had as much human reason for boasting as anyone, reminded himself and others, "By the grace of God I am what I am" (1 Cor. 15:10).

He also notes that a godly lifestyle will normally produce a healthy life, and that a generous spirit — especially one that faithfully supports the Lord's work — will normally bring God's material blessings on one's life as well as spiritual (note also 2 Cor. 9:6–8; Mal. 3:10–12; etc.). The motivation for such generosity, of course, should be to "honour the LORD," not to bargain with the Lord.

It may be noted in passing that since the "new wine" mentioned here is fresh from the wine presses, it is healthful grape juice, still unfermented. Thus there is no conflict with Proverbs 23:29–35, which severely warns against intoxicating wine.

Proverbs 3:11–20

11. *My son, despise not the chastening of the LORD; neither be weary of His correction:*
12. *For whom the LORD loveth He correcteth; even as a father the son in whom he delighteth.*

13. *Happy is the man that findeth wisdom, and the man that getteth understanding.*
14. *For the merchandise of it is better than the merchandise of silver, and the gain thereof than fine gold.*
15. *She is more precious than rubies; and all the things thou canst desire not to be compared unto her.*
16. *Length of days is in her right hand; and in her left hand riches and honour.*
17. *Her ways are ways of pleasantness, and all her paths are peace.*
18. *She is a tree of life to them that lay hold upon her: and happy is every one that retaineth her.*
19. *The LORD by wisdom hath founded the earth; by understanding hath He established the heavens.*
20. *By His knowledge the depths are broken up, and the clouds drop down the dew.*

This sixth sermon for "*my son*" begins with two verses quoted (with interpretation) in the New Testament, as follows, "My son, despise not thou the chastening of the Lord, nor faint when thou art rebuked of Him: For whom the Lord loveth, He chasteneth, and scourgeth every son whom He receiveth" (Heb. 12:5-6).

This usage not only validates the Old Testament exhortation to chasten children when needed but also validates the fact that Solomon's instruction to his son in these verses (and thus by implication, all the Book of Proverbs) was considered by the apostles of Christ to be divinely inspired and authoritative. Furthermore, it is probable that Solomon himself was referring to the statement of Eliphaz in Job 5:17, and thus *that* passage is also accepted as inspired by God.

The Hebrew word for "chastening" here is the same word as "instruction." Thus God's chastening is always for purposes of instruction, and should not be ignored or resented. One would infer that Rehoboam did on occasion need corporal correction by his father Solomon — as well as, later, by God.

Then Solomon again returns to the great importance of finding the true Wisdom, once again bringing in the metaphor of the godly woman. "She is more precious than rubies," he says, and then even goes to the extreme of calling her value greater than anything one could desire — better even than the long life, riches, and honor which she can provide.

Verse 17 is especially intriguing. Remember that Solomon's wife was Naamah, and no doubt she also was very interested in her son's instruction (note Prov. 1:8). As he was writing these words of divine wisdom, he may well have been glancing occasionally at his beautiful wife, perhaps visualizing in her the model (physically, at least) of the metaphorical woman about whom he was writing.

The reason for speculating thus is that in verse 17, speaking of the godly woman personifying Wisdom, Solomon wrote, "Her ways are ways of pleasantness (Hebrew word *noam*) and all her paths are peace" (Hebrew *shalom*). Now *Naamah* which is very similar, also means "pleasantness" and "the Shulamite" (Solomon's designation for Naamah in his Song of Solomon) also means "peaceful." Thus, it would be a simple but meaningful play on words if Solomon were to render his verse 17 as: "Her ways are the ways of Naamah, and her paths are the ways of the Shulamite."

That may be far-fetched, and Solomon surely would not intend his comparison to be sacrilegious, but the similarity of words could hardly escape his notice at least. In any case, Solomon then goes on to compare the godly woman to the very tree of life back in the Garden of Eden. Then, he goes even further, again climaxing his eulogy by recognizing Wisdom not only as the spiritual tree of life but also as the agent by whom God created heaven and earth and by whom life is maintained on earth via the marvelous hydrologic cycle.

The word "depths" in verse 20 is the same as "deep" in Genesis 1:2 and Genesis 7:11; etc. The "dew" (that is, the water covering the land's plant life each day) actually originates mostly in the deep ocean, when the sun and wave spray break up its surface, allowing the water to rise and be translated inland to accumulate in clouds which eventually descend, in various forms, to the waiting land.

Proverbs 3:21–26

21. *My son, let not them depart from thine eyes: keep sound wisdom and discretion;*
22. *So shall they be life unto thy soul, and grace to thy neck.*
23. *Then shalt thou walk in thy way safely, and thy foot shall not stumble.*
24. *When thou liest down, thou shalt not be afraid: yea, thou shalt lie down, and thy sleep shall be sweet:*
25. *Be not afraid of sudden fear, neither of the desolation of the wicked, when it cometh.*
26. *For the* LORD *shall be thy confidence, and shall keep thy foot from being taken.*

Solomon's seventh sermon to his son continues with his praise of true wisdom, as found only in the Creator and His revealed Word. The assurances given in these verses obviously come not from "wisdom" as a mere human character attribute, but from God himself who, in Christ, is "made unto us wisdom" (1 Cor. 1:30). This is finally made clear in verse

26: "For the LORD shall be thy confidence, and shall keep thy foot from being taken."

Proverbs 3:27–35

27. *Withhold not good from them to whom it is due, when it is in the power of thine hand to do it.*
28. *Say not unto thy neighbour, Go, and come again, and to morrow I will give, when thou hast it by thee.*
29. *Devise not evil against thy neighbour, seeing he dwelleth securely by thee.*
30. *Strive not with a man without cause, if he hath done thee no harm.*
31. *Envy thou not the oppressor, and choose none of his ways.*
32. *For the froward is abomination to the LORD: but His secret is with the righteous.*
33. *The curse of the LORD is in the house of the wicked: but He blesseth the habitation of the just.*
34. *Surely He scorneth the scorners, but He giveth grace to the lowly.*
35. *The wise shall inherit glory: but shame shall be the promotion of fools.*

These closing verses of the seventh sermon indicate practical ways in which the assurances of the preceding verses should manifest themselves in daily living. Our relations with our neighbors should be characterized by generosity, helpfulness, and patience.

Since we have all the blessings of the divine wisdom which had created the earth itself and maintains life on it, there is certainly no reason ever to be envious of the occasional prosperity of the wicked, for that is very temporary at best (note Ps. 37:1–2). Verse 34 is applied beautifully in the New Testament by both James and Peter. "God resisteth the proud, but giveth grace to the humble" (James 4:6; 1 Pet. 5:5).

Finally we are promised that "the wise shall inherit glory." The Lord Jesus Christ, who not only personifies but is God's perfect wisdom, and in whom we also find our wisdom, will be "appointed heir of all things" (Heb. 1:2), and we who have received Him by faith as our "way," our "truth," and our "life" (John 14:6) have been made "joint-heirs with Christ" (Rom. 8:17). That will, indeed, be an inheritance of *glory!*

Proverbs 4:1–9

1. *Hear, ye children, the instruction of a father, and attend to know understanding.*
2. *For I give you good doctrine, forsake ye not my law,*

3. *For I was my father's son, tender and only beloved in the sight of my mother.*

4. *He taught me also, and said unto me, Let thine heart retain my words: keep my commandments, and live.*

5. *Get wisdom, get understanding: forget it not; neither decline from the words of my mouth.*

6. *Forsake her not, and she shall preserve thee: love her, and she shall keep thee.*

7. *Wisdom is the principal thing; therefore get wisdom: and with all thy getting, get understanding.*

8. *Exalt her, and she shall promote thee: she shall bring thee to honour, when thou dost embrace her.*

9. *She shall give to thine head an ornament of grace: a crown of glory shall she deliver to thee.*

This eighth lesson, or sermon, is the first one addressed by Solomon to "ye children," instead of just to "my son." We could surmise that his two daughters, Taphath and Basmath, were included. The renewed emphasis on wisdom and understanding in this particular section assures that Solomon (and therefore the Lord God himself, since the Holy Spirit was the divine mover behind these words of Solomon — note 2 Pet. 1:21) is urging both young men and young women to seek true wisdom and understanding.

There is evidently a subtle distinction here between the words "understanding" and "wisdom." Probably the key is that "understanding" implies placing the various items of one's factual knowledge into proper perspective with each other, so as to comprehend the broad significance of all of them in one's world view. "Wisdom," then, is the art and skill of applying one's understanding of the facts to make good judgments and decisions in life situations. Solomon desired both for his children, as does our Heavenly Father for all *His* children.

Interestingly, Solomon here refers to his own father and mother, David and Bathsheba. They were the ones who first inculcated a desire for wisdom in Solomon, and this was undoubtedly one main incentive behind Solomon's famous prayer to God for wisdom (1 Kings 3:5–14). Solomon, in fact, seems actually to be quoting the words of his father David here in the remainder of this lesson (verses 4–9).

Note also that the metaphor of Wisdom as a godly and virtuous woman was repeatedly used by David in these words. Note, for example: "love her, and she shall keep thee" (verse 6); "Exalt her, and she shall promote thee" (verse 8); "a crown of glory shall she give to thee" (verse 9); etc. No wonder he says, "Wisdom is the principal thing; therefore get wisdom: and with all thy getting, get understanding" (verse 7). Solomon may, therefore, first have heard this figure of speech from David, and then adopted the same for his instructions to his own children.

Proverbs 4:10–19

10. *Hear, O my son, and receive my sayings; and the years of thy life shall be many.*
11. *I have taught thee in the way of wisdom; I have led thee in right paths.*
12. *When thou goest, thy steps shall not be straitened; and when thou runnest, thou shalt not stumble.*
13. *Take fast hold of instruction; let her not go: keep her, for she is thy life.*
14. *Enter not into the path of the wicked, and go not in the way of evil men.*
15. *Avoid it, pass not by it, turn from it, and pass away.*
16. *For they sleep not, except they have done mischief; and their sleep is taken away, unless they cause some to fall.*
17. *For they eat the bread of wickedness, and drink the wine of violence.*
18. *But the path of the just is as the shining light, that shineth more and more into the perfect day.*
19. *The way of the wicked is as darkness: they know not at what they stumble.*

Solomon here directs his attention back especially to "my son," and thus indirectly to young men in general. Returning to the type of warnings and promises in his first three sermons, he reiterates his assurance that obedience to his words will enhance the prospect of a long life (as well as eternal life in God's kingdom). Note Proverbs 3:1–2.

He also returns in these verses to the figure of the two paths — "the path of the wicked" (verse 14) and "the path of the just" (verse 18). "I have led thee in right paths," says Solomon (verse 11), and there is "shining light" along that path, which will lead one finally to the land of "perfect day" (verse 18), where there shall be life everlasting and "no night there" (Rev. 21:25).

On the other hand, "the way of the wicked is as darkness" (verse 19). When men try to seduce you to follow *that* path, "avoid it, pass not by it, turn from it, and pass away" (verse 15). "For the LORD knoweth the way of the righteous: but the way of the ungodly shall perish" (Ps. 1:6).

The path of ungodliness is often made to appear beautiful and pleasurable, whereas the path of godliness is derided as harsh and restrictive by most people. But the words of the Lord Jesus Christ (who, we must never forget, was our Creator and Redeemer, and will eventually be our judge and King of all kings) are very plain and pointed. "Enter ye in at the strait gate: for wide is the gate, and broad is the way, that leadeth to destruction, and many there be which go in thereat: Because strait is the gate, and narrow is the way, which leadeth unto life, and few there be that find it" (Matt. 7:13–14).

Proverbs 4:20–27

20. *My son, attend to my words; incline thine ear unto my sayings.*
21. *Let them not depart from thine eyes; keep them in the midst of thine heart.*
22. *For they are life unto those that find them, and health to all their flesh.*
23. *Keep thy heart with all diligence; for out of it are the issues of life.*
24. *Put away from thee a froward mouth, and perverse lips put far from thee.*
25. *Let thine eyes look right on, and let thine eyelids look straight before thee.*
26. *Ponder the path of thy feet, and let all thy ways be established.*
27. *Turn not to the right hand nor to the left: remove thy foot from evil.*

In this sermon to his son, King Solomon continues to stress the importance of obeying his words, which actually are coming as from God himself. Sadly, in later life, Rehoboam either forgot or deliberately decided to reject much of his father's counsel, and largely wrecked his life and his kingdom because of it.

Nevertheless, they are still good words and need to be heeded and followed. It is interesting to note the different members of the body about which Solomon centers his counsel, noting that obedience brings "life to those that find them, and health to all their flesh" (verse 22).

Don't let them get away from your "eyes," he says, and keep them in your "heart" (verse 21). Avoid developing a "froward mouth, and perverse lips" (verse 24). Keep straight "the path of thy feet" and "turn not to the right hand nor to the left" (verses 26–27).

The heart, of course, is most important, for it controls all the rest. Therefore, "keep thy heart with all diligence; for out of it are the issues of life" (verse 23).

Proverbs 5:1–6

1. *My son, attend unto my wisdom, and bow thine ear to my understanding;*

2. *That thou mayest regard discretion, and that thy lips may keep
    knowledge.*
3. *For the lips of a strange woman drop as an honeycomb, and her
    mouth is smoother than oil:*
4. *But her end is bitter as wormwood, sharp as a twoedged
    sword.*
5. *Her feet go down to death; her steps take hold on hell.*
6. *Lest thou shouldest ponder the path of life, her ways are move-
    able, that thou canst not know them.*

This section comprises Solomon's 11th sermon to his son, and he
again urges strict attention to his words. He is introducing a new and
very important subject — the dangerous influences of strange (that is,
foreign) women in Israel. He had briefly alluded to this danger in his 4th
sermon (Prov. 2:16–19), but now would be discussing it in more detail in
his remaining sermons (especially in Prov. 5 and 7, with additional seg-
ments in Prov. 6 and 9).

When Israel entered the Promised Land, God had told them not only
to conquer but also to destroy the nations then inhabiting it, knowing
that otherwise they would eventually be led into the idolatrous religions
and immoral lifestyles of those nations. They finally did complete the
conquest, but not the destruction, and were therefore continually being
led into these heathen systems.

The first example was in the countries of Moab and Midian, even
before the Children of Israel crossed the Jordan River into Canaan proper.
"And Israel abode in Shittim, and the people began to commit whoredom
with the daughters of Moab" (Num. 25:1). Similar problems surfaced
repeatedly during the days of the judges. The pagan women of the various
Canaanite tribes, having been raised in religious systems which not only
condoned but even fostered immorality, were a continual temptation to
the Israelites among whom they were now living.

The Kingdom of Israel had been extended to its greatest dimensions
under David and Solomon, and there were many of these "strange women"
with their pagan cultures living within its borders. Unless they had been
converted to the worship of the true God, it would not be surprising that
they became a serious problem to the men of Israel. Many, no doubt,
would have desired to be a wife, or even a mistress, to an Israelite, whose
station in life in general would normally be well above that of the men
of the conquered nations.

This situation, presumably, was the background of Solomon's warnings to his son and other young men against being tempted by the "strange
woman." Not only were God's commandments against adultery and
fornication being broken, but also the people were being drawn into the

pagan religions thereby. This eventually became a problem even to Solomon himself in his old age, though he probably rationalized the situation in his case, until God directly rebuked him.

At the time of writing these exhortations to his children, however, he had evidently not yet become involved with foreign women to any significant degree.

With one exception, of course! The mother of Rehoboam (who was in full agreement with Solomon in writing these sermons — note Prov. 1:8; etc.) was herself from the nation of Ammon, one of the nations subjugated by David. Furthermore, Solomon's mother was Bathsheba, who had previously been married to a Hittite, and so might even have been an ethnic Hittite herself.

Undoubtedly, however, both Naamah (mother of Rehoboam) and Bathsheba (mother of Solomon) had become converts to the true Lord and His worship and had tried diligently to raise their children in the faith of their fathers. In fact, Uriah the Hittite, Bathsheba's earlier husband, had an Israelite name (meaning "Flame of Jah") and had been one of David's specially chosen "mighty men" (2 Sam. 23:8, 39), and he was certainly a believer in Jehovah.

There was also an Ammonite among David's mighty men by the name of Zelek (2 Sam. 23:37), and it seems reasonable to infer that he could have been the father of Naamah, Rehoboam's mother. He also, no doubt, was an Israeli proselyte. In any case, Naamah surely was a sincere believer in Jehovah and, as we have seen in chapter 2, almost certainly was the Shulamite maiden of the Song of Solomon, the first and only true love of King Solomon.

Bathsheba and Naamah were thus no longer "strange women" themselves, of course, and very probably would have been in hearty agreement with Solomon in his warnings against such women. They would have been well aware of the depravities of the pagan religions of the Hittites, Ammonites, and others, and would surely have wanted their own sons and grandsons not to become entangled therein.

When Solomon warned Rehoboam that such entanglements would lead to death and hell (verse 5), he was concerned not only with the dangers of physical death but also — probably even more — with the fate of eternal death and hell to which the worship of false gods would lead. As his father David had warned, "The wicked shall be turned into hell, and all the nations that forget God" (Ps. 9:17).

Solomon concludes this sermon by warning those who would consider following *this* path of life as proposed by the alien temptress, that her own life was very unstable and was not a way of life to which they could relate at all. It could only lead to heartbreak and death and hell.

Proverbs 5:7–14

7. Hear me now, therefore, O ye children, and depart not from the words of my mouth.
8. Remove thy way far from her, and come not nigh the door of her house:
9. Lest thou give thine honour unto others, and thy years unto the cruel:
10. Lest strangers be filled with thy wealth; and thy labours be in the house of a stranger;
11. And thou mourn at the last, when thy flesh and thy body are consumed,
12. And say, How have I hated instruction, and my heart despised reproof;
13. And have not obeyed the voice of my teachers, nor inclined mine ear to them that instructed me!
14. I was almost in all evil in the midst of the congregation and assembly.

Solomon's warnings concerning the influence of foreign women continues in this sermon, except that now he extends it to his "children" as well as his son. There was evidently even significant danger to young Israeli women who became too familiar with these pagan women. Human nature, both male and female, is inherently sinful, and easily led astray by worldly and ungodly influences. There might also be some danger to the daughters of Israel from pagan men, but the subjugated state of the latter might not be as tempting to them as the seductive beauty of the pagan women, whose lifestyles some might wish to emulate. Hence Solomon included his daughters, as well as his son, in this warning.

Such warnings are needed today more than ever, when both young men and young women are being led into immoral infidelity by evil influences of all kinds, especially by peer pressure of pagan acquaintances and friends, as well as by godless teachers and liberal religionists. Multitudes of young people today would rather follow the pseudo-intellectualism and the hedonistic pleasures of the pagan world (not the foreign influences, as in Solomon's day but the home-grown paganism of our post-Christian civilization). One day soon they may well find "strangers . . . filled with thy wealth" and themselves serving "in the house of a stranger" (verse 10). God will not be mocked forever.

Proverbs 5:15–23

15. Drink waters out of thine own cistern, and running waters out of thine own well.

16. *Let thy fountains be dispersed abroad, and rivers of waters in the streets.*

17. *Let them be only thine own, and not strangers' with thee.*

18. *Let thy fountain be blessed: and rejoice with the wife of thy youth.*

19. *Let her be as the loving hind and pleasant roe; let her breasts satisfy thee at all times; and be thou ravished always with her love.*

20. *And why wilt thou, my son, be ravished with a strange woman, and embrace the bosom of a stranger?*

21. *For the ways of man are before the eyes of the Lord, and He pondereth all his goings.*

22. *His own iniquities shall take the wicked himself, and he shall be holden with the cords of his sins.*

23. *He shall die without instruction; and in the greatness of his folly he shall go astray.*

Although still addressing all his children, Solomon again is thinking particularly of young men, and especially his own son. To prevent the sad end foreseen in verses 12–14, Solomon specifically urges young men to find and be content with the one woman with whom each will spend his life.

Using the colorful imagery of life-giving waters as symbolic of sexual activity and procreation, he urges that one be satisfied with his own cistern and well. Verse 16 should probably be understood as a rhetorical question: "Should you disperse your seed abroad, with illegitimate and homeless children running in the streets like rivers?" Far better would it be to beget, care for and train one's own children, borne just by one faithful wife.

When Solomon advises his son to "rejoice with the wife of thy youth," he most likely was thinking of his own beautiful and beloved Naamah. It is almost inconceivable that he could have written the words in verses 18–20 after he had begun acquiring other wives. When he uses the figures of "the loving hind and pleasant roe," he is going back to the pictures drawn in his Song of Songs (Song of Sol. 2:7; 3:5; 4:5; 7:3). When he speaks of being "ravished always with her love," he seems to be thinking in terms of Song of Solomon 4:9.

Then, when he asks his son how he could possibly "embrace the bosom of a stranger?" even reminding him that this would be done "before the eyes of the Lord" (verse 21), whose laws strictly forbade such things, there seems no way that Solomon could have said this while he himself was involved in sexual intimacies with his own "strange wives."

Therefore, these words must have been written well before "Solomon loved many strange wives, together with the daughter of Pharaoh" (1 Kings 11:1). God could never have countenanced such hypocrisy otherwise.

This "daughter of Pharaoh" had been married (or at least espoused) to Solomon rather early in his reign (1 Kings 3:1), but this was clearly a political marriage and nothing more. He later built a "house for Pharaoh's daughter" (1 Kings 7:8), rather than to have her in his own house. There is no mention in the Bible of any children from this marriage, as there almost certainly would have been *had* there been any children.

Furthermore, there is no record at all of children from any of Solomon's seven hundred wives and three hundred concubines. This is very strange, if these women were in Solomon's harem for anything other than political and/or prestige purposes. The only children mentioned are Rehoboam, Taphath, and Basmath, all probably born of Naamah, the "wife of his youth."

This odd scribal reticence was not true of the records of either Solomon's father or his son. The names of David's seven named wives and 19 sons are given in 1 Chronicles 3:1–9. Then it is recorded that Rehoboam "took eighteen wives, and threescore concubines; and begat twenty and eight sons, and threescore daughters" (2 Chron. 11:21).

Not only are no other children of Solomon mentioned in either book of Chronicles, but neither are his seven hundred wives and three hundred concubines mentioned there. Yet these books are especially concerned with details of families and genealogies in Judah. This omission is odd, to say the least — unless, that is, the multitude of Solomonic wives and concubines were there for political and prestige purposes only. Most of them, if not all except the Egyptian princess, were apparently acquired when he was old, and this may have also been an inhibiting factor. His "love" for these foreign wives was platonic rather than romantic, most likely.

Solomon's challenge to Rehoboam and other young men to love only the wife of his youth is clearly given in all urgent sincerity, with no suggestion that he himself had not followed his own counsel. In any case, the counsel is good, for it was divinely inspired, later confirmed by Christ himself (Matt. 19:3–6).

Proverbs 6:1–11

1. *My son, if thou be surety for thy friend, if thou hast stricken thy hand with a stranger,*
2. *Thou art snared with the words of thy mouth, thou art taken with the words of thy mouth.*
3. *Do this now, my son, deliver thyself, when thou art come into the hand of thy friend; go, humble thyself, and make sure thy friend.*
4. *Give not sleep to thine eyes, nor slumber to thine eyelids.*
5. *Deliver thyself as a roe from the hand of the hunter, and as a bird from the hand of the fowler.*

6. *Go to the ant, thou sluggard; consider her ways, and be wise:*
7. *Which having no guide, overseer, or ruler,*
8. *Provideth her meat in the summer, and gathereth her food in the harvest.*
9. *How long wilt thou sleep, O sluggard? when wilt thou arise out of thy sleep?*
10. *Yet a little sleep, a little slumber, a little folding of the hands to sleep:*
11. *So shall thy poverty come as one that travelleth, and thy want as an armed man.*

The next sermon to "my son," which is the 13th in the series of 17 contained in Proverbs 6:1–9, begins with warnings against two particular weaknesses that affect believers — that of gullibility (verses 1–5) and slothfulness (verses 6–11). Seemingly unrelated, the connection may be that the sin of laziness is most commonly the unacknowledged reason why either friends or strangers will come to an industrious person requesting him to act as surety (that is, as a guarantor) in connection with a financial commitment he wants to make. This warning is repeated several times in Proverbs (11:15; 17:18; 20:16; 22:26–27).

If the person is really worthy of help, if the proposal is sound, and if the one to whom the request is made is able to help without going into debt himself, it would normally be better simply to give that person the needed money or else to make repayment optional and non-interest-bearing (note 1 John 3:17; Lev. 25:35–38). While it may seem harsh to refuse to co-sign a note for a Christian brother, for example, the very real possibility of default (otherwise he would not need a co-signer) may well lead to later estrangement and bitterness, as well as hardship for the family of the one acting as surety.

The sin of idleness, of course, is highly unbecoming to a Christian, and should certainly not be encouraged by well-meaning and generous but gullible Christian friends or relatives (2 Thess. 3:6–12).

The reference to the ant as showing commendable industrious foresight is one of numerous suggestions that the God-created instinctive behaviors of animals, as well as other aspects of creation, can serve as good examples to human beings. Note also such Scriptures as Job 12:7–10; Proverbs 30:24–28; Joel 1:4; Jeremiah 8:7; Matthew 6:26-30; etc.

Proverbs 6:12–19

12. *A naughty person, a wicked man, walketh with a froward mouth.*
13. *He winketh with his eyes, he speaketh with his feet, he teacheth with his fingers;*

14. *Frowardness is in his heart, he deviseth mischief continually; he soweth discord.*

15. *Therefore shall his calamity come suddenly; suddenly shall he be broken without remedy.*

16. *These six things doth the LORD hate; yea, seven are an abomination unto him:*

17. *A proud look, a lying tongue, and hands that shed innocent blood,*

18. *An heart that deviseth wicked imaginations, feet that be swift in running to mischief,*

19. *A false witness that speaketh lies, and he that soweth discord among brethren.*

Verses 12–15 of this sermon describe the character and destiny of "a naughty person," which Solomon makes synonymous with "a wicked man." The Hebrew word translated "naughty" means "worthless," and was properly rendered "naughty" by the King James translators, since the English word "naughty" was originally derived from "naught" (meaning "nothing") and thus was an adjective implying "useless" or "without value." Such a person is wicked in the sight of God. He is good for nothing but to plan and cause trouble. The actual Hebrew word rendered "naughty" is *belial*, which in some passages is used as a name for the devil, who is, of course, good for nothing but evil.

Even the body language of the wicked person tends to identify his character, and certainly the "frowardness" of his talk, full of complaint and criticism and slander, reveals the frowardness of his heart.

This naughty person, against whom Solomon is warning his son, evidently personifies in his entire attitude seven types of personal behavior that are especially hateful in God's sight. These seven, of course, are especially descriptive of Belial, or Satan himself. Note the listed attributes:

(1) "A proud look." Pride is "the condemnation of the devil" (1 Tim. 3:6).

(2) "A lying tongue." Jesus said that Satan "is a liar, and the father of it" (John 8:44).

(3) "Hands that shed innocent blood." Jesus also said that Satan "was a murderer from the beginning" (John 8:44).

(4) "A heart that deviseth wicked imaginations." The most wicked imagination ever devised was when Satan said in his heart, "I will be like the most High" (Isa. 14:14).

(5) "Feet . . . swift in running to mischief." Peter said the devil "as a roaring lion, walketh about, seeking whom he may devour" (1 Pet. 5:8).

(6) "A false witness that speaketh lies." Satan is the ultimate of all liars and deceivers, for he is "the Devil, and Satan, which deceiveth the whole world" (Rev. 12:9).

(7) "He that soweth discord among believers." He is also called "the accuser of our brethren, which accuses them before our God day and night" (Rev. 12:10).

It is no wonder that these seven sins "are an abomination unto Him," for they stem directly from the wicked desire of Satan to dethrone God. He is continually tempting all men to do these things, so we must "be sober, be vigilant," continually resisting him "stedfast in the faith" (1 Pet. 5:8–9).

Proverbs 6:20–35

20. *My son, keep thy father's commandment, and forsake not the law of thy mother.*
21. *Bind them continually upon thine heart, and tie them about thy neck.*
22. *When thou goest, it shall lead thee; when thou sleepest, it shall keep thee; and when thou awakest, it shall talk with thee.*
23. *For the commandment is a lamp: and the law is light; and reproofs of instruction are the ways of life.*
24. *To keep thee from the evil woman, from the flattery of the tongue of a strange woman.*
25. *Lust not after her beauty in thine heart; neither let her take thee with her eyelids.*
26. *For by means of a whorish woman a man is brought to a piece of bread: and the adulteress will hunt for the precious life.*
27. *Can a man take fire in his bosom, and his clothes not be burned?*
28. *Can one go upon hot coals, and his feet not be burned?*
29. *So he that goeth in to his neighbour's wife; whosoever toucheth her shall not be innocent.*
30. *Men do not despise a thief, if he steal to satisfy his soul when he is hungry;*
31. *But if he be found, he shall restore sevenfold; he shall give all the substance of his house.*
32. *But whoso committeth adultery with a woman lacketh understanding: he that doeth it destroyeth his own soul.*
33. *A wound and dishonour shall he get; and his reproach shall not be wiped away.*
34. *For jealousy is the rage of a man: therefore he will not spare in the day of vengeance.*

*35. He will not regard any ransom; neither will he rest content
    though thou givest many gifts.*

Once again, as Solomon begins his 14th lesson for his son, also with
the supporting authority of his son's mother, Naamah, he urges Rehoboam
to remember continually their instructions and warnings, especially about
involvement with immoral women. Such warnings are as relevant today
as then, although they now could apply equally well, if not more so, to
young women in danger from predatory men. In Solomon's time, with so
many pagan women from the conquered nation around seeking husbands
or lovers, such a man as Rehoboam, son of the king, would be especially
desirable and vulnerable.

But such liaisons are always dangerous, and often deadly. The Bible
is full of warnings against adultery and fornication, whether heterosexual
or homosexual. The pagan world of antiquity was exceedingly wicked in
this as well as other aspects, but no more so than today's world. Christian
young men and women today are also very vulnerable, and warnings such
as those of Solomon and Naamah to Rehoboam are urgently relevant.
They are in constant danger of tragedy in this life and judgment in the
future life. "Marriage is honourable in all, and the bed undefiled: but
whoremongers [same word in the Greek as 'fornicators'] and adulterers
God will judge" (Heb. 13:4).

Apparently, in addition to youthful fornication, adultery with the
pagan wives of the pagan men in the conquered tribes in Israel was also
common, especially in view of the servile status of the men, but Solomon
warned that "whoso committeth adultery with a woman . . . destroyeth his
own soul." Even if he does not become a victim of a husband's revenge,
he must at least answer to God in the Day of Judgment. Any sin (except
permanent rejection of God and His salvation) can be forgiven, of course,
but no man can "take fire in his bosom, and his clothes not be burned."

Proverbs 7:1–23

1. *My son, keep my words, and lay up my commandments with
    thee.*
2. *Keep my commandments, and live; and my law as the apple of
    thine eye.*
3. *Bind them upon thy fingers, write them upon the table of thine
    heart.*
4. *Say unto wisdom, Thou art my sister; and call understanding
    thy kinswoman:*
5. *That they may keep thee from the strange woman, from the
    stranger which flattereth with her words.*
6. *From the window of my house, I looked through my casement*

7. *And beheld among the simple ones, I discerned among the youths a young man void of understanding,*

8. *Passing through the street near her corner, and he went the way to her house,*

9. *In the twilight, in the evening, in the black and dark night:*

10. *And, behold, there met him a woman with the attire of an harlot, and subtil of heart.*

11. *(She is loud and stubborn; her feet abide not in her house:*

12. *Now is she without, now in the streets, and lieth in wait at every corner.)*

13. *So she caught him, and kissed him, and with an impudent face said unto him,*

14. *I have peace offerings with me; this day have I payed my vows.*

15. *Therefore came I forth to meet thee, diligently to seek thy face, and I have found thee.*

16. *I have decked my bed with coverings of tapestry, with carved works, with fine linen of Egypt.*

17. *I have perfumed my bed with myrrh, aloes and cinnamon.*

18. *Come, let us take our fill of love until the morning: let us solace ourselves with loves.*

19. *For the goodman is not at home, he is gone a long journey:*

20. *He hath taken a bag of money with him, and will come home at the day appointed.*

21. *With her much fair speech, she caused him to yield, with the flattering of her lips she forced him.*

22. *He goeth after her straightway, as an ox goeth to the slaughter, or as a fool to the correction of the stocks;*

23. *Till a dart strike through his liver; as a bird hasteth to the snare, and knoweth not that it is for his life.*

This 15th lesson continues the warning against immorality, but more intensely and graphically than ever. This apparently was proving a serious temptation to Rehoboam, and Solomon was greatly concerned about it. And, of course, that implies that God is also intensely concerned about the dangerous attraction of sexual sins for all *His* sons, as well as His daughters, and for those of this day as well as Solomon's day. Again, the lesson begins with reminding Rehoboam (and us!) that the authority for these warnings is God himself. It is vital that we "keep [His] commandments and live," even though we know that the grace of God in Christ can provide forgiveness and salvation. One of the very last promises of the Bible is, "Blessed are they that do His commandments, that they may have right to the tree of life" (Rev. 22:14).

The commandments in particular view here, of course, are those enjoining sexual purity. Solomon was particularly concerned with the danger from the "strange woman," the foreign woman living among the people of God while still serving her own pagan gods. His son was in urgent need of true wisdom, personified by "thy kinswoman."

It seems that Solomon had actually observed from his own window such a foreign woman in the act of tempting a young man, and he wanted his own son to be forewarned. The scene he described was graphic and realistic and obviously very seductive to the young victim. Though the woman is married, presumably to a man of the conquered peoples, she is promiscuous, and her dalliances have somehow apparently provided luxuries that might otherwise be unavailable to these captive peoples. One wonders if her husband might even be complicit with her in her actions, since his own system of morality would probably be at least as flexible as that of his wife.

Her reference to "peace offerings" and "vows" is intriguing. She may indeed have offered sacrifices and vows to her pagan gods, but here she seems rather to be hypocritically using the peace offerings required of Israelites as a further inducement to the young man. These offerings implied that she was at peace with God and thus her invitation was quite appropriate. The meat of the peace offerings had to be eaten that same night or the next (Lev. 7:15–16), so the invitation included a good meal as well as "making love." How could a virile, but naïve and foolish, young man refuse?

"The goodman" [literally "the man" or "the husband"] would not be there to interfere, she assured him, so he followed her into the house, like an ox being led to the slaughter! But he is sinning not only against God, but against his own soul, and so is she.

Proverbs 7:24–27

24. *Hearken unto me now therefore, O ye children, and attend to the words of my mouth.*
25. *Let not thine heart decline to her ways, go not astray in her paths.*
26. *For she hath cast down many wounded: yea, many strong men have been slain by her.*
27. *Her house is the way to hell, going down to the chambers of death.*

The last two lessons are addressed to "ye children," as Solomon proceeds from warning against the strange woman (Folly) to eulogizing the godly kinswoman (Wisdom), and so are vital for both sons and daughters.

The first four verses, however, rehearse once again the stern warning against yielding to the immoral sexual temptations of paganism. Daughters need this warning as well as sons, because the lifestyles of many women who succeed in seducing desirable men into marriage or cohabitation with such methods could well be tempting them to do the same. In any case, and however the variables work in different times and places, young people should be constantly reminded that this kind of lifestyle is "the way to hell, going down to the chambers of death."

Proverbs 8:1–12

1. *Doth not wisdom cry? and understanding put forth her voice?*
2. *She standeth in the top of high places, by the way in the places of the paths.*
3. *She crieth at the gates, at the entry of the city, at the coming in at the doors.*
4. *Unto you, O men, I call and my voice is to the sons of man.*
5. *Ye simple, understand wisdom, and ye fools, be ye of an understanding heart.*
6. *Hear, for I will speak of excellent things; and the opening of my lips shall be right things.*
7. *For my mouth shall speak truth; and wickedness is an abomination to my lips.*
8. *All the words of my mouth are in righteousness; there is nothing froward or perverse in them.*
9. *They are all plain to him that understandeth, and right to them that find knowledge.*
10. *Receive my instruction, and not silver, and knowledge rather than choice gold.*
11. *For wisdom is better than rubies; and all the things that may be desired are not to be compared to it.*
12. *I wisdom dwell with prudence, and find out knowledge of witty inventions.*

At this point in the sermon to his children, Solomon once again (as in Prov. 1:20–33) is no longer just giving his own counsel, divinely inspired though it be, but has become the direct spokesman for God, recording words dictated, as it were, by the personified Wisdom, the godly kinswoman. And, as noted in the former instance, these words are actually the words of God himself, for He alone, in the person of the divine Word, is all wisdom (1 Cor. 1:30; Col. 2:3).

Note the claims made by God, personified as Wisdom, concerning the words which He speaks. The things of which He speaks are "excellent things" (verse 6), "right things" (verse 6), "truth[ful]" things (verse 7), and "plain" things (verse 9). Conversely, nothing God says in His word can, therefore, be either trivial things, wrong things, false things, or things impossible to understand. Therefore, anyone can understand God's Word if he or she is willing to study it, believe it, obey it, and honor it. The teachings of Scripture are better than silver or gold or rubies, or anything else that could ever be desired. It is, in fact, the one thing in this present world that can never pass away (Matt. 24:35).

Verse 12 is fascinating. Wisdom and prudence (that is, clever discretion) are roommates, as it were. They live and work together. The wisdom that comes from God is not naïve gullibility (as skeptics often view Christian faith) but insightful and true understanding. They produce "witty inventions" (one word in the Hebrew) — that is, ingenious ways of proving the truth of their faith — sharing it effectively with others, and responding knowledgeably to the witty inventions of those who would destroy our faith.

Proverbs 8:13–21

13. *The fear of the* LORD *is to hate evil: pride and arrogancy, and the evil way, and the froward mouth, do I hate.*
14. *Counsel is mine, and sound wisdom: I am understanding; I have strength.*
15. *By me kings reign, and princes decree justice.*
16. *By me princes rule, and nobles, even all the judges of the earth.*
17. *I love them that love me; and those that seek me early shall find me.*
18. *Riches and honour are with me; yea, durable riches and righteousness.*
19. *My fruit is better than gold, yea, than fine gold; and my revenue than choice silver.*
20. *I lead in the way of righteousness, in the midst of the paths of judgment:*
21. *That I may cause those that love me to inherit substance; and I will fill their treasures.*

This very potent phrase, "the fear of the LORD" occurs no less than 15 times in the Book of Proverbs, in each instance either adding to the definition of what the fear of Jehovah is, or what it does, for the one who truly manifests it in his faith and life. The personified Wisdom (actually God the Word) reminds us in verse 13 that God hates arrogant pride, as well as evil deeds and words, so that one who truly fears God (not as a vengeful tyrant, but as an all-knowing righteous Father) will likewise hate these things — in his own life as well as in others.

Note that the implied speaker, who had just said "I wisdom" (verse 12) now also says "I am understanding." Remember that Solomon had written, "Wisdom is the principal thing; therefore get wisdom: and with all thy getting get understanding" (Prov. 4:7). The divine speaker is here claiming that He (God the Son, here symbolized as the godly kinswoman contrasted with the ungodly strange woman) is, personally, both the true wisdom and the true understanding.

He then notes that it must be by this God-given wisdom and understanding that kings and other leaders must rule if they would be successful in their leadership. "The powers that be are ordained of God," we are reminded by the apostle Paul (Rom. 13:1). We have the responsibility to obey them, but they first of all have the greater responsibility to reign in terms of God's wisdom, as now revealed most clearly and explicitly in the Bible. God had greatly honored Solomon's prayer to grant him wisdom in leading his people, and now surely Solomon would desire the same thing for his son Rehoboam.

The promise applies to all the rest of us as well. "Those that seek me early shall find me." "If any of you lack wisdom, let him ask of God, that giveth to all men liberally, and upbraideth not; and it shall be given him" (James 1:5).

God also gave Solomon riches and honor as a result of his prayer for wisdom, and these verses tell us that they are available also to "them that love me," subject, of course, to the will of God for each individual. In the light of the New Testament, we know that the "true riches" (Luke 16:11) ("durable riches," as they are called here) are spiritual riches. "For ye know the grace of our Lord Jesus Christ, that, though He was rich, yet for your sakes He became poor, that ye through His poverty might be rich" (2 Cor. 8:9). As far as "honour" is concerned, the Lord Jesus has said, "If any man serve me, him will my Father honour" (John 12:26). Whether on earth or in heaven, *that* honor is what really counts!

Proverbs 8:22–26

22. *The Lord possessed me in the beginning of His way, before His works of old.*
23. *I was set up from everlasting, from the beginning, or ever the earth was.*
24. *When there were no depths, I was brought forth; when there were no fountains abounding with water.*
25. *Before the mountains were settled, before the hills was I brought forth:*
26. *While as yet He had not made the earth, nor the fields, nor the highest part of the dust of the world.*

Verses 8–31 of this eighth chapter of Proverbs constitute one of the most remarkable passages in the Bible, rehearsing in a different way the account of creation in Genesis chapter 1. "Wisdom" is still speaking, but now more clearly than ever in words that could only be from the eternal Son of God, the divine Word. He brings us back to the "time" before the creation of time or space or matter, back to "the beginning of His way, before His works of old." The New Testament revelation is similar. It says, "In the beginning was the Word, and the Word was with God, and the Word was God. The same was in the beginning with God" (John 1:1–2).

"I was set up from everlasting," He says, "from the beginning, or ever the earth was." When, in the fulness of time, "the Word was made flesh, and dwelt among us" (John 1:14), then the Lord Jesus could pray to His Father, as He was almost ready to return to heaven, "Now, O Father, glorify thou me with thine own self with the glory which I had with thee before the world was" (John 17:5). "For thou lovedst me before the foundation of the world" (John 17:24).

When we compare this passage in Proverbs with the New Testament revelation of the eternal Son of God, we almost have to conclude that the Lord Jesus Christ, in His pre-incarnate existence, is really the one speaking through Solomon in this section.

When He says that "I was set up from everlasting," He is using an unusual Hebrew word for "set up" (*nasak*). It is the same word used prophetically in Psalm 2:6 when God, in response to the determination of the world's leaders to break the control of the Lord and His Christ over the world, says, "Yet have I set my king upon my holy hill of Zion." Its basic meaning and most common use, however, is to "pour" or "pour out," as used, for example, in connection with the pouring out of drink offerings at the base of an altar. It can also mean "anointed."

Therefore, the divine Word is saying, in effect, that "I was poured out as an offering from everlasting." This remarkable prophecy throws light on the reference in Revelation 13:8 to "the Lamb slain from the foundation of the world" and also to Peter's marvelous statement concerning our redemption by "the precious blood of Christ, as of a lamb without blemish and without spot: Who verily was foreordained before the foundation of the world, but was manifest in these last times for you" (1 Pet. 1:19–20).

What a tremendous revelation it is to realize that, in the purposes of the triune God, the second person had planned to pour out His shed blood for our redemption before He ever created the mighty universe! What a Savior we have!

Note also the amazing revelation that He was "brought forth" from eternity. That is, He is eternally being brought forth from the Father as

His only begotten Son. There was never a time when He was created, for He himself is the Creator of all things in heaven and earth (Col. 1:16; John 1:3). Yet He exists always in relation to the Father as the Son brought forth from the Father. His "goings forth have been from of old, from everlasting" (Mic. 5:2). Like the Father, the Son also is "The mighty God, the everlasting Father" (Isa. 9:6), for, said Jesus, "I and the Father are one" (John 10:30).

One is awed by the fact that this revelation was written hundreds of years before John or Micah or Isaiah, by none other than *Solomon*! This obviously came not out of Solomon's own store of human wisdom, great as that was, but by very direct revelation through God's Holy Spirit — yet it was included in one of the "sermons" to his son. Truly, God's "wisdom and knowledge" are "unsearchable," and "His ways past finding out!" (Rom. 11:33).

But no matter how this amazing truth reached us, we can simply rejoice that we have it! God knew us and had provided the means of our eternal salvation before He ever created the world, for He himself, in Christ, would pay the price in His own blood.

The Lord Jesus then, in this primeval revelation, actually reviews some of the events recorded in the Genesis account of creation. The word "depths" is the same as "deep," and clearly refers to the primordial boundless world ocean of Genesis 1:2. This great deep was soon formed into a network of "seas" which supplied a vast subterranean reservoir feeding the "fountains of waters" through which great artesian springs would produce the rivers of Eden and, no doubt, of the rest of the "very good" world which God would create.

Then the gentle mountains and hills of the primeval world were formed, all of them simply spoken into existence by the Word of God — that is, by our Lord Jesus Christ.

But He reminds us again that He himself was eternally "brought forth" before any of these were created and made. The reference to "the highest part of the dust of the world" is intriguing, and it is difficult to determine its precise meaning. The "dust" refers to the smallest particles of matter, and "world" refers to the inhabited parts of the earth. "The highest part" is one word in the original (*rosh*), translated in various ways, most often as "head" or "top." One possible meaning is that of the small particles of dust, salt, etc., in the atmosphere. Another possibility might be that of the most complex arrangements of matter, all composed ultimately of very small particles, "dust," or even the atomic elements. The most complex of all systems in the habitable world is man himself — especially the human brain — and the creation record tells us that he was formed "of the dust of the ground" (Gen. 2:7).

Proverbs 8:27–31

27. *When He prepared the heavens, I was there: when He set a compass upon the face of the depth.*
28. *When He established the clouds above: when He strengthened the fountains of the deep:*
29. *When He gave to the sea His decree, that the waters should not pass His commandment: when He appointed the foundations of the earth:*
30. *Then I was by Him, as one brought up with Him: and I was daily His delight, rejoicing always before Him;*
31. *Rejoicing in the habitable part of His earth; and my delights were with the sons of men.*

He next recalls the preparation of the heavens. First, God created "space" and "matter" and "time" — that is, heaven and earth in the beginning (Gen. 1:1). The infinite heaven is as unending as space (what could be beyond the end of space, except more space?). The Genesis record speaks of the heaven where the stars shine and the heaven where birds fly — that is, the sidereal heaven and the atmospheric heaven — but beyond all these is the infinite heaven where God has His throne.

The word for "compass" (Hebrew *khug*) is the same as "circle" in Isaiah 40:22, as well as "compassed" in Job 26:10. All three references are to the roundness of the earth, especially to the approximately spherical nature of sea level defining the global shape of the earth. The Bible nowhere suggests that the earth is flat, though skeptics often make this careless charge.

The word "clouds" in verse 28 is the same word as "sky" or "vapor." This most likely is a reference to the "waters above the firmament" in the original creation, probably an extensive canopy of invisible water vapor. Note again that the words "depth" (verses 24, 27) and "deep" (verses 28) are the same in the Hebrew, referring to the waters created on day 1 and placed in their positions and functions relative to the earth on days 2 and 3 of creation week. It was also on day 3 that Christ made the "fountains of the deep" strong enough to carry out their mission of delivering water from the subterranean reservoir to the earth's surface and also provided solid "foundations of the earth" to support the continents and other structures of the earth's crust when the dry lands were separated from the global waters. It was then also that the original worldwide ocean was constrained at the edges of the lands, with sea level maintained globally by the necessity of water everywhere to seek its own level.

And throughout all the mighty events of creation week the divine wisdom was there, implementing with His spoken words (as the Word of God) the creative purposes of the triune God. There was joyful fellowship — "delight" — within the Godhead throughout the wonderful project of creation.

Then, finally, when Adam and Eve were created and told to multiply and fill the earth (Gen. 1:28), there was great rejoicing over all God's finished work in the "habitable parts" (that is, the "world") of the earth. No doubt the angels rejoiced, Adam and Eve rejoiced, and God rejoiced, especially that person of the Godhead who would one day become a man himself. "My delights," He said, "were with the sons of men." That is, literally, "with the sons of Adam."

The Lord surely knew the immediate sorrow that Cain would soon cause, and then, through the centuries, many other sons of Adam. But plans to redeem these lost men, or at least those who would receive the gift of redemption, had already been set and God would look beyond the immediate ages of suffering to the future ages of fellowship, and rejoice.

This specially inspired and revealed perspective on creation concludes Solomon's 16th sermon, this one addressed not just to "my son" but to "ye children."

The 17th and final sermon, or lesson, is addressed also to all his children. The last two sermons are profoundly significant, not just to Rehoboam, Taphath, and Basmath, of course, but also to all God's children everywhere and in every age.

Proverbs 8:32–36

32. *Now therefore hearken unto me, O ye children: for blessed are they that keep my ways.*
33. *Hear instruction, and be wise, and refuse it not.*
34. *Blessed is the man that heareth me, watching daily at my gates, waiting at the posts of my doors.*
35. *For whoso findeth me findeth life, and shall obtain favour of the* LORD.
36. *But he that sinneth against me wrongeth his own soul: all they that hate me love death.*

Solomon begins his last message to his children by reminding them again how urgently important it is to keep God's ways, heed his instruction, and be spiritually wise. He is doing this by citing the words of the divine wisdom, mediated through him, as it were, to his children. Such obedience is not only important as a matter of general lifestyle, but one that requires *daily* attention. We must hear the Lord daily, watching and waiting daily, if we would receive His true blessing and guidance. This we do, of course, through daily Bible study and prayer, not only hearing His words, but believing and obeying them.

This is no take-it-or-leave-it choice, either, but a matter of life and death. "Whoso findeth me findeth life," but "all they that hate me love death."

It is wisdom who is speaking but, as we have seen, wisdom really is none other than the Lord Jesus Christ. He is the One who created us and who paid the awful price of His unspeakably precious blood to redeem us. To fail to appreciate His great gift of creation and His even greater gift of redemption is to "love death."

It was Christ, in His human incarnation, who said, "He that believeth on him is not condemned: but he that believeth not is condemned already, because he hath not believed in the name of the only begotten Son of God" (John 3:18).

Proverbs 9:1–6

1. *Wisdom hath builded her house, she hath hewn out her seven pillars:*
2. *She hath killed her beasts; she hath mingled her wine; she hath also furnished her table.*
3. *She hath sent forth her maidens: she crieth upon the highest places of the city,*
4. *Whoso is simple, let him turn in hither: as for him that wanteth understanding, she saith to him,*
5. *Come, eat of my bread, and drink of the wine which I have mingled.*
6. *Forsake the foolish, and live; and go in the way of understanding.*

Once again, in this last message to his children, Solomon personifies Wisdom as the wise, godly, virtuous kinswoman, as opposed to the foolish alien woman. As the latter had invited the simple young man into her house of death (Prov. 7:6–27), so Wisdom invited him to enter her house of life. "Forsake the foolish, and live" she says, "go in the way of understanding."

Her house is constructed sturdily on seven strong pillars, perhaps visualized as one central pillar, with six at 60-degree intervals on the periphery. The number seven throughout the Bible represents completeness, stability, and perfection.

But what exactly are the seven pillars of wisdom? Solomon does not define or describe them, but perhaps the answer is in the New Testament book of wisdom, the epistle of James. James also contrasts the foolish wisdom of death with the wisdom of life. His emphasis, however, is not on the outward sins of immorality and the like, but on the inward sins of the mind and heart.

"Who is a wise man and endued with knowledge?" he asks. "Let him shew out of a good conversation his works with meekness of wisdom. But if ye have bitter envying and strife in your hearts, glory not, and lie not against the truth. This wisdom descendeth not from above, but is earthly, sensual, devilish. For where envying and strife is, there is confusion and every evil work" (James 3:13–16).

Yes, but what are the seven pillars of this house of true wisdom? "The wisdom that is from above is first pure, then peaceable, gentle, and easy to be entreated, full of mercy and good fruits, without partiality, and without hypocrisy" (James 3:17).

Without being dogmatic (since there is no specific scriptural quote to that effect), it does seem that these seven characteristics of heavenly wisdom could well serve as the seven pillars of the house of real wisdom. We can describe them very simply, as follows.

(1) Purity. This attribute, stressed so strongly in Proverbs, could be taken as the central pillar, combining its strength with each of the other six. Without purity of life and doctrine, the other pillars will fail.

(2) Peaceableness. "Blessed are the peacemakers," Jesus said (Matt. 5:9).

(3) Gentleness. The Greek word here is also translated "mild" or "patient." A Christian should be a gentleman, or a gentle-woman.

(4) Reasonableness. This is the implication of the phrase "easy to be entreated."

(5) Helpfulness. Being "full of mercy and good fruits" implies that one always tries to be helpful, charitable, and loving in deed as well as word.

(6) Humility. The phrase "without partiality" translates a Greek word used only this one time in the New Testament. It suggests a genuine lack of arrogance and judgmentalism.

(7) Sincerity. A person "without hypocrisy" is sincere and reliable in his words and actions.

Whether or not James intended these fruits of Christian wisdom to correspond to Solomon's seven pillars, they are certainly attributes worth cultivating by any believer who really desires to manifest true wisdom in his life. Returning to the Proverbs passage, Wisdom is presented as having prepared a wonderful feast for all who accept her invitation — a banquet of excellent meat, bread, and wine. The wine is "mingled" and should be understood, of course, as mixed with much water and spices so as to be non-intoxicating and healthful, as well as delicious.

Proverbs 9:7–12

7. He that reproveth a scorner getteth to himself shame: and he
    that rebuketh a wicked man getteth himself a blot.
8. Reprove not a scorner, lest he hate thee: rebuke a wise man, and
    he will love thee.
9. Give instruction to a wise man, and he will be yet wiser: teach
    a just man, and he will increase in learning.
10. The fear of the LORD is the beginning of wisdom: and the knowl-
    edge of the holy is understanding.
11. For by me thy days shall be multiplied, and the years of thy life
    shall be increased.
12. If thou be wise, thou shalt be wise for thyself: but if thou scor-
    nest, thou alone shalt bear it.

These instructions are apparently presented by Solomon as the counsel
given by the godly woman Wisdom to those who enter her seven-pillared
house for the promised banquet. Those who are intrinsically or potentially
wise among the young people are the ones who will pay heed to instruction and profit from rebuke and correction. Those who are fools in God's
sight are those who scoff at wise counsel and react angrily and arrogantly
when rebuked or criticized. A wise person can profit from reproofs even
if they are not warranted. As Peter said, "If when ye do well, and suffer
for it, ye take it patiently, this is acceptable with God" (1 Pet. 2:20).

Now even a strong house supported by seven strong pillars will not
stand if it does not have a strong foundation, for its pillars must be supported by a foundation that can carry their loads. So Solomon recognizes
this by reminding his children — and us — that "the fear of the LORD is
the beginning of wisdom." That is, reverence for God and His authoritative Word is the ultimate foundation of all true wisdom.

In the introduction to his 17 sermons, Solomon had stressed that "the
fear of the LORD is the beginning of knowledge" (Prov. 1:7). Here, in the
closing section of his sermons, he emphasizes that "the fear of the LORD
is the beginning of wisdom."

These two verses are probably the key verses of the entire Book of
Proverbs. And both, of course, point us to the Lord Jesus Christ, for "in
[Him] are hid all the treasures of wisdom and knowledge" (Col. 2:3). "O
the depth of the riches both of the wisdom and knowledge of God!"
(Rom. 11:33).

Proverbs 9:13–18

13. A foolish woman is clamorous: she is simple, and knoweth
    nothing.

14. For she sitteth at the door of her house, on a seat in the high places of the city,

15. To call passengers who go right on their ways:

16. Whoso is simple, let him turn in hither: and as for him that wanteth understanding, she saith to him,

17. Stolen waters are sweet, and bread eaten in secret is pleasant.

18. But he knoweth not that the dead are there; and that her guests are in the depths of hell.

Just before ending his last sermon to his children, especially his son, Solomon wanted to add one last warning of the danger of following a "foolish" woman instead of the "wise" woman. Both have houses, and both issue invitations to "the simple" and to "him that wanteth understanding" (verses 1 and 14; 4 and 16). But the wise woman promises eternal life as well as true wisdom; the foolish woman promises sweetness but such stolen waters flow down into hell. Both literally and symbolically, a pure life centered in Christ and eschewing immorality leads to true happiness and everlasting life. A life of temporary pleasure and immorality results in a wasted life and eternal death in hell. Therefore, Solomon would say, "Choose life."

4

Putting Proverbs into Practice

Proverbs 10:1–22:16

The second major section of the Book of Proverbs, comprising chapter 10 through most of chapter 22, begins with the simple title, "The Proverbs of Solomon." According to 1 Kings 4:32, wise King Solomon "spake three thousand proverbs," so this section contains 375 of them, or exactly one-eighth of the total.

When it says that Solomon "spake" these proverbs, it does not necessarily mean that he composed all of them himself. The Hebrew word *dabar* means simply "communicated" or "arranged." It is frequently translated "communed." But whether Solomon wrote them himself or collected them from various sources, their present form is properly attributed to him, as guided by the Holy Spirit.

Unlike the "sermons" or "lessons" in the earlier chapters, and with very few exceptions, each of these 375 proverbs stands on its own, with no apparent connection to those before or after. They are all what has been called "pithy maxims," pertinent in every age as practical guidelines for successful living to those who believe in the true God and want to serve and honor Him in all they do.

Many of them are self-explanatory, and need no particular exposition. Others warrant closer individual analysis and comparison with other Scriptures to get their full impact. Thus the treatment of these 375 proverbs may be selective and uneven, but we trust will be helpful and challenging as we seek to live lives that are both pleasing to God and practical in our human relationships. The text of each of these 13 chapters will therefore be quoted in full, with commentary only as appropriate and needful.

Proverbs 10

1. *The proverbs of Solomon. A wise son maketh a glad father: but a foolish son is the heaviness of his mother.*

2. *Treasures of wickedness profit nothing: but righteousness delivereth from death.*

3. *The LORD will not suffer the soul of the righteous to famish: but He casteth away the substance of the wicked.*

4. *He becometh poor that dealeth with a slack hand: but the hand of the diligent maketh rich.*

5. *He that gathereth in summer is a wise son: but he that sleepeth in harvest is a son that causeth shame.*

6. *Blessings are upon the head of the just: but violence covereth the mouth of the wicked.*

7. *The memory of the just is blessed: but the name of the wicked shall rot.*

8. *The wise in heart will receive commandments: but a prating fool shall fall.*

9. *He that walketh uprightly walketh surely: but he that perverteth his ways shall be known.*

10. *He that winketh with the eye causeth sorrow: but a prating fool shall fall.*

11. *The mouth of a righteous man is a well of life: but violence covereth the mouth of the wicked.*

12. *Hatred stirreth up strifes: but love covereth all sins.*

13. *In the lips of him that hath understanding wisdom is found: but a rod is for the back of him that is void of understanding.*

14. *Wise men lay up knowledge: but the mouth of the foolish is near destruction.*

15. *The rich man's wealth is his strong city: the destruction of the poor is their poverty.*

16. *The labour of the righteous tendeth to life: the fruit of the wicked to sin.*

17. *He is in the way of life that keepeth instruction: but he that refuseth reproof erreth.*

18. *He that hideth hatred with lying lips, and he that uttereth a slander, is a fool.*

19. *In the multitude of words there wanteth not sin: but he that refraineth his lips is wise.*

20. *The tongue of the just is as choice silver: the heart of the wicked is little worth.*

21. *The lips of the righteous feed many: but fools die for want of wisdom.*

22. *The blessing of the* LORD, *it maketh rich, and He addeth no sorrow with it.*
23. *It is as sport to a fool to do mischief: but a man of understanding hath wisdom.*
24. *The fear of the wicked, it shall come upon him: but the desire of the righteous shall be granted.*
25. *As the whirlwind passeth, so is the wicked no more: but the righteous is an everlasting foundation.*
26. *As vinegar to the teeth, and as smoke to the eyes, so is the sluggard to them that send him.*
27. *The fear of the* LORD *prolongeth days: but the years of the wicked shall be shortened.*
28. *The hope of the righteous shall be gladness: but the expectation of the wicked shall perish.*
29. *The way of the* LORD *is strength to the upright: but destruction shall be to the workers of iniquity.*
30. *The righteous shall never be removed: but the wicked shall not inhabit the earth.*
31. *The mouth of the just bringeth forth wisdom: but the froward tongue shall be cut out.*
32. *The lips of the righteous know what is acceptable: but the mouth of the wicked speaketh frowardness.*

As we enter this section of the remarkable Book of Proverbs, we notice immediately that most of the individual proverbs are in the form of "antithetic" couplets, each contrasting two ways of belief or behavior, one right way and one wrong way. This format continues, with a few exceptions, through chapter 15 of Proverbs. Then, in Proverbs 16:1–22:16, the couplets are mostly "synthetic," with the second statement simply supplementing and strengthening the first. No reason is given for organizing the proverbs in the form of couplets, but it does at least facilitate memorization.

The first verse re-emphasizes a theme prominent in Proverbs 1–9 — that is, the concern of Solomon and Naamah for Rehoboam's character development, as well as for that of all young people with God-fearing and concerned parents.

Another principle becomes obvious as we read the proverbs. They are often cast in the form of generalizations, not as inflexible rules that allow no exceptions. This is illustrated in verse 3. There have, no doubt, been some occasions when righteous men and innocent children have gone hungry or even starved, and when wicked men have acquired and kept great riches all their lives, but these are exceptions. Furthermore, the principle becomes perfectly true when applied to the future life. These two constraints should be kept in mind when interpreting each of these antithetical proverbs.

Verse 4 also illustrates these constraints. There are some slothful people who become rich through inheritance or gambling or some other means, and some industrious and intelligent people who never get rich. The principle is only generally true in this present life but becomes absolutely true in eternity.

Verse 6b probably means that a devious planner of violence will "cover" his mouth so as to conceal his intentions. Verses 8b and 10b both use the colorful phrase, "a prating fool shall fall." The Hebrew word for "prating" is usually translated "lips," and the meaning seems to be that a man using his lips foolishly will eventually come to grief.

The statement that "violence covereth the mouth of the wicked" is repeated in verse 11 (note verse 6). In contrast, "the mouth" of a righteous man is like a well of life-giving water. It was said prophetically of Christ that "grace is poured into thy lips" (Ps. 45:2), and He should be our example. Note how many of the proverbs in this chapter have to do with our speech (Prov. 10:6, 8, 10–11, 13–14, 18–21, and 31–32).

Verse 12 is reflected in the "love chapter" of the Pauline epistles (1 Cor. 13:4–7), and is partially quoted by Peter, when he says that "charity (Greek *agape*) shall cover the multitude of sins" (1 Pet. 4:8), and also by James, when he says that a faithful witness who brings a sinning brother back to repentance and faith "shall hide a multitude of sins" (James 5:20).

The "rod" mentioned in verse 13 can be understood as symbolic of punishment in general, whatever type is appropriate and lawful in relation to the crime committed by those who refuse or neglect to "get understanding" (Prov. 4:7) — that is, understanding of what is acceptable behavior in the sight of God or the God-ordained governmental system.

As noted earlier, many of these verses are so self-explanatory that commentary or exposition is not needed. Verse 19, however, seems so untypical of normal human activity that it is worth special emphasis. "He that refraineth his lips is wise." This reminds us of Jesus' admonition: "But I say unto you, That every idle word that men shall speak, they shall give account thereof in the day of judgment" (Matt. 12:36). And James says, "Let every man be swift to hear, slow to speak, slow to wrath" (James 1:19).

As verse 24 implies, the minds of wicked men are occupied with fear that they will have to pay someday for their evil, and that fear will indeed be realized. In contrast, the minds of the righteous are occupied with hope and desire for good, and their prayers will indeed be answered.

When Solomon penned verse 27, he may have remembered God's promise to him to "lengthen thy days" provided he would "keep my statutes and my commandments" (1 Kings 3:14). The sad fact is that Solomon did not remember long enough, for sometime later he began to bring pagan wives into his harem and even to build shrines for their pagan religions. The result was that God actually shortened his days, and he died at about 60 years of age.

Proverbs 11

1. *A false balance is abomination to the LORD: but a just weight is His delight.*
2. *When pride cometh, then cometh shame: but with the lowly is wisdom.*
3. *The integrity of the upright shall guide them: but the perverseness of transgressors shall destroy them.*
4. *Riches profit not in the day of wrath: but righteousness delivereth from death.*
5. *The righteousness of the perfect shall direct his way: but the wicked shall fall by his own wickedness.*
6. *The righteousness of the upright shall deliver them: but transgressors shall be taken in their own naughtiness.*
7. *When a wicked man dieth, his expectation shall perish: and the hope of unjust men perisheth.*
8. *The righteous is delivered out of trouble: and the wicked cometh in his stead.*
9. *An hypocrite with his mouth destroyeth his neighbour: but through knowledge shall the just be delivered.*
10. *When it goeth well with the righteous, the city rejoiceth: and when the wicked perish, there is shouting.*
11. *By the blessing of the upright, the city is exalted: but it is overthrown by the mouth of the wicked.*
12. *He that is void of wisdom despiseth his neighbour: but a man of understanding holdeth his peace.*
13. *A talebearer revealeth secrets: but he that is of a faithful spirit concealeth the matter.*
14. *Where no counsel is, there the people fall: but in the multitude of counsellors there is safety.*
15. *He that is surety for a stranger shall smart for it: and he that hateth suretyship is sure.*
16. *A gracious woman retaineth honour: and strong men retain riches.*
17. *The merciful man doeth good to his own soul: but he that is cruel troubleth his own flesh.*

18. *The wicked worketh a deceitful work: but to him that soweth righteousness shall be a sure reward.*

19. *As righteousness tendeth to life; so he that pursueth evil pursueth it to his own death.*

20. *They that are of a froward heart are abomination to the LORD: but such as are upright in their way are His delight.*

21. *Though hand join in hand, the wicked shall not be unpunished: but the seed of the righteous shall be delivered.*

22. *As a jewel of gold in a swine's snout, so is a fair woman without discretion.*

23. *The desire of the righteous is only good: but the expectation of the wicked is wrath.*

24. *There is that scattereth, and yet increaseth; and there is that withholdeth more than is meet, but it tendeth to poverty.*

25. *The liberal soul shall be made fat: and he that watereth shall be watered also himself.*

26. *He that withholdeth corn, the people shall curse him: but blessing shall be upon the head of him that selleth it.*

27. *He that diligently seeketh good procureth favour: but he that seeketh mischief, it shall come unto him.*

28. *He that trusteth in his riches shall fall: but the righteous shall flourish as a branch.*

29. *He that troubleth his own house shall inherit the wind: and the fool shall be servant to the wise of heart.*

30. *The fruit of the righteous is a tree of life; and he that winneth souls is wise.*

31. *Behold, the righteous shall be recompensed in the earth: much more the wicked and the sinner.*

The first verse of this 11th chapter of Proverbs deals with the specific question of honesty in weighing items for sale, but it can be considered as representative of business and commerce in general. Dishonesty in business practices has been all too common all over the world throughout history, and God says this is abominable in His sight. Christians should be scrupulously honest and fair in all business and financial matters if they want to be among those who delight the Lord.

Verse 2 is echoed in the New Testament by both James and Peter. "God resisteth the proud, but giveth grace unto the humble" (James 4:6; 1 Pet. 5:5; see also Prov. 3:34).

The future "day of wrath" is mentioned in verse 4 as a time of coming judgment on the ungodly, when a man's riches will not deliver him. This day of wrath is mentioned first in Job 20:28 and again in Psalm 110:5, this being the third reference. It is a common theme in the prophets and in the New Testament. At that time only the righteousness of Christ, imputed to the believer on the basis of faith in Christ's substitutionary sacrifice, will avail.

The term "naughtiness" in verse 6 should be understood in terms of its original English connotation — that is, as something of "naught," utterly worthless. The Hebrew word means "perverseness" or "base wickedness."

Verses 7–12 are self-explanatory. Remember, however, that all these maxims are general rules, not necessarily applicable in every individual case.

The word "talebearer" in verse 13 is translated from two Hebrew words meaning "one who goes around slandering." Malicious gossip, even if based on fact, is best left unsaid.

Verse 14 stresses the importance of basing important decisions not just on one person's opinion, no matter how well qualified, but on the consensus of several qualified people. Even though one person may actually have to make the decision, he or she should first consult with others whose qualifications are appropriate. A pure dictatorship, whether in a nation, a business, a church, or even a family, will sooner or later fall.

The warning against suretyship in verse 15 revisits the strong counsel given by Solomon to his son in Proverbs 6:1–5. The penalty cited is being made to "smart," with two similar Hebrew words literally meaning something like "get evil in return for evil."

One of the more colorfully expressive proverbs is verse 22, comparing a beautiful, but indiscreet (literally "tasteless") woman to a golden jewel adorning the snout of a pig. This is not an outlandish comparison, as many women of that day did actually wear nose jewels.

Paul's testimony to the Corinthians parallels Solomon's observation in verse 24. Paul said, "He which soweth sparingly shall reap also sparingly; and he which soweth bountifully shall reap also bountifully" (2 Cor. 9:6). "For whatsoever a man soweth, that shall he also reap" (Gal. 6:7).

The reference to the "liberal soul" in verse 25, of course, applies to the original meaning of "liberal" — that is, generous, or liberating. The word in modern times has come to apply to those who are seeking to change society or religion or any existing system away from its traditional ("conservative") practices or beliefs.

The phrase "inherit the wind" in verse 29 was adopted as the title of the grossly inaccurate motion picture based on the famous 1925 Scopes trial. The picture made a hero out of the atheistic lawyer who was attacking the biblical record of creation and a buffoon out the Christian statesman defending it. Actually, the verse itself was twisted out of context when it was applied in this way to the Scopes trial. The real "troublers of their own house" are the evolutionists who are trying to undermine the basic Christian faith of the nation's founders in favor of modern evolutionary humanism.

Verse 30 is the second of the four metaphorical references to the Edenic "tree of life" in Proverbs. See also Proverbs 3:18; 13:12; and 15:4. The truly righteous person — a man or woman to whom the perfect righteousness of Christ has been imputed (2 Cor. 5:21) and who is therefore seeking by God's grace to be one "that doeth righteousness...even as he is righteous" (1 John 3:7) is justly pictured as a "tree of life," since his fruit can be the winning of souls to eternal life in Christ if he is spiritually "wise." And the Holy Spirit assures us, through Solomon, that "he that winneth souls is wise."

Proverbs 12

1. *Whoso loveth instruction loveth knowledge: but he that hateth reproof is brutish.*
2. *A good man obtaineth favour of the LORD: but a man of wicked devices will he condemn.*
3. *A man shall not be established by wickedness: but the root of the righteous shall not be moved.*
4. *A virtuous woman is a crown to her husband: but she that maketh ashamed is as rottenness in his bones.*
5. *The thoughts of the righteous are right: but the counsels of the wicked are deceit.*
6. *The words of the wicked are to lie in wait for blood: but the mouth of the upright shall deliver them.*
7. *The wicked are overthrown, and are not: but the house of the righteous shall stand.*
8. *A man shall be commended according to his wisdom: but he that is of a perverse heart shall be despised.*
9. *He that is despised, and hath a servant, is better than he that honoureth himself, and lacketh bread.*
10. *A righteous man regardeth the life of his beast: but the tender mercies of the wicked are cruel.*
11. *He that tilleth his land shall be satisfied with bread: but he that followeth vain persons is void of understanding.*
12. *The wicked desireth the net of evil men: but the root of the righteous yieldeth fruit.*
13. *The wicked is snared by the transgression of his lips: but the just shall come out of trouble.*
14. *A man shall be satisfied with good by the fruit of his mouth: and the recompence of a man's hands shall be rendered unto him.*

15. *The way of a fool is right in his own eyes: but he that hearkeneth unto counsel is wise.*
16. *A fool's wrath is presently known: but a prudent man covereth shame.*
17. *He that speaketh truth sheweth forth righteousness: but a false witness deceit.*
18. *There is that speaketh like the piercings of a sword: but the tongue of the wise is health.*
19. *The lip of truth shall be established for ever: but a lying tongue is but for a moment.*
20. *Deceit is in the heart of them that imagine evil: but to the counsellors of peace is joy.*
21. *There shall no evil happen to the just: but the wicked shall be filled with mischief.*
22. *Lying lips are abomination to the LORD: but they that deal truly are his delight.*
23. *A prudent man concealeth knowledge: but the heart of fools proclaimeth foolishness.*
24. *The hand of the diligent shall bear rule: but the slothful shall be under tribute.*
25. *Heaviness in the heart of man maketh it stoop: but a good word maketh it glad.*
26. *The righteous is more excellent than his neighbour: but the way of the wicked seduceth them.*
27. *The slothful man roasteth not that which he took in hunting: but the substance of a diligent man is precious.*
28. *In the way of righteousness is life; and in the pathway thereof there is no death.*

The first verse of Proverbs 12 returns again to Solomon's thesis on the importance of knowledge and related topics. The words for "knowledge" are used 42 times in Proverbs and 7 times in Ecclesiastes, as a total of 7 x 7 times. "Instruction," also translated occasionally as "correction," or "chastening," occurs 30 times in Proverbs.

Many of the verses in this chapter, as throughout Proverbs in general, contrast the ways and ultimate fate of the "righteous" and the "wicked" (note verses 2–3, 5–7, 10, 12–13, 21, and 26). As noted before, Jesus was the only truly "righteous" man in all history, but His righteousness has been imputed to all who believe God's Word and come to Him through faith in His provision of a substitutionary sacrifice. (The Old Testament offerings served as temporary provisions until Christ could come and offer himself as the one perfect sacrifice for sins forever.) Those who thus receive His righteousness then seek to live righteously, in accord with God's commands, thereby demonstrating their thanks for His gift of forgiveness and eternal life, and also showing its reality.

The term "wicked" or "wickedness" is used 8 times in this chapter, starting in verses 2 and 3, and over 90 times in Proverbs altogether, as well as 12 times in Ecclesiastes. The Hebrew word *rasha* means, "habitually immoral person or lifestyle." Solomon obviously encountered much wickedness in his reign and so felt constrained often to warn against it in his writings. The immorality of his pagan wives and others eventually affected even him.

Verse 4 extols the merits of a "virtuous woman," a theme elaborated at length in the last 22 verses of Proverbs. The Hebrew word conveys the idea of strength and valor, as well as high moral standards. Symbolically, the "virtuous woman" can be considered as another synonym for the godly kinswoman Wisdom, in contrast to the strange woman personifying Folly.

In verse 9, the word "hath" is not in the original, so the verse could better be understood in the sense of "He that is despised and *is* a servant (that is, works to supply his own needs) is really better than one who praises himself but does not earn his living."

Verse 10 reminds us that God cares for His animal creation as well as for men and women, and desires us to do the same. When God placed the animals under man's dominion (Genesis 1:26–28), this was a stewardship, not a license for cruelty. God has a purpose for every creature, and even though man can use them for food, clothing, etc., they should be respected as creatures of God. On the other hand, animals should not be regarded as human ancestors or as gods to worship, and should not be allowed to become harmful to man.

The word for "net" in verse 12 is translated various ways, most commonly as something like "defense" or "stronghold." The idea seems to be that wicked men find their own defensive support in the company of other wicked men. The defense of the righteous, on the other hand, who root their lives firmly in the truth of God, is the good fruit they produce.

Most of the verses in this chapter explain themselves just by their obvious common sense. Further emphasis on the truthful, helpful use of our words (and warnings about their misuse) is noted in verses 6, 13–14, 17–19, and 22. As Paul said, "Let no corrupt communication proceed out of your mouth, but that which is good to the use of edifying, that it may minister grace unto the hearers" (Eph. 4:29).

When verse 21 notes that "there shall no evil happen to the just," we have to remember that the proverbs are generalizations which usually (but not always — think of all the abuses suffered by Job and by Paul, for example) hold true in this life, but must await their complete fulfillment in the future life.

"Abomination" is another word which occurs frequently in Proverbs — here at verse 22, but also about 20 other times. "Lying lips are an abomination to the LORD" but so also are "a froward heart" (Prov. 3:32; 11:20), "a false balance" (Prov. 11:1), and even "the sacrifice of the wicked" (Prov. 15:8; 21:27), as well as various other evils. Recall the seven "abominations" of Proverbs 6:16–19.

On the other hand, there are a number of things that "delight" the Lord. Verse 22 says He is delighted with those "that deal truly." Some of the others are "a just weight" (Prov. 11:1), and "the prayer of the upright" (Prov. 15:8).

There are very few references in the Bible to hunting, but verse 27 is one of them. It suggests that hunting for food is permissible, but not if the hunter is too lazy or indifferent to cook and eat it. The only hunters mentioned by name in the Bible are Nimrod and Esau (Gen. 10:9; 25:27), and both were rebels against God and His will.

The 12th chapter closes with a beautiful promise: "In the way of righteousness is life; and in the pathway thereof there is no death" (verse 28). This points us, of course, to the Lord Jesus Christ, who is both "the way" and "the life" (John 14:6).

Proverbs 13

1. *A wise son heareth his father's instruction: but a scorner heareth not rebuke.*
2. *A man shall eat good by the fruit of his mouth: but the soul of the transgressors shall eat violence.*
3. *He that keepeth his mouth keepeth his life: but he that openeth wide his lips shall have destruction.*
4. *The soul of the sluggard desireth, and hath nothing: but the soul of the diligent shall be made fat.*
5. *A righteous man hateth lying: but a wicked man is loathsome, and cometh to shame.*
6. *Righteousness keepeth him that is upright in the way: but the wickedness overthroweth the sinner.*
7. *There is that maketh himself rich, yet hath nothing: there is that maketh himself poor, yet hath great riches.*
8. *The ransom of a man's life are his riches: but the poor heareth not rebuke.*
9. *The light of the righteous rejoiceth: but the lamp of the wicked shall be put out.*

10. *Only by pride cometh contention: but the well advised is wisdom.*

11. *Wealth gotten by vanity shall be diminished: but he that gathereth by labour shall increase.*

12. *Hope deferred maketh the heart sick: but when the desire cometh, it is a tree of life.*

13. *Whoso despiseth the word shall be destroyed: but he that feareth the commandment shall be rewarded.*

14. *The law of the wise is a fountain of life, to depart from the snares of death.*

15. *Good understanding giveth favour: but the way of transgressors is hard.*

16. *Every prudent man dealeth with knowledge: but a fool layeth open his folly.*

17. *A wicked messenger falleth into mischief: but a faithful ambassador is health.*

18. *Poverty and shame shall be to him that refuseth instruction: but he that regardeth reproof shall be honoured.*

19. *The desire accomplished is sweet to the soul: but it is abomination to fools to depart from evil.*

20. *He that walketh with wise men shall be wise: but a companion of fools shall be destroyed.*

21. *Evil pursueth sinners: but to the righteous good shall be repayed.*

22. *A good man leaveth an inheritance to his children's children: and the wealth of the sinner is laid up for the just.*

23. *Much food is in the tillage of the poor: but there is that is destroyed for want of judgment.*

24. *He that spareth his rod hateth his son: but he that loveth him chasteneth him betimes.*

25. *The righteous eateth to the satisfying of his soul: but the belly of the wicked shall want.*

The "wise son" is mentioned three times in Proverbs. Here, in verse 1, God (through Solomon) tells us that such a son will heed the teachings of his father. A wise son thus makes a "glad father," according to Proverbs 10:1 and 15:20.

Another warning against talkativeness is given in verse 3 and against laziness in verse 4, both themes occurring often in the Proverbs. Verse 7 deals with the true riches, and is echoed in 2 Corinthians 6:10, which tells us that God's true servants are "as poor, yet making many rich; as having nothing, and yet possessing all things." And, of course, it is especially illustrated by Christ himself who, "though he was rich, yet for your sakes he became poor, that ye through his poverty might be rich" (2 Cor. 8:9).

Verse 8 notes that a rich man may have to use his riches as a ransom to persuade captors to spare his life. The Lord Jesus also warned, "What is a man profited, if he shall gain the whole world, and lose his own soul?" (Matt. 16:26). Solomon himself came perilously close to such an end; with all his immense wealth, he finally concluded that it was all "vanity and vexation of spirit, and there was no profit under the sun" (Eccles. 2:11).

Verse 9 means that to the wicked there shall finally be "the blackness of darkness for ever" (Jude 13), but for the righteous "there shall be no night there . . . for the Lord God giveth them light" (Rev. 22:5), and "they shall obtain joy and gladness, and sorrow and sighing shall flee away" (Isa. 35:10).

The third metaphorical reference in Proverbs to Eden's "tree of life" is found in verse 12. Fulfilled hope — especially answers to faithful and persistent prayer — like true wisdom and righteousness is so vitalizing as to seem like God's very tree of life.

But terrible is the ultimate fate of those who despise God's Word. According to verse 13, they "shall be destroyed," when they are judged by the very Word they despised (John 12:48; Rev. 20:12; 22:19).

Verse 14 says that "the law of the wise is a fountain of life," and then Proverbs 14:27 echoes back that "the fear of the LORD is a fountain of life." In the new earth, the Lord Jesus promises to "give unto him that is athirst of the fountain of the water of life freely" (Rev. 21:6).

"A good man leaveth an inheritance to his children's children." This testimony in verse 22 would indicate that it is appropriate for believers to provide financially for their children and grandchildren when they die, provided they have assurance that the heirs will use it properly. On the other hand, the more real and lasting inheritance is that of godly teaching and example, as well as answered prayer for the family.

Verse 24 is the first of several proverbs that tell us that children can and should profit from corporal punishment if it is applied out of love and concern for their future development, and, of course, in such a way as not to inflict lasting injury. It is surprising to note that failure to use "the rod" when needed is a mark of "hatred" rather than love — modern child psychologists and liberal religionists to the contrary notwithstanding.

Proverbs 14

1. *Every wise woman buildeth her house: but the foolish plucketh it down with her hands.*
2. *He that walketh in his uprightness feareth the Lord: but he that is perverse in his ways despiseth him.*

3. *In the mouth of the foolish is a rod of pride: but the lips of the wise shall preserve them.*

4. *Where no oxen are, the crib is clean: but much increase is by the strength of the ox.*

5. *A faithful witness will not lie: but a false witness will utter lies.*

6. *A scorner seeketh wisdom, and findeth it not: but knowledge is easy unto him that understandeth.*

7. *Go from the presence of a foolish man, when thou perceivest not in him the lips of knowledge.*

8. *The wisdom of the prudent is to understand his way: but the folly of fools is deceit.*

9. *Fools make a mock at sin: but among the righteous there is favour.*

10. *The heart knoweth his own bitterness; and a stranger doth not intermeddle with his joy.*

11. *The house of the wicked shall be overthrown: but the tabernacle of the upright shall flourish.*

12. *There is a way which seemeth right unto a man, but the end thereof are the ways of death.*

13. *Even in laughter the heart is sorrowful; and the end of that mirth is heaviness.*

14. *The backslider in heart shall be filled with his own ways: and a good man shall be satisfied from himself.*

15. *The simple believeth every word: but the prudent man looketh well to his going.*

16. *A wise man feareth, and departeth from evil: but the fool rageth, and is confident.*

17. *He that is soon angry dealeth foolishly: and a man of wicked devices is hated.*

18. *The simple inherit folly: but the prudent are crowned with knowledge.*

19. *The evil bow before the good: and the wicked at the gates of the righteous.*

20. *The poor is hated even of his own neighbour: but the rich hath many friends.*

21. *He that despiseth his neighbour sinneth: but he that hath mercy on the poor, happy is he.*

22. *Do they not err that devise evil? but mercy and truth shall be to them that devise good.*

23. *In all labour there is profit: but the talk of the lips tendeth only to penury.*

24. *The crown of the wise is their riches: but the foolishness of fools is folly.*
25. *A true witness delivereth souls: but a deceitful witness speaketh lies.*
26. *In the fear of the LORD is strong confidence: and his children shall have a place of refuge.*
27. *The fear of the LORD is a fountain of life, to depart from the snares of death.*
28. *In the multitude of people is the king's honour: but in the want of people is the destruction of the prince.*
29. *He that is slow to wrath is of great understanding: but he that is hasty of spirit exalteth folly.*
30. *A sound heart is the life of the flesh: but envy the rottenness of the bones.*
31. *He that oppresseth the poor reproacheth his Maker: but he that honoureth him hath mercy on the poor.*
32. *The wicked is driven away in his wickedness: but the righteous hath hope in his death.*
33. *Wisdom resteth in the heart of him that hath understanding: but that which is in the midst of fools is made known.*
34. *Righteousness exalteth a nation: but sin is a reproach to any people.*
35. *The king's favour is toward a wise servant: but his wrath is against him that causeth shame.*

The opening verse of Proverbs 14 reminds the reader once again of the two symbolic women so often discussed in Proverbs — the godly kinswoman and the sinful alien woman, Wisdom and Folly, respectively. Here two literal kinds of women are contrasted — a wise woman who makes a good home for her family, like the seven-pillared house of Proverbs 9:1, and the foolish woman, who destroys her home by "brawling" (Prov. 21:9) or pleasure-seeking (1 Tim. 5:6).

Verse 4 expresses in a rather colorful way the fact that real accomplishment in life involves hard, and sometimes distasteful, work. One wonders if Solomon was thinking here of his having to execute Adonijah, Shimei, and Joab at the beginning of his reign in order to establish a stable base for the great kingdom he developed.

The contrast drawn in verse 6 between the scorner and one who seeks true knowledge has a very modern ring to it. Scoffers may put great stock in their college degrees and intellectual veneer, deriding those who believe in God and His Word, but they can never achieve true wisdom without the fear of the Lord (Prov. 9:10). They can never find ultimate meaning in life or genuine fulfillment and peace of soul, for "he that cometh to

God must believe that He is" (Heb. 11:6). Verse 7 then indicates that it is pointless even to argue with such a person; better just to leave him alone. He is even deceiving himself, as well as others, as implied in verse 8.

Because of his intellectual pride, he even ridicules those who oppose sinful behavior and thus in God's sight is one of the "fools" who "make a mock at sin" (verse 9).

Incidentally, the Book of Proverbs uses the two Hebrew words translated as "fool" more than in all the rest of the Bible combined. Altogether the word and its derivatives ("foolish," "folly," etc.) occur more than 90 times in Proverbs. Note in passing the very pointed usage in verse 24: "The foolishness of fools is folly."

Verse 12 is often cited in refutation of the opinion that sincerity in one's beliefs is all that matters. One can sincerely believe in atheism or any of the pagan religions or even in his own moral judgments, but they will end in death, not salvation and life eternal with God. God's Word, not man's opinion, is the criterion. No humanistically oriented reasoning can ever lead to true life. Note that this warning is repeated again in Proverbs 16:25.

Verse 13 would remind us that laughter is only a temporary and artificial device that cannot characterize a truly useful and godly life. The Bible never records an instance of Jesus laughing, for example, though he is frequently observed weeping. The only references to God laughing show him laughing in derision at those who oppose Him (e.g., Ps. 2:4; Prov. 1:26).

One who is a "backslider" is self-centered rather than God-centered, according to verse 14. Then verse 15 cautions against taking the words of an unbeliever (even a very intellectual unbeliever) at face value. Above all, one should test every teaching by their fidelity to God's Word (Isa. 8:20).

Verse 19, speaking of evil bowing to good, is a generalization which often seems not to work in this present life. Nevertheless, it will be fulfilled quite literally in the future (note, for example, Phil. 2:10; Rom. 14:11; Rev. 3:9; etc.).

An encouraging verse for those who try to witness for Christ is verse 25: "A true witness delivereth souls." Sometimes the "deliverance" seems long in coming, but if our witness is true to the Word of God and given in love and sincerity, God promises it will bear fruit (Isa. 55:11).

On the "fountain of life" mentioned in verse 27, see Proverbs 13:14. On "the fear of the LORD," see especially Proverbs 1:7; 8:13; 9:10.

Verse 34 is familiar, and should certainly be taken to heart today more than ever. The unique blessings of God on the American nation are primarily attributable to the spiritual convictions and motivations of so many of its founders and early leaders. Its present moral decline and religious apathy and apostasy are an ominous portent for the future.

Proverbs 15

1. *A soft answer turneth away wrath: but grievous words stir up anger.*
2. *The tongue of the wise useth knowledge aright: but the mouth of fools poureth out foolishness.*
3. *The eyes of the LORD are in every place, beholding the evil and the good.*
4. *A wholesome tongue is a tree of life: but perverseness therein is a breach in the spirit.*
5. *A fool despiseth his father's instruction: but he that regardeth reproof is prudent.*
6. *In the house of the righteous is much treasure: but in the revenues of the wicked is trouble.*
7. *The lips of the wise disperse knowledge: but the heart of the foolish doeth not so.*
8. *The sacrifice of the wicked is an abomination to the LORD: but the prayer of the upright is His delight.*
9. *The way of the wicked is an abomination unto the LORD: but He loveth him that followeth after righteousness.*
10. *Correction is grievous unto him that forsaketh the way: and he that hateth reproof shall die.*
11. *Hell and destruction are before the LORD: how much more then the hearts of the children of men?*
12. *A scorner loveth not one that reproveth him: neither will he go unto the wise.*
13. *A merry heart maketh a cheerful countenance: but by sorrow of the heart the spirit is broken.*
14. *The heart of him that hath understanding seeketh knowledge: but the mouth of fools feedeth on foolishness.*
15. *All the days of the afflicted are evil: but he that is of a merry heart hath a continual feast.*
16. *Better is little with the fear of the LORD than great treasure and trouble therewith.*
17. *Better is a dinner of herbs where love is, than a stalled ox and hatred therewith.*
18. *A wrathful man stirreth up strife: but he that is slow to anger appeaseth strife.*
19. *The way of the slothful man is as an hedge of thorns: but the way of the righteous is made plain.*

20. *A wise son maketh a glad father: but a foolish man despiseth his mother.*

21. *Folly is joy to him that is destitute of wisdom: but a man of understanding walketh uprightly.*

22. *Without counsel purposes are disappointed: but in the multitude of counsellors they are established.*

23. *A man hath joy by the answer of his mouth: and a word spoken in due season, how good is it!*

24. *The way of life is above to the wise, that he may depart from hell beneath.*

25. *The LORD will destroy the house of the proud: but he will establish the border of the widow.*

26. *The thoughts of the wicked are an abomination to the LORD: but the words of the pure are pleasant words.*

27. *He that is greedy of gain troubleth his own house; but he that hateth gifts shall live.*

28. *The heart of the righteous studieth to answer: but the mouth of the wicked poureth out evil things.*

29. *The LORD is far from the wicked: but he heareth the prayer of the righteous.*

30. *The light of the eyes rejoiceth the heart: and a good report maketh the bones fat.*

31. *The ear that heareth the reproof of life abideth among the wise.*

32. *He that refuseth instruction despiseth his own soul: but he that heareth reproof getteth understanding.*

33. *The fear of the LORD is the instruction of wisdom; and before honour is humility.*

The 15th chapter begins with still more exhortations on the right use of our divinely given gift of speech. Verse 1 urges the use of "soft" (literally "tender") responses to a confrontive challenge, the object being not to win an argument but to win a soul (compare 2 Tim. 2:24–26; Colossians 4:6; etc.).

God is omnipresent, according to verse 3, for His "eyes" metaphorically are everywhere. See 2 Chronicles 16:9 and Zechariah 4:10 for further confirmation of the all-seeing eyes of the Lord, which "run to and fro throughout the whole earth."

Then, verse 4 assures us that a "wholesome" (literally "healing" or "healthy") tongue is like a "tree of life," the fourth and final reference in Proverbs to the "tree of life" (see also 3:18; 11:30; 13:12).

Proverbs 13:1 had asserted that "a wise son heareth his father's instruction." Now Solomon gives us the obverse truth: "A fool despiseth his father's instruction" (verse 5).

Both the sacrifices and the ways of the wicked are abominable to the Lord, but the Lord loves both the prayers and the ways of "the upright" (verses 8–9).

"Hell and destruction" (that is, *sheol and abaddon*, deep in the heart of the earth where lost souls are awaiting judgment) are open to God's all-seeing eyes, so there is no doubt that He can "see" into the very "hearts of the children of men" (note Acts 1:24). This is the message of verse 11.

The "merry heart" mentioned in verse 13 does not mean a frivolously laughing heart, but a "rejoicing" or "joyful" heart, thankful for God's many blessings; such a heart is indeed reflected in a "cheerful countenance." The "merry heart" in verse 15 is from a different Hebrew word, meaning essentially a "good heart."

Verse 18 supplements the truth in verse 1. "A wrathful man stirreth up strife" but "a soft answer turneth away wrath." "Let not the sun go down upon your wrath," Paul admonishes us in Ephesians 4:26. Verse 20 is almost identical to the very first verse of this section of Proverbs (Prov. 10:1), thus stressing again the deep concern of Solomon and Naamah for their own son and for all sons who care for their parents.

The importance of good "counsellors" is stressed again in verse 22 (see also Prov. 11:14; 12:20; 24:6), but these are not to be understood as professional counselors in the modern sense. The latter are, too often, simply professional psychologists, whose training has been mainly in some form of humanistic psychology.

The counselors referred to in these and other Scriptures were understood to be simply wise men, mature in the faith and knowledgeable in the words, will, and ways of God.

Note, in verse 24, that "hell" is "beneath," while the "way" leading to life is "above." Hell (that is, *sheol*) is always described in the Old Testament as deep in the center of the earth. Heaven is away from the earth, and the true way of life leads there.

Chapter 15 closes with still another reference to "the fear of the LORD" (verse 33) — what it is, and what it does. In this case, the fear of the Lord is not only the beginning of wisdom (Prov. 9:10) but also the instruction of wisdom. Note, incidentally, that Solomon always refers to God as "the LORD" — that is, as *Jehovah* or *Yahweh*. He never, for some reason, uses the name *Adonai*, always thinking of his God in the sense of His self-existent character and of His redemptive work for His people. *Jehovah* occurs in Proverbs over 85 times. Even *Elohim* ("God") is used only 6 times in Proverbs.

One final note in the chapter is that "humility" must come "before honour" (verse 33). This, of course, is exactly the teaching also of the Lord Jesus Christ (Matt. 23:12).

Proverbs 16

1. The preparations of the heart in man, and the answer of the tongue, is from the LORD.
2. All the ways of a man are clean in his own eyes; but the LORD weigheth the spirits.
3. Commit thy works unto the LORD, and thy thoughts shall be established.
4. The LORD hath made all things for Himself: yea, even the wicked for the day of evil.
5. Every one that is proud in heart is an abomination to the LORD: though hand join in hand, he shall not be unpunished.
6. By mercy and truth iniquity is purged: and by the fear of the LORD men depart from evil.
7. When a man's ways please the LORD, he maketh even his enemies to be at peace with him.
8. Better is a little with righteousness than great revenues without right.
9. A man's heart deviseth his way: but the LORD directeth his steps.
10. A divine sentence is in the lips of the king: his mouth transgresseth not in judgment.
11. A just weight and balance are the LORD's: all the weights of the bag are His work.
12. It is an abomination to kings to commit wickedness: for the throne is established by righteousness.
13. Righteous lips are the delight of kings; and they love him that speaketh right.
14. The wrath of a king is as messengers of death: but a wise man will pacify it.
15. In the light of the king's countenance is life; and his favour is as a cloud of the latter rain.
16. How much better is it to get wisdom than gold! and to get understanding rather to be chosen than silver!
17. The highway of the upright is to depart from evil: he that keepeth his way preserveth his soul.
18. Pride goeth before destruction, and an haughty spirit before a fall.
19. Better it is to be of an humble spirit with the lowly, than to divide the spoil with the proud.

20. He that handleth a matter wisely shall find good: and whoso trusteth in the LORD, happy is he.
21. The wise in heart shall be called prudent: and the sweetness of the lips increaseth learning.
22. Understanding is a wellspring of life unto him that hath it: but the instruction of fools is folly.
23. The heart of the wise teacheth his mouth, and addeth learning to his lips.
24. Pleasant words are as an honeycomb, sweet to the soul, and health to the bones.
25. There is a way that seemeth right unto a man, but the end thereof are the ways of death.
26. He that laboureth laboureth for himself: for his mouth craveth it of him.
27. An ungodly man diggeth up evil: and in his lips there is as a burning fire.
28. A froward man soweth strife: and a whisperer separateth chief friends.
29. A violent man enticeth his neighbour, and leadeth him into the way that is not good.
30. He shutteth his eyes to devise froward things: moving his lips he bringeth evil to pass.
31. The hoary head is a crown of glory, if it be found in the way of righteousness.
32. He that is slow to anger is better than the mighty; and he that ruleth his spirit than he that taketh a city.
33. The lot is cast into the lap; but the whole disposing thereof is of the LORD.

Proverbs 16 contains many insightful and familiar maxims. Verse 2, for example, notes the natural tendency of people to justify their own actions, no matter how contrary to the laws of God or man they may be. However, the Lord is the true judge, and we must all give an account to Him someday (Rom. 14:12). Note also Proverbs 21:2.

The perennial question as to why God created us in the first place is at least partially answered in verse 4. It was simply His will and pleasure to do so (Rev. 4:11), and that is all we really have to know right now. He has assured us that in the ages to come He will show us the exceeding riches of His grace in His kindness to us through Christ Jesus (Eph. 2:7). In the meantime, there is even a divine purpose in His ordaining a day of judgment for which the wicked were made, thereby eliciting yet greater love and thanksgiving in the hearts of the redeemed and more perfect fellowship between them and their Maker in eternity.

What God thinks of our self-justifying pride is pungently set forth in verse 5: it is an abomination! Although all godly men and women will have enemies when they take a strong stand for the truth and integrity of Scripture and the saving gospel of Christ, the Lord will mollify any who harbor enmity for any other reasons, if we live and act in ways that please the Lord. As Peter says, "If ye be reproached for the name of Christ, happy are ye. . . . But let none of you suffer as a murderer, or as a thief, or as an evildoer, or as a busybody in other men's matters. Yet if any man suffer as a Christian, let him not be ashamed; but let him glorify God on this behalf" (1 Pet. 4:14–16).

Verse 11 again stresses that the Lord expects His people to be scrupulously honest in business as well as in personal life. See Proverbs 11:1.

Verses 10 and 12–15 all relate to the thoughts and actions of a king in relation to his subjects. Solomon was probably thinking of his own experience here, and was sensitive to his great responsibility in being "able to judge this thy so great a people," as he had once prayed to the Lord (1 Kings 3:9). But these verses are even more applicable to the thoughts and judgments of Christ himself as ultimate King of all kings.

Returning yet again in verse 16 to the theme of wisdom and understanding, Solomon points out that they are better than silver and gold, as he had stressed in Proverbs 3:13–14. He had an abundance of all of these, as God had promised, and thus he would surely be able to appreciate their relative values.

One of the most famous warnings against pride is found in verse 18. Pride, in fact, was the primeval sin of Satan which led to his fall (1 Tim. 3:6). In 1 Corinthians 10:12 Paul likewise warns, "Let him that thinketh he standeth take heed lest he fall." "Whosoever exalteth himself shall be abased," Jesus said, and He said it at least twice (Luke 14:11; 18:14).

"Whoso trusteth in the LORD, happy is he," we read in verse 20. Solomon here is, in effect, echoing the testimony of his father David (see Ps. 2:12; 34:8). In either case, it is forever true that true happiness — true blessedness — comes only to those who truly trust the Lord Jesus Christ as their Creator, Savior, and King.

Verse 21 speaks of "the sweetness of his lips" as conducive to learning, a concept containing excellent advice for those who are, or who desire to be, teachers. "Pleasant words are as an honeycomb, sweet to the soul, and health to the bones" (verse 24).

Proverbs 16:25 is an important truth, repeated here from Proverbs 14:12. The "broad way" often seems very attractive, even in a spiritual sense, for there are more traveling on that road, and thus more who need to hear the truth. Nevertheless, it leads only to destruction and death, and believers who are tempted to stay on it for only a little while may later find it very difficult, if not impossible, to change directions when they want to do so.

Verse 31 indicates that long life is, at least to many, a reward for those who are regularly found "in the way of righteousness." Such had been promised to Solomon (1 Kings 3:14), and he remained in that "way" for many years. When he later fell into serious disobedience, however, God seems to have shortened his life. He was only 20 years old or younger when he became king, and he reigned 40 years, thus dying at age 60 or less (1 Kings 11:42). Nevertheless, he apparently died in peace.

The closing verse of the chapter, verse 33, refers to the casting of lots as a means of deciding between different possible courses of action. Apparently God, in grace, sanctioned this procedure on occasion, and indicated His will by controlling the outcome. In no place, however, do we ever read of His directing or authorizing such a procedure. The only New Testament example, apart from the Roman soldiers casting lots for Christ's vesture at the cross, was in the selection of a new apostle to take the place of Judas (Acts 1:23–26). It is significant that, before the lots were cast, the 11 prayed that God would direct the procedure so as to accomplish His will. This was in the spirit, at least, of this 33rd verse, and God apparently honored it. Whether or not any such procedure should be used today, now that we have God's complete Word, is at least doubtful.

Proverbs 17

1. *Better is a dry morsel, and quietness therewith, than an house full of sacrifices with strife.*
2. *A wise servant shall have rule over a son that causeth shame, and shall have part of the inheritance among the brethren.*
3. *The fining pot is for silver, and the furnace for gold: but the LORD trieth the hearts.*
4. *A wicked doer giveth heed to false lips; and a liar giveth ear to a naughty tongue.*
5. *Whoso mocketh the poor reproacheth his Maker: and he that is glad at calamities shall not be unpunished.*
6. *Children's children are the crown of old men; and the glory of children are their fathers.*
7. *Excellent speech becometh not a fool: much less do lying lips a prince.*
8. *A gift is as a precious stone in the eyes of him that hath it: whithersoever it turneth, it prospereth.*
9. *He that covereth a transgression seeketh love; but he that repeateth a matter separateth very friends.*

10. *A reproof entereth more into a wise man than an hundred stripes into a fool.*

11. *An evil man seeketh only rebellion: therefore a cruel messenger shall be sent against him.*

12. *Let a bear robbed of her whelps meet a man, rather than a fool in his folly.*

13. *Whoso rewardeth evil for good, evil shall not depart from his house.*

14. *The beginning of strife is as when one letteth out water: therefore leave off contention, before it be meddled with.*

15. *He that justifieth the wicked, and he that condemneth the just, even they both are an abomination to the LORD.*

16. *Wherefore is there a price in the hand of a fool to get wisdom, seeing he hath no heart to it?*

17. *A friend loveth at all times, and a brother is born for adversity.*

18. *A man void of understanding striketh hands, and becometh surety in the presence of his friend.*

19. *He loveth transgression that loveth strife: and he that exalteth his gate seeketh destruction.*

20. *He that hath a froward heart findeth no good: and he that hath a perverse tongue falleth into mischief.*

21. *He that begetteth a fool doeth it to his sorrow: and the father of a fool hath no joy.*

22. *A merry heart doeth good like a medicine: but a broken spirit drieth the bones.*

23. *A wicked man taketh a gift out of the bosom to pervert the ways of judgment.*

24. *Wisdom is before him that hath understanding; but the eyes of a fool are in the ends of the earth.*

25. *A foolish son is a grief to his father, and bitterness to her that bare him.*

26. *Also to punish the just is not good, nor to strike princes for equity.*

27. *He that hath knowledge spareth his words: and a man of understanding is of an excellent spirit.*

28. *Even a fool, when he holdeth his peace, is counted wise: and he that shutteth his lips is esteemed a man of understanding.*

Note that the proverbs in chapter 16 were not of the "antithetical" type, as they had been in chapters 10–15, with two opposing concepts being paired against each other. Rather, these were each "synthetic" couplets, with the second thought supporting the first. That will also be found true in Proverbs 17, as well as in the remaining chapters of this segment of the

Book of Proverbs. That is, all of the proverbs in Proverbs 16:1 through 22:16 are of this style.

Most of the proverbs in chapter 17 are self-explanatory and require no interpretive comments. Nevertheless, each is profoundly true, well worth pondering and applying in one's life. For example, verse 1 sets forth the superiority in God's sight of a peaceful and loving home with no luxuries and even very little of life's necessities in comparison to a materially prosperous home full of bitterness and dissension.

The "fining pot" of verse 3 was a refining pot or crucible. They can be used to purify metals, but only the Lord can cleanse the heart.

Verse 6 notes the ideal relationships within families and generations. Grandparents have a great incentive for godly living in order to set a good example for their children and grandchildren, that they may indeed "glory" in their parents.

One who accepts a bribe (which is the meaning of the "gift" mentioned in verse 8) will be very pleased to have it, at least for a time, but verse 23 indicates that it will pervert his judgment and actually identify him in God's sight as a "wicked man."

A man who foments rebellion against either God's truth or God's divinely called authorities will, sooner or later according to verse 11, be called to account by a "cruel messenger." As a matter of fact, the Hebrew word for "messenger" is the usual word for "angel." It is thus quite possible that the cruel messenger may be an avenging angel sent by God to stop his subversion.

The "letting out of water" mentioned in verse 14 seems to refer to opening a small breach in a water tank. A dispute may seem small at first, but unless it is quickly halted can quickly develop into a break which will, like the breach in the tank, completely inundate the participants and destroy the relationship.

The familiar maxim of verse 22 is supported by modern health science (assuming that the "merry heart" is understood in its real sense as a "cheerful heart" rather than as a joking heart provoking irresponsible hilarity) which has shown that a person's mental and spiritual health tends to be strongly correlated with physical health.

When verse 24 states that "the eyes of a fool are in the ends of the earth," when he searches for wisdom, the idea is that fools will search out all manner of earthly philosophies in vain before they will accept the true wisdom which would be right "before him" if he would only see it. Such a "foolish son" grieves his father and is "bitterness" to his mother (verse 25).

The closing verses of the chapter, verses 27 and 28, again bring up the importance of being careful and sparing in our words. Christians need to cultivate the grace of quietness, instead of loquacity. "Be not rash with thy mouth" (Eccles. 5:2) and "study to be quiet" (1 Thess. 4:11), for Christ warned that "every idle word that men shall speak, they shall give account thereof in the day of judgment" (Matt. 12:36). Note also Proverbs 10:19; 13:2; 15:2; 17:28; 21:23; James 1:19; Ephesians 5:4; etc.

Proverbs 18

1. *Through desire a man, having separated himself, seeketh and intermeddleth with all wisdom.*
2. *A fool hath no delight in understanding, but that his heart may discover itself.*
3. *When the wicked cometh, then cometh also contempt, and with ignominy reproach.*
4. *The words of a man's mouth are as deep waters, and the wellspring of wisdom as a flowing brook.*
5. *It is not good to accept the person of the wicked, to overthrow the righteous in judgment.*
6. *A fool's lips enter into contention, and his mouth calleth for strokes.*
7. *A fool's mouth is his destruction, and his lips are the snare of his soul.*
8. *The words of a talebearer are as wounds, and they go down into the innermost parts of the belly.*
9. *He also that is slothful in his work is brother to him that is a great waster.*
10. *The name of the LORD is a strong tower: the righteous runneth into it, and is safe.*
11. *The rich man's wealth is his strong city, and as an high wall in his own conceit.*
12. *Before destruction the heart of man is haughty, and before honour is humility.*
13. *He that answereth a matter before he heareth it, it is folly and shame unto him.*
14. *The spirit of a man will sustain his infirmity; but a wounded spirit who can bear?*
15. *The heart of the prudent getteth knowledge; and the ear of the wise seeketh knowledge.*
16. *A man's gift maketh room for him, and bringeth him before great men.*
17. *He that is first in his own cause seemeth just; but his neighbour cometh and searcheth him.*

18. *The lot causeth contentions to cease, and parteth between the mighty.*
19. *A brother offended is harder to be won than a strong city: and their contentions are like the bars of a castle.*
20. *A man's belly shall be satisfied with the fruit of his mouth; and with the increase of his lips shall he be filled.*
21. *Death and life are in the power of the tongue: and they that love it shall eat the fruit thereof.*
22. *Whoso findeth a wife findeth a good thing, and obtaineth favour of the* LORD.
23. *The poor useth intreaties; but the rich answereth roughly.*
24. *A man that hath friends must shew himself friendly: and there is a friend that sticketh closer than a brother.*

This is a fairly short chapter and, once again, most of the verses are their own commentary. Verse 1 indicates that a man who rejects sound wisdom from helpful counselors and separates himself from them does so in order to satisfy his own selfish desires, and thus he is fully responsible when they fail. He is the fool of verse 2, who reveals his own wicked heart thereby. Then follows the deserved contempt and reproach from others, as noted in verse 3. On the other hand, the counsel of a godly man with long experience can, as stressed in verse 4, be like an inexhaustible well or stream of life-giving water.

The proverb of verse 8 is repeated in Proverbs 26:22. The "wounds" mentioned in these verses probably should be understood as self-wounds; the whispers of the tale-bearer may hurt others, but may well hurt himself most of all.

The Lord is often symbolized as a "strong tower," as in verse 10. See Psalm 18:2; 61:3; 144:2. Note their emphasis on "running" to that place of safety from sin. One should "run," not hesitate, to the Lord. Those who are said to have "run" to the Lord Jesus include the demon-possessed man seeking deliverance (Mark 5:6), the young man seeking eternal life (Mark 10:17), the unhappy wealthy man (Luke 19:4), the concerned observer at the cross (Mark 15:36), and John and Peter on hearing of the opened tomb (John 20:4, 8).

Verse 12 picks up parts of Proverbs 16:18 and 15:33. Indeed pride *does* lead eventually to destruction, and true honor will indeed go to the humble.

Verse 14 notes the poignant truth that it is easier to endure bodily pain or sickness than a broken spirit. God, of course, can give sustaining grace in both situations to those who look to Him (1 Pet. 5:7; 1 Cor. 10:13).

Verse 18 seems to suggest that casting lots (or, presumably, some equivalent way of settling differences or making decisions between alternatives) can be a God-approved way. It is noteworthy that the casting of lots is mentioned often in Scripture, always in a positive sense (see Esther 3:7; Prov. 16:33; Acts 1:26; etc.), though it is never directly ordered by God.

Verses 20 and 21 again stress the importance of thoughtful and gracious speech. The tongue can be, as James says, "an unruly evil, full of deadly poison" (James 3:8). How much better that it be "alway with grace, seasoned with salt, that ye may know how ye ought to answer every man" (Col. 4:6).

When Solomon says that "whoso findeth a wife findeth a good thing, and obtaineth favour of the LORD" in verse 22, it is reasonable to assume he was thinking of his own beautiful and gracious wife Naamah, mother of his son Rehoboam.

Whether these words were written before he married all his foreign princess-wives we do not know, but in any case none could usurp the place of "the wife of [his] youth" (Prov. 5:18) in his love and admiration. Note also Proverbs 19:14.

God had said in the beginning, "It is not good that the man should be alone" (Gen. 2:18). In an age when life-long monogamous marriage between a man and a woman is increasingly being denigrated, it is important for believers to stand firm on this vital truth.

The chapter closes in praise of making good friends. And, of course, the Lord Jesus Christ is the truest friend of all, because He laid down His life for us (see John 15:13–15).

Proverbs 19

1. Better is the poor that walketh in his integrity, than he that is perverse in his lips, and is a fool.
2. Also, that the soul be without knowledge, it is not good; and he that hasteth with his feet sinneth.
3. The foolishness of man perverteth his way: and his heart fretteth against the LORD.
4. Wealth maketh many friends, but the poor is separated from his neighbour.
5. A false witness shall not be unpunished, and he that speaketh lies shall not escape.
6. Many will intreat the favour of the prince: and every man is a friend to him that giveth gifts.
7. All the brethren of the poor do hate him: how much more do his friends go far from him? he pursueth them with words, yet they are wanting to him.
8. He that getteth wisdom loveth his own soul: he that keepeth understanding shall find good.

9. A false witness shall not be unpunished, and he that speaketh lies shall perish.
10. Delight is not seemly for a fool; much less for a servant to have rule over princes.
11. The discretion of a man deferreth his anger; and it is his glory to pass over a transgression.
12. The king's wrath is as the roaring of a lion; but his favour is as dew upon the grass.
13. A foolish son is the calamity of his father: and the contentions of a wife are a continual dropping.
14. House and riches are the inheritance of fathers: and a prudent wife is from the LORD.
15. Slothfulness casteth into a deep sleep; and an idle soul shall suffer hunger.
16. He that keepeth the commandment keepeth his own soul; but he that despiseth his ways shall die.
17. He that hath pity upon the poor lendeth unto the LORD; and that which he hath given will He pay him again.
18. Chasten thy son while there is hope, and let not thy soul spare for his crying.
19. A man of great wrath shall suffer punishment: for if thou deliver him, yet thou must do it again.
20. Hear counsel, and receive instruction, that thou mayest be wise in thy latter end.
21. There are many devices in a man's heart; nevertheless the counsel of the LORD, that shall stand.
22. The desire of a man is his kindness: and a poor man is better than a liar.
23. The fear of the LORD tendeth to life: and he that hath it shall abide satisfied; he shall not be visited with evil.
24. A slothful man hideth his hand in his bosom, and will not so much as bring it to his mouth again.
25. Smite a scorner, and the simple will beware: and reprove one that hath understanding, and he will understand knowledge.
26. He that wasteth his father, and chaseth away his mother, is a son that causeth shame, and bringeth reproach.
27. Cease, my son, to hear the instruction that causeth to err from the words of knowledge.
28. An ungodly witness scorneth judgment: and the mouth of the wicked devoureth iniquity.
29. Judgments are prepared for scorners, and stripes for the back of fools.

According to verse 2 of this 19th chapter, it is actually a sin to proceed carelessly on a course without knowledge of the factors involved and without due caution and consideration. Then verse 3 notes an unpleasant aspect of fallen human nature. When a foolish man makes a foolish mistake, he compounds his foolishness by blaming it on the Lord.

Verses 5 and 9 are almost identical, emphasizing the awful judgment awaiting those who bear false witness. There are several other warnings in Proverbs against bearing false witness (Prov. 6:19; 12:17; 14:5; 21:28; 25:18). The ninth commandment also deals with this crime, and the last great warnings against it are found in Revelation 21:27 and 22:15. Jesus Christ is "the truth" and God's "Word is truth" (John 14:6; 17:17), so God hates "a false witness that speaketh lies" (Prov. 6:16, 19).

Verse 11 commends as "glory" the attitude of one who maintains a forgiving spirit in regard to personal wrongs committed against him. This was also the teaching of Christ (Matt. 5:24) and Paul (Eph. 4:32).

Verses 13 and 14 contrast the nagging of a contentious wife with the blessing of a prudent wife. One wonders whether Solomon here might have been thinking of his political wife, the Egyptian princess, for whom he had to build a separate palace, in comparison to his beloved wife, Naamah, who had given him the son who would one day succeed him on the throne.

An interesting insight is provided in verse 17. When we give to the poor (or, presumably, to charitable and faith-building ministries in general), we are not really giving money away. The gift is, rather, a loan to the Lord, who in the future will repay it with interest, if not in material blessings, at least spiritually — probably both. Compare Malachi 3:10–12; 2 Corinthians 9:6–11.

Verse 18 is one of several verses in Proverbs endorsing the use of corporal punishment for disobedient and disrespectful children. Note also Proverbs 13:24; 22:15; 23:14. Pain is often a good teacher, if administered in love and in such a way as not to cause injury or greater rebellion. Note Colossians 3:21. Actually the Hebrew word translated "crying" in this verse really means "kill," or "slay," or "death," and is so translated many times, being rendered "crying" only in this one verse. Thus the injunction means to chasten the son when needed, but not in such anger and severity as to endanger his life.

The fact that God's wisdom and God's Word will always be better than any human philosophy or program is stated clearly in verse 21. "The word of our God shall stand for ever" (Isa. 40:8), and no man-devised stratagem or system can ever prevail against it in the long run.

One of the many references in Proverbs to "the fear of the LORD" is found in verse 23. At least in general, this attitude toward God leads to longer life, abiding satisfaction with life, and a peaceful life.

Solomon urges Rehoboam in verse 27 (and inferentially all other sons) not to heed those that would teach against the words of God. Perhaps Rehoboam was inclined to listen to such false teachers, and Solomon wanted him to stop. How urgently this counsel is needed today for our young people, especially in the colleges and universities.

Proverbs 20

1. *Wine is a mocker, strong drink is raging: and whosoever is deceived thereby is not wise.*
2. *The fear of a king is as the roaring of a lion: whoso provoketh him to anger sinneth against his own soul.*
3. *It is an honour for a man to cease from strife: but every fool will be meddling.*
4. *The sluggard will not plow by reason of the cold; therefore shall he beg in harvest, and have nothing.*
5. *Counsel in the heart of man is like deep water; but a man of understanding will draw it out.*
6. *Most men will proclaim every one his own goodness: but a faithful man who can find?*
7. *The just man walketh in his integrity: his children are blessed after him.*
8. *A king that sitteth in the throne of judgment scattereth away all evil with his eyes.*
9. *Who can say, I have made my heart clean, I am pure from my sin?*
10. *Divers weights, and divers measures, both of them are alike abomination to the LORD.*
11. *Even a child is known by his doings, whether his work be pure, and whether it be right.*
12. *The hearing ear, and the seeing eye, the LORD hath made even both of them.*
13. *Love not sleep, lest thou come to poverty; open thine eyes, and thou shalt be satisfied with bread.*
14. *It is naught, it is naught, saith the buyer: but when he is gone his way, then he boasteth.*
15. *There is gold, and a multitude of rubies: but the lips of knowledge are a precious jewel.*
16. *Take his garment that is surety for a stranger: and take a pledge of him for a strange woman.*
17. *Bread of deceit is sweet to a man; but afterwards his mouth shall be filled with gravel.*

18. *Every purpose is established by counsel: and with good advice make war.*

19. *He that goeth about as a talebearer revealeth secrets: therefore meddle not with him that flattereth with his lips.*

20. *Whoso curseth his father or his mother, his lamp shall be put out in obscure darkness.*

21. *An inheritance may be gotten hastily at the beginning; but the end thereof shall not be blessed.*

22. *Say not thou, I will recompense evil; but wait on the LORD, and He shall save thee.*

23. *Divers weights are an abomination unto the LORD; and a false balance is not good.*

24. *Man's goings are of the LORD; how can a man then understand his own way?*

25. *It is a snare to the man who devoureth that which is holy, and after vows to make enquiry.*

26. *A wise king scattereth the wicked, and bringeth the wheel over them.*

27. *The spirit of man is the candle of the LORD, searching all the inward parts of the belly.*

28. *Mercy and truth preserve the king: and his throne is upholden by mercy.*

29. *The glory of young men is their strength: and the beauty of old men is the grey head.*

30. *The blueness of a wound cleanseth away evil: so do stripes the inward parts of the belly.*

It is difficult to justify even so-called social drinking by Christian believers in light of verse 1 of this chapter. Those who argue that drinking in moderation is all right are "not wise" and their "wine is a mocker." Even very small amounts of alcohol have been shown to result in permanent brain damage. Note also Proverbs 23:20; 23:29-35.

Verse 4 provides yet another warning against slothfulness (see also Prov. 6:6; 6:9; 10:26; 12:24; 13:4; 15:19; 18:9; 19:24; etc.). The illustration in this particular proverb is that of a lazy farmer quick to find excuses not to work, but the principle applies to any vocation. As Paul said, "If any would not work, neither should he eat" (2 Thess. 3:10).

A striking commentary on human nature is provided in verse 6. Faithfulness is a precious jewel, rare but valuable when found, whereas the attitude of self-righteousness and the practice of self-justification are as common clay, even among professing Christians.

If a father would desire God's blessings on his children, then — according to verse 7 — he must be a man of consistent righteousness in his life and, particularly, a man of true integrity in all his dealings with others. A reference standard of integrity is that of honest weights and measures in sales transactions, as stressed in verse 10. Note also Proverbs 11:1; 16:11; 20:23.

Verse 9 raises the question: "Who can say . . . I am pure from my sin?" The answer, of course, is as Solomon later wrote, "There is not a just man upon earth, that doeth good, and sinneth not" (Eccles. 7:20). However, one can now have the righteousness and purity of Christ himself imputed to him by faith in Christ as his Savior and Lord. For though "all have sinned, and come short of the glory of God," yet we can be "justified freely by his grace through the redemption that is in Christ Jesus . . . through faith in his blood" (Rom. 3:23–25).

Verse 11 indicates that even young children can understand right and wrong and can be judged accordingly. It is thus never too early to indoctrinate them in the Word of God, especially the saving gospel of the Lord Jesus Christ.

The overwhelming evidence of intelligent design in nature, especially in the human body, is stressed in verse 12. How absurd it is for foolish unbelievers to argue that such marvelous instruments as eyes and ears have evolved by chance mutations and natural selection over imaginary millions of years. It is far more likely that a cyclone blowing through a lumber yard will erect a beautiful home out of the scattering timbers.

Verses 14 and 17 are unusually picturesque in their expressions, one referring to haggling over a sale and its aftermath, the other to the bitter aftertaste of dishonest gain. Both have a very modern ring; human nature has not changed in three thousand years!

On the warning in verse 19 against talebearers (that is, slanderous gossips), see also Proverbs 11:13. This verse indicates that those who use flattery may well also use slander.

Again in verse 20 Solomon stresses the importance of honoring one's parents. Those who actually "curse" (and this word could also mean "despise" or "make light of") their parents have committed a grievous sin in God's sight. In fact, God had established it as a capital crime in Israel (Exod. 21:17; Lev. 20:9) under the Mosaic law system.

We are reminded in verse 22 that we should not return evil for evil, for "vengeance is mine; I will repay, saith the Lord" (Rom. 12:19).

Verse 27 speaks of "the spirit of man." The human "spirit" (Hebrew *neshamah* in this verse) has been imparted to man directly by God himself (Gen. 2:7), and is part of the "image" of God (Gen. 1:26). That image has been severely marred by sin, but is still there, serving as God's "candle" to illuminate his thoughts and to enable him to respond in saving faith to God's provision of salvation and restoration.

Verse 29 provides a measure of comfort to men who have grown old and gray-headed, for their gray hair is called here their "glory" or "splendor." They may no longer have the strength of youth but "the hoary head is a crown of glory, if it be found in the way of righteousness" (Prov. 16:31).

The last verse of the chapter, verse 30, has sometimes been misused to justify flogging of sinners, even by certain cults who enforce their standards of obedience by flogging members who break them. The translation is difficult, but the analogy seems to be that as the infection in a wound is cleansed by blood flowing through it, so chastening by God (or a father) will, if rightly applied, remove evil thoughts and behavior from the life.

Proverbs 21

1. *The king's heart is in the hand of the LORD, as the rivers of water: He turneth it whithersoever He will.*
2. *Every way of a man is right in his own eyes: but the LORD pondereth the hearts.*
3. *To do justice and judgment is more acceptable to the LORD than sacrifice.*
4. *An high look, and a proud heart, and the plowing of the wicked, is sin.*
5. *The thoughts of the diligent tend only to plenteousness; but of every one that is hasty only to want.*
6. *The getting of treasures by a lying tongue is a vanity tossed to and fro of them that seek death.*
7. *The robbery of the wicked shall destroy them; because they refuse to do judgment.*
8. *The way of man is froward and strange: but as for the pure, his work is right.*
9. *It is better to dwell in a corner of the housetop, than with a brawling woman in a wide house.*
10. *The soul of the wicked desireth evil: his neighbour findeth no favour in his eyes.*
11. *When the scorner is punished, the simple is made wise: and when the wise is instructed, he receiveth knowledge.*
12. *The righteous man wisely considereth the house of the wicked: but God overthroweth the wicked for their wickedness.*
13. *Whoso stoppeth his ears at the cry of the poor, he also shall cry himself, but shall not be heard.*
14. *A gift in secret pacifieth anger: and a reward in the bosom strong wrath.*

15. *It is joy to the just to do judgment: but destruction shall be to the workers of iniquity.*
16. *The man that wandereth out of the way of understanding shall remain in the congregation of the dead.*
17. *He that loveth pleasure shall be a poor man: he that loveth wine and oil shall not be rich.*
18. *The wicked shall be a ransom for the righteous, and the transgressor for the upright.*
19. *It is better to dwell in the wilderness, than with a contentious and an angry woman.*
20. *There is treasure to be desired and oil in the dwelling of the wise; but a foolish man spendeth it up.*
21. *He that followeth after righteousness and mercy findeth life, righteousness, and honour.*
22. *A wise man scaleth the city of the mighty, and casteth down the strength of the confidence thereof.*
23. *Whoso keepeth his mouth and his tongue keepeth his soul from troubles.*
24. *Proud and haughty scorner is his name, who dealeth in proud wrath.*
25. *The desire of the slothful killeth him; for his hands refuse to labour.*
26. *He coveteth greedily all the day long: but the righteous giveth and spareth not.*
27. *The sacrifice of the wicked is abomination: how much more, when he bringeth it with a wicked mind?*
28. *A false witness shall perish: but the man that heareth speaketh constantly.*
29. *A wicked man hardeneth his face: but as for the upright, he directeth his way.*
30. *There is no wisdom nor understanding nor counsel against the LORD.*
31. *The horse is prepared against the day of battle: but safety is of the LORD.*

"The powers that be are ordained of God" (Rom. 13:1), and we are exhorted to pray "for kings and all that are in authority" (1 Tim. 2:2). Verse 1 of Proverbs 21 assures that God can control the hearts (or minds) of kings as easily as He can direct the flow of water in a river, so that He can indeed answer our prayers concerning the actions of kings.

Then verse 2 reminds us again that man's ways may not be God's ways (Prov. 14:12; 16:25). Even imprisoned criminals are commonly found still to be justifying themselves and blaming others for the sinful acts which caused their problems. The human "heart is deceitful above all things, and desperately wicked" (Jer. 17:9). It takes God himself, the Holy Spirit, to bring true conviction and repentance to the heart of a sinner (John 16:7–11).

Although the sacrificial offerings of Leviticus had been prescribed by God as the means that God's people could be saved from the eternal penalty of their sins, they were of no avail unless the one offering the sacrifice was truly repentant and resolved to sin no more (note Mic. 6:6–8; Hos. 6:6). Verse 3 points up this truth.

Not only pride but even "the plowing of the wicked is sin," according to verse 4. A very similar Hebrew word is translated "lamp," and some translations use this reading. The point in either case is that even activities or guidelines which normally would be meritorious are sinful when serving the devices of the wicked. Even "the sacrifice of the wicked is an abomination unto the LORD" (Prov. 15:8; 21:27), and so are his "thoughts" (Prov. 15:26). God does not mince words!

Solomon mentions in verse 9 the misery of trying to live in the same house — even in a corner of the roof — with "a brawling woman." Again we wonder if he had the Egyptian princess in mind (2 Chron. 8:11). In any case, the sentiment is understandable and valid. Then in verse 19 Solomon says it would even be better to go out and live in the desert!

As is frequently noted, many of the proverbs in this chapter, while pungently true, are quite clear without any further explanation or necessary comment. However, "the congregation of the dead," mentioned in verse 16 refers to the lost souls awaiting judgment down in the great pit called *sheol*, in the heart of the earth. Their bodies are in the grave, but their spirits are quite conscious. Note the graphic description of this "congregation" in Ezekiel 32:18–32.

The truth that godly wisdom is superior to physical strength is the message of verse 22. Then note again in verse 27 that God rejects even the sacrificial offerings of those who offer them "with a wicked mind." Pious adherence to rules of religious ritualism is hypocrisy without a godly life. It is here called an "abomination," a word often used to describe idolatry. Thus, even religious practices ordained by God can become equivalent to idolatry under such circumstances. Note also Proverbs 28:9.

Verse 30 reminds us that those intellectuals who reject the Lord as Creator and Savior, despite their pretense of superior wisdom, are actually fools (Ps. 14:1). The very foundation of real "wisdom" and "understanding" and "counsel" is "the fear of the LORD" (Prov. 1:7; 9:10), and in the Lord Jesus Christ alone are "hid all the treasures of wisdom and knowledge" (Col. 2:3).

Finally, we need to remember, as verse 31 tells us, that true "safety is of the LORD," not in military, physical, or intellectual prowess.

Proverbs 22:1–16

1. *A good name is rather to be chosen than great riches, and loving favour rather than silver and gold.*
2. *The rich and poor meet together: the LORD is the maker of them all.*
3. *A prudent man foreseeth the evil, and hideth himself: but the simple pass on, and are punished.*
4. *By humility and the fear of the LORD are riches, and honour, and life.*
5. *Thorns and snares are in the way of the froward: he that doth keep his soul shall be far from them.*
6. *Train up a child in the way he should go: and when he is old, he will not depart from it.*
7. *The rich ruleth over the poor, and the borrower is servant to the lender.*
8. *He that soweth iniquity shall reap vanity: and the rod of his anger shall fail.*
9. *He that hath a bountiful eye shall be blessed; for he giveth of his bread to the poor.*
10. *Cast out the scorner, and contention shall go out; yea, strife and reproach shall cease.*
11. *He that loveth pureness of heart, for the grace of his lips the king shall be his friend.*
12. *The eyes of the LORD preserve knowledge, and He overthroweth the words of the transgressor.*
13. *The slothful man saith, There is a lion without, I shall be slain in the streets.*
14. *The mouth of strange women is a deep pit: he that is abhorred of the LORD shall fall therein.*
15. *Foolishness is bound in the heart of a child; but the rod of correction shall drive it far from him.*
16. *He that oppresseth the poor to increase his riches, and he that giveth to the rich, shall surely come to want.*

The first 16 verses of chapter 22 constitute the final portion of the section of Proverbs called "The proverbs of Solomon" (Prov. 10:1). At verse 17 a new section begins, either written by or associated with someone or some group called "the wise." This section will be dealt with in chapter 5 of this book.

King Solomon had "great riches" and an abundance of "silver and gold." However, in verse 1 he says that "a good name" and "loving favour" were better than these. He later elaborated much further on the vanity of riches in Ecclesiastes 2:4–11. Note also Paul's comparison of riches with the better things of life in 1 Timothy 6:3–10. The Lord will judge both rich and poor according to His standards, not those of the world, as implied in verse 3. The statement in verse 3 was considered important enough to repeat in Proverbs 27:12. A prudent man — that is, one who is knowledgeable in the Scriptures and also about human events — can often be forewarned when troubles are imminent, and make adequate preparations. Those who are self-centered and indifferent to important developments will often be overcome by them.

One of the most familiar verses in Proverbs is verse 6, which in the King James Bible reads, "Train up a child in the way he should go: and when he is old, he will not depart from it." However, the popular understanding of the verse is not quite correct. The words "Train up" are from a Hebrew verb which is elsewhere always translated "dedicate." The phrase "the way he should go" should be understood as "to go his way" — that is, the way his talents and interests, as given him by God, have prepared him to go. Parents should seek to ascertain these in a child's nature, and then dedicate him or her to that sacred cause, so that the child, when grown, can make the optimum contribution to the kingdom of God.

The true-to-life situation expressed in verse 7 with respect to the danger in borrowing money is expressed in the New Testament as an actual command to the believer through Paul, who said, "Owe no man anything, but to love one another" (Rom. 13:8).

The word translated "bountiful" in verse 9 is usually rendered simply "good," which is its basic meaning. The phrase "good eye" is evidently used here to mean "generous." A like promise is found in 2 Corinthians 9:6–7: "He which soweth bountifully shall reap also bountifully . . . for God loveth a cheerful giver."

Verse 12 is our assurance that the Lord will preserve truth, whereas all the high-sounding words of false philosophy and sinful practices will eventually be overthrown and forgotten.

The danger in following the words of "strange women" — that is, foreign women with their pagan religions and morality — is noted in verse 14. Solomon apparently either copied or wrote this warning before he had accumulated many of his seven hundred "strange wives." He could hardly have considered himself "abhorred of the LORD" when he wrote it, in view of the great blessings God had bestowed on him. Eventually, however, God had to rebuke him severely for allowing the pagan religions of his strange wives to take root in Israel (1 Kings 11:4–11), especially in Jerusalem.

According to verse 15, modern theories of child-raising which allow children full freedom of expression when they are not yet wise or experienced enough to make intelligent choices are self-defeating. Note again Proverbs 13:24.

The last of the 375 proverbs in the collection called "The proverbs of Solomon" (Prov. 10:1–22:16) is here at verse 16. Warning against either exploiting the poor or bribing the rich, or both, God threatens bankruptcy and poverty to those who hope to gain by such practices.

As we have seen, practically all of the proverbs in this section stand alone and, for the most part, are self-explanatory. Many have become familiar sayings in everyday modern life, and all are still pithy, pungent, practical maxims even three thousand years after they were written. Human nature does not change, regardless of the changes in our technological civilization. Solomon indeed had a marvelous divine gift of wisdom, even though he himself later failed seriously in practicing what he preached, at least for a good part of his later life. As noted before, we have some reason to hope and believe that he finally repented of these failures and returned to the faith of his father before he died. We shall see some of the evidence for this in chapter 7, when we study his last book, Ecclesiastes.

5

Words and Ways of Wisdom

Ⅰt was pointed out in chapter 3 that the Book of Proverbs consists of several distinct sections. The third section can be called "the words of the wise" (Prov. 22:17) and extends from Proverbs 22:17 through 24:34. It follows the 17 lessons to "my son," in Proverbs 1–9 and then a section called simply "The proverbs of Solomon" (Prov. 10:1) going from Proverbs 10:1 through 22:16.

Apparently this present section is a collection later added to the two original compilations, with no direct statement as to its author. These proverbs are not a group of one-verse-long individual couplets, as in the previous section, but are paragraphs of two or more verses each, with each paragraph focussed on a specific exhortation by "the wise."

Although the author or authors are not named, that very fact may suggest that the compiler (whoever *he* may have been) simply assumed the readers would know that the proverbs came from Solomon (after all, who was more likely to be called "the wise" than Solomon himself!). In any case, the author seems to have been an individual rather than a group of men, for the admonitions are often addressed to "my son" (Prov. 23:15; 23:19; 23:26; 24:13; 24:21), just as Solomon had done in the first section of the book.

Therefore, as we look at these particular proverbs, they — like the others — will be considered as coming from (or through) Solomon to the unknown compiler into what he has called "the words of the wise." As in chapter 4, each particular chapter of the Book of Proverbs will be set forth first, followed by such interpretive or explanatory comments as might be helpful. It will be obvious, however, that many of the paragraphs — just as in the previous section — are so clear and pungently practical as to need no further comment, except, perhaps, just a short "Amen!"

Proverbs 22:17–29

17. *Bow down thine ear, and hear the words of the wise, and apply thine heart unto my knowledge.*
18. *For it is a pleasant thing if thou keep them within thee; they shall withal be fitted in thy lips.*
19. *That thy trust may be in the LORD, I have made known to thee this day, even to thee.*
20. *Have not I written to thee excellent things in counsels and knowledge,*
21. *That I might make thee know the certainty of the words of truth; that thou mightest answer the words of truth to them that send unto thee?*
22. *Rob not the poor, because he is poor: neither oppress the afflicted in the gate:*
23. *For the LORD will plead their cause, and spoil the soul of those that spoiled them.*
24. *Make no friendship with an angry man; and with a furious man thou shalt not go.*
25. *Lest thou learn his ways, and get a snare to thy soul.*
26. *Be not thou one of them that strike hands, or of them that are sureties for debts.*
27. *If thou hast nothing to pay, why should he take away thy bed from under thee?*
28. *Remove not the ancient landmark, which thy fathers have set.*
29. *Seest thou a man diligent in his business? he shall stand before kings; he shall not stand before mean men.*

It is quickly seen that the proverbs in these verses were not written to people in general, but to an individual, as counsel to guide that individual in his own ways. This is evident from the continual use of the second-person-singular pronouns ("thou," "thee," "thine," etc.) instead of the second-person-plural ("you," "your," etc.). This is a characteristic of the King James Bible, the translators seeking to be meticulously true to the sense of the original languages.

The person to whom the exhortations are addressed is undoubtedly "my son," as noted above. Thus it seems most probable that — as in Proverbs 1–9 — King Solomon was thinking particularly of his son Rehoboam as he wrote these words. That does not mean, of course, that they are not of equal, or even greater, application to all "sons" and daughters of all times and places.

The author (presumably Solomon) begins this section with an urgent plea (verses 17–21) to hear his words and apply his heart to the knowledge he was about to impart. He strongly implies that these "excellent things" he is imparting are actually words inspired by God, for they are "words of truth." Perhaps this is the reason he does not identify himself by name, because he recognizes that the term "the wise" can properly be ascribed only to the omniscient Creator of all knowledge.

Incidentally, in this section as well as throughout the whole Book of Proverbs God is identified always as "LORD" (note verses 19, 23), that is, as *Jehovah* (or *Yahweh*).

Solomon's purpose in stressing the urgency of hearing his words was threefold: (1) "that thy trust may be in the LORD," not in some humanistic or pantheistic philosophy; (2) that he would "know the certainty of the words of truth," being assured that they were God's words, not just those of men, even such a wise man as Solomon; and (3) "that thou mightest answer the words of truth to them that send unto thee," an exhortation echoed centuries later by the apostle Peter when he exhorted Christian believers to "be ready always to give an answer to every man that asketh you a reason of the hope that is in you with meekness and fear" (1 Pet. 3:15).

Following this initial exhortation to know and then use the words of truth (which, by obvious implication, are to be understood as the words of God as written in the Scriptures, the "wise" counselor sets forth a series of practical instructions for successful godly living, many of these being extensions or applications of earlier proverbs. First, in verses 22 and 23 is a sober warning against exploiting the poor or the afflicted, the penalty for which may ultimately be the spoiling of the soul of the exploiter (this could as well be translated as taking the life).

Then follows a warning (verses 24 and 25) against being infected by the anger of men who have become embittered about something. Earlier warnings against acting as surety for others are then reiterated in verse 26 and 27 (compare Prov. 6:1–5 and 20:16).

There is an intriguing reference to the sanctity of "the ancient landmark" in verse 28 (also in 23:10). The lands of the earth were originally divided up by the Lord himself (Gen. 10:32) when He "set the bounds of the people" (Deut. 32:8). "The earth is the LORD's" (Ps. 24:1), and He can give and transfer its lands according to His will (Acts 17:26). These God-given boundaries should be respected (Deut. 19:14; 27:17).

The chapter ends (verse 29) with an exhortation to be diligent in business. A corresponding New Testament exhortation is Romans 12:11, which tells us to be "not slothful in business; fervent in spirit; serving the Lord."

Proverbs 23

1. *When thou sittest to eat with a ruler, consider diligently what is before thee:*

2. *And put a knife to thy throat, if thou be a man given to appetite.*

3. *Be not desirous of his dainties: for they are deceitful meat.*

4. *Labour not to be rich: cease from thine own wisdom.*

5. *Wilt thou set thine eyes upon that which is not? for riches certainly make themselves wings: they fly away as an eagle toward heaven.*

6. *Eat thou not the bread of him that hath an evil eye, neither desire thou his dainty meats:*

7. *For as he thinketh in his heart, so is he: Eat and drink, saith he to thee; but his heart is not with thee.*

8. *The morsel which thou hast eaten shalt thou vomit up, and lose thy sweet words.*

9. *Speak not in the ears of a fool: for he will despise the wisdom of thy words.*

10. *Remove not the old landmark; and enter not into the fields of the fatherless:*

11. *For their redeemer is mighty; He shall plead their cause with thee.*

12. *Apply thine heart unto instruction, and thine ears to the words of knowledge.*

13. *Withhold not correction from the child: for if thou beatest him with the rod, he shall not die.*

14. *Thou shalt beat him with the rod, and shalt deliver his soul from hell.*

15. *My son, if thine heart be wise, my heart shall rejoice, even mine.*

16. *Yea, my reins shall rejoice, when thy lips speak right things.*

17. *Let not thine heart envy sinners: but be thou in the fear of the LORD all the day long.*

18. *For surely there is an end; and thine expectation shall not be cut off.*

19. *Hear thou, my son, and be wise, and guide thine heart in the way.*

20. *Be not among winebibbers; among riotous eaters of flesh:*

21. *For the drunkard and the glutton shall come to poverty: and drowsiness shall clothe a man with rags.*

22. *Hearken unto thy father that begat thee, and despise not thy mother when she is old.*

23. *Buy the truth, and sell it not; also wisdom, and instruction, and understanding.*

24. *The father of the righteous shall greatly rejoice: and he that begetteth a wise child shall have joy of him.*

25. *Thy father and thy mother shall be glad, and she that bare thee shall rejoice.*

26. *My son, give me thine heart, and let thine eyes observe my ways.*

27. *For a whore is a deep ditch; and a strange woman is a narrow pit.*

28. *She also lieth in wait as for a prey, and increaseth the transgressors among men.*

29. *Who hath woe? who hath sorrow? who hath contentions? who hath babbling? who hath wounds without cause? who hath redness of eyes?*

30. *They that tarry long at the wine; they that go to seek mixed wine.*

31. *Look not thou upon the wine when it is red, when it giveth his colour in the cup, when it moveth itself aright.*

32. *At the last it biteth like a serpent, and stingeth like an adder.*

33. *Thine eyes shall behold strange women, and thine heart shall utter perverse things.*

34. *Yea, thou shalt be as he that lieth down in the midst of the sea, or as he that lieth upon the top of a mast.*

35. *They have stricken me, shalt thou say, and I was not sick; they have beaten me, and I felt it not: when shall I awake? I will seek it yet again.*

The first three verses of this chapter (verses 23:1–3) constitute a warning to be very careful when asked to dine with a ruler — that is, anyone in a position of authority or special influence — for it would be quite possible that such a "ruler" would have some ulterior motive in extending the invitation. Then verses 4 and 5 bring further warning against an inordinate desire to be rich, for riches can be not only dangerous, but also very ephemeral.

The "evil eye" mentioned in verse 6 is not a reference to an occult power of some sort, nor is it a "miser" or "selfish person" as some Bible versions try to paraphrase it. Proverbs 28:22 says, "He that hasteth to be rich hath an evil eye." The eye is said to be the window of the soul. Thus, a greedy person or lustful person or a person with evil thoughts can often be discerned as such by the look in his eyes. Note Matthew 6:22–23.

The statement in verse 7 — "as he thinketh in his heart, so is he" — was in effect applied by Christ (Matt. 12:35; Mark 7:20–23) when rebuking the Pharisees.

There is another warning in verse 10 (see Prov. 22:28) against removing old landmarks — that is, boundaries set in ancient times by God when He divided the earth's land areas or as later authorized by Him.

Verses 13 and 14, provide yet another emphasis on corporal punishment for disobedient children. See Proverbs 13:24. These verses do not, of course, endorse child-beating in the modern sense of the term. The Hebrew word for "beat" is the same as used in 2 Kings 11:12 ("they clapped their hands"). It has a range of meanings, from "strike lightly" to "strike lethally," depending on context. Similarly, the word for "rod" can mean anything from a flexible switch to a weapon of war. This and other passages in Proverbs do provide divine authorization for spanking or whipping — not in anger or revenge or so severely as to risk injury — but in concern for developing character and to discourage future wrongdoing.

Verse 14 is a remarkable promise — namely, that the right type of physical punishment will contribute to the child's salvation, by discouraging him from future rebellion against his parents and his Creator. The word "hell" here, of course, is the Hebrew *sheol*, the great pit in the center of the earth where the souls of the dead await either deliverance by Christ or ultimate judgment by God.

The term "reins" in verse 16 is an old term for the kidneys, and was used to indicate the center of deep feelings.

Verses 20 and 21, and verses 29–35, especially the latter passage, contain probably the strongest warnings against drinking intoxicating beverages, especially to the point of becoming drunk, to be found anywhere in the Bible. Verse 21 also warns against gluttony and revelry. Note also Proverbs 20:1 and Ephesians 5:18. Verse 31 warns against even looking at the wine, lest it tempt one to drink.

Verses 22–26 once again urge "my son" (and by extension, all children) to honor and heed their parents, even after they are old (verse 22), for it will give their mother and father great joy in their old age. He also warns his son again to stay away from prostitutes and pagan women in general (verses 26–28), comparing them in a vivid metaphor to a "deep ditch" and a "narrow pit."

Proverbs 24

1. *Be not thou envious against evil men, neither desire to be with them.*
2. *For their heart studieth destruction, and their lips talk of mischief.*
3. *Through wisdom is an house builded; and by understanding it is established:*
4. *And by knowledge shall the chambers be filled with all precious and pleasant riches.*
5. *A wise man is strong; yea, a man of knowledge increaseth strength.*

6. *For by wise counsel thou shalt make thy war: and in multitude of counsellors there is safety.*

7. *Wisdom is too high for a fool: he openeth not his mouth in the gate.*

8. *He that deviseth to do evil shall be called a mischievous person.*

9. *The thought of foolishness is sin: and the scorner is an abomination to men.*

10. *If thou faint in the day of adversity, thy strength is small.*

11. *If thou forbear to deliver them that are drawn unto death, and those that are ready to be slain;*

12. *If thou sayest, Behold, we knew it not; doth not He that pondereth the heart consider it? and He that keepeth thy soul, doth not He know it? and shall not He render to every man according to his works?*

13. *My son, eat thou honey, because it is good; and the honeycomb, which is sweet to thy taste:*

14. *So shall the knowledge of wisdom be unto thy soul: when thou hast found it, then there shall be a reward, and thy expectation shall not be cut off.*

15. *Lay not wait, O wicked man, against the dwelling of the righteous; spoil not his resting place:*

16. *For a just man falleth seven times, and riseth up again: but the wicked shall fall into mischief.*

17. *Rejoice not when thine enemy falleth, and let not thine heart be glad when he stumbleth:*

18. *Lest the LORD see it, and it displease Him, and He turn away His wrath from him.*

19. *Fret not thyself because of evil men, neither be thou envious at the wicked;*

20. *For there shall be no reward to the evil man; the candle of the wicked shall be put out.*

21. *My son, fear thou the LORD and the king: and meddle not with them that are given to change:*

22. *For their calamity shall rise suddenly; and who knoweth the ruin of them both?*

23. *These things also belong to the wise. It is not good to have respect of persons in judgment.*

24. *He that saith unto the wicked, Thou art righteous; him shall the people curse, nations shall abhor him:*

25. *But to them that rebuke him shall be delight, and a good blessing shall come upon them.*

26. *Every man shall kiss his lips that giveth a right answer.*

27. *Prepare thy work without, and make it fit for thyself in the field; and afterwards build thine house.*

28. *Be not a witness against thy neighbour without cause; and deceive not with thy lips.*

29. *Say not, I will do so to him as he hath done to me: I will render to the man according to his work.*

30. *I went by the field of the slothful, and by the vineyard of the man void of understanding;*

31. *And, lo, it was all grown over with thorns, and nettles had covered the face thereof, and the stone wall thereof was broken down.*

32. *Then I saw, and considered it well: I looked upon it, and received instruction.*

33. *Yet a little sleep, a little slumber, a little folding of the hands to sleep:*

34. *So shall thy poverty come as one that travelleth; and thy want as an armed man.*

The further admonishments of "the wise" (presumably Solomon himself) are included in this chapter. Many of its proverbs deal with matters discussed in earlier chapters, but repetition, reinforcement, and application of important teachings are always salutary. It opens with another reminder not to envy or emulate evil men (verses 1–2).

Verses 3 and 4 then use the picture of a well-built house as an illustration of a well-planned and soundly developed life. The main factors in erecting such a house or such a life are wisdom and knowledge and understanding. A similar figure is used in Psalm 127:1 and especially in 1 Corinthians 3:9–17.

Prosecution of warfare demands similar careful planning and implementation (verses 5–6), whether actual military action or conflict with humanistic programs or spiritual wickedness. "Wise counsel" is essential, even a "multitude of counsellors" (see also Prov. 11:14; 15:22; 20:18).

The reference in verse 7 to "the gate" probably refers to the city gate where the wise men and rulers of the town would gather to address problems and make decisions. Foolish men who have not bothered to learn knowledge and develop wisdom are well advised to remain silent in such situations.

Verses 10–12 inform us that ignorance of God's Word is never an adequate excuse for failure to do what is right, especially going to the defense of those under attack, physically or spiritually. God will judge such action on the basis of works, not knowledge or lack of knowledge. "To him that knoweth to do good, and doeth it not, to him it is sin" (James 4:17).

A precious truth for the Christian believer is derived from verse 16. One who is "just" — that is righteous before God — will never fall permanently.

"Seven times," of course, is a metaphor for fulness, so it refers to any number of times. Even though Solomon elsewhere recognized that "there is not a just man upon earth" (Eccles. 7:20), the wonderful truth is that we are "not justified by the works of the law, but by the faith of Jesus Christ" and thus have been made "just," or "righteous" because "He is made unto us . . . righteousness" (Gal. 2:16; 1 Cor. 1:30). Therefore, "if any man sin, we have an advocate with the Father, Jesus Christ the righteous: And He is the propitiation for our sins" (1 John 2:1–2). "If we confess our sins, he is faithful and just to forgive us our sins" (1 John 1:9).

The "wicked" are not necessarily those who are flagrant and open sinners, but all those who have not been justified by faith in Christ. Since the Lord Jesus has paid the penalty for their sins, they can be saved by believing on Him. If they die in their sins, however, "the candle of the wicked shall be put out" (verse 20).

Therefore, we are told to "fret not thyself because of evil men, neither be thou envious of the wicked" (verse 19). What little "reward" they have is limited to this life only. (Compare Psalm 37:1–2; Matthew 6:2, 5, 16). Remember also that the Christian who does fall back and sin, perhaps many times, may lose his potential rewards in heaven, "but he himself will be saved" (1 Cor. 3:14–15).

The wise writer, presumably Solomon, again addresses "my son" in verse 21, advising him to fear the Lord and the king and to "meddle not with them that are given to change." The latter clause is somewhat ambiguous, but the thought seems to be that there is no point in wasting time arguing with people who are agitating against the words of God or of the God-ordained king. God will deal with them in His own way and time.

Verse 23 again mentions "the wise" (see comment on Prov. 22:17), again calling attention to the writer's divine authority in giving his counsel. There are many warnings in the Bible against having "respect of persons in judgment" (verse 23). Note Leviticus 19:15; Deuteronomy 1:17; 16:19; 2 Chronicles 19:7; Proverbs 28:21; Romans 2:11; Ephesians 6:9; Colossians 3:25; and James 2:1, remembering that "God is no respecter of persons" (Acts 10:34). This is evidently an important principle that God wants maintained in His economy.

The admonition to "kiss his lips that giveth a right answer" (verse 26), at least in our present culture, would mean to express appropriate appreciation when a person gives a straightforward (as opposed to devious or equivocal) answer to an honest question.

Verse 27 tells us not to begin building a house — whether a literal house or a family — without first making proper and adequate preparations for all the responsibilities involved.

Personal retribution to one who has injured us is not appropriate for one who would please God (verse 29). "Vengeance is mine, I will repay, saith the Lord" (Rom. 12:19). God has dealt with us in grace; we should manifest grace in dealing with others, even when they don't merit it. The practice of personal payback, though widely prevalent among the world's nations and tribes, is not scriptural. See also Matthew 5:39–44.

The last several verses of the chapter — and of the section of Proverbs written by "the wise" (Prov. 22:17) — constitute a graphic rebuke to those who are "slothful" or "void of understanding." There is no excuse for either, with the exception of those who have serious physical or mental handicaps, and either will lead to poverty.

Proverbs 25

1. *These are also proverbs of Solomon, which the men of Hezekiah king of Judah copied out.*
2. *It is the glory of God to conceal a thing: but the honour of kings is to search out a matter.*
3. *The heaven for height, and the earth for depth, and the heart of kings is unsearchable.*
4. *Take away the dross from the silver, and there shall come forth a vessel for the finer.*
5. *Take away the wicked from before the king, and his throne shall be established in righteousness.*
6. *Put not forth thyself in the presence of the king, and stand not in the place of great men:*
7. *For better it is that it be said unto thee, Come up hither; than that thou shouldest be put lower in the presence of the prince whom thine eyes have seen.*
8. *Go not forth hastily to strive, lest thou know not what to do in the end thereof, when thy neighbour hath put thee to shame.*
9. *Debate thy cause with thy neighbour himself; and discover not a secret to another:*
10. *Lest he that heareth it put thee to shame, and thine infamy turn not away.*
11. *A word fitly spoken is like apples of gold in pictures of silver.*
12. *As an earring of gold, and an ornament of fine gold, so is a wise reprover upon an obedient ear.*
13. *As the cold of snow in the time of harvest, so is a faithful messenger to them that send him: for he refresheth the soul of his masters.*
14. *Whoso boasteth himself of a false gift is like clouds and wind without rain.*

15. *By long forbearing is a prince persuaded, and a soft tongue breaketh the bone.*

16. *Hast thou found honey? eat so much as is sufficient for thee, lest thou be filled therewith, and vomit it.*

17. *Withdraw thy foot from thy neighbour's house; lest he be weary of thee, and so hate thee.*

18. *A man that beareth false witness against his neighbour is a maul, and a sword, and a sharp arrow.*

19. *Confidence in an unfaithful man in time of trouble is like a broken tooth, and a foot out of joint.*

20. *As he that taketh away a garment in cold weather, and as vinegar upon nitre, so is he that singeth songs to a heavy heart.*

21. *If thine enemy be hungry, give him bread to eat; and if he be thirsty, give him water to drink:*

22. *For thou shalt heap coals of fire upon his head, and the LORD shall reward thee.*

23. *The north wind driveth away rain: so doth an angry countenance a backbiting tongue.*

24. *It is better to dwell in the corner of the housetop, than with a brawling woman and in a wide house.*

25. *As cold waters to a thirsty soul, so is good news from a far country.*

26. *A righteous man falling down before the wicked is as a troubled fountain, and a corrupt spring.*

27. *It is not good to eat much honey: so for men to search their own glory is not glory.*

28. *He that hath no rule over his own spirit is like a city that is broken down, and without walls.*

This fourth section of the Book of Proverbs, extending from Proverbs 25 through 29, is headed by the definitive statement, "These are also proverbs of Solomon, which the men of Hezekiah king of Judah copied out" (verse 1). They contain 138 verses, which means essentially 138 more proverbs, since practically every verse represents an independent proverb (in a few cases, a specific theme is covered in two or more verses, but even each verse of these can also stand independently).

One wonders how these proverbs failed to appear in one of the earlier collections, since they are plainly said to be "proverbs of Solomon" and include many of the most familiar and most salient proverbs in the whole book. King Hezekiah was descended from Solomon, of course, but there had been 12 kings of Judah in between the two, covering about 254 years, and many of these were years of apostasy.

Hezekiah's reign, however, was a time of great revival in Judah. In spite of the apostasies of his father Ahaz, Hezekiah still had a great nucleus of the followers of Jehovah available to participate in the restoration of the ancient worship. Most importantly, they still had the Scriptures — not only "in the law, and in the commandments" (2 Chron. 31:21), but also "the commandment of the LORD by his prophets" (2 Chron. 29:25), and were even able "to sing praise unto the LORD with the words of David, and of Asaph the seer" (2 Chron. 29:30). Evidently they had all the Scriptures which had been written up to that time, and this would include the writings of Solomon.

Now, somewhere Solomon "spake three thousand proverbs" (1 Kings 4:32), but only a fraction of these had been incorporated in the three collections we have discussed. One can only assume that the rest of them had been filed away somewhere in the temple (after all, some scribe must have counted them, and he would never have been so presumptuous as to discard any of the great king's books). Possibly this particular group was written later in Solomon's career and, then, in the turmoil of his later years and the following years when Rehoboam was king and the Egyptians were invading Israel, they just remained hidden in the temple files.

Until Hezekiah's men discovered them, that is, when they were renovating the temple at the king's orders. Then, as they had opportunity, they chose the proverbs that seemed most meaningful out of this collection, and compiled them into what are now chapters 25–29 of the Book of Proverbs.

Whether this is how it really happened or not, somehow these godly servants of Hezekiah did copy out these proverbs in a new collection, and they soon were assimilated into the Book of Proverbs as we now have it. And a wonderful collection it is!

Incidentally, the fact that the men of Hezekiah had access to and copied Solomon's writings so long after his reign lends weight to the related suggestion that the 15 "songs of degrees" (Ps. 120–134) were actually written and/or collected by King Hezekiah. Fifteen years had been added to Hezekiah's life when he prayed and God answered by causing the shadow on his sundial to go back ten degrees. Five of the songs of degrees had been written by David, the other ten by Hezekiah, who had promised, as a result of the miracle, that "we will sing my songs . . . all the days of our life in the house of the LORD" (Isa. 38:20).

The first of the proverbs copied by Hezekiah's men is particularly fascinating (verse 2). In the dominion mandate, God commissioned Adam and his descendants to "subdue" the earth (Gen. 1:28). This command authorizes every honorable human occupation — especially that of research to understand the systems and processes of nature, so that they can be ordered and utilized for God's glory and man's good. These systems and processes are almost innumerable and all are incredibly complex in their structure and working. When studied in depth, they all should cause their researchers to give glory to God, who has designed and made them. It is almost like a divine game. God's "glory" is "concealed," as it were, in His creations, and He has challenged men to search these things out. There is, then, great joy in such discoveries, and great scientists such as Kepler, Newton, and Maxwell have all recognized that their scientific revelations were merely "thinking God's thoughts after Him," and they gave Him the glory. But how incredibly absurd are the claims of evolutionary scientists that all these wonders somehow just happened without God being involved at all.

There are certain things, however, that human research can never uncover (verse 3). Astronomers can never penetrate the height of heaven: even the physical heavens are infinite (Isa. 55:9). Geophysicists will never probe the depths of the earth, though they have published guesses about its composition. And psychologists will never understand the mind and heart of the most ignorant savage, let alone that of a great king.

Verse 7 beautifully anticipates the wise counsel of Jesus, when He said, "When thou art bidden of any man to a wedding, sit not down in the highest room; lest a more honourable man than thou be bidden of him; And he . . . say to thee, Give this man place. . . . But when thou art bidden, go and sit down in the lowest room; that when he that bade thee cometh, he may say unto thee, Friend, go up higher" (Luke 14:8–10).

Verse 9 is surely good advice in terms both of one's own reputation (lest otherwise he or she be considered a gossip or scandal monger) and also in terms of better relationships with others and avoiding misunderstandings.

Then verse 11 is a beautiful simile, encouraging careful choice of one's words. The "pictures" referred to are actually images carved in relief. In any case, as Paul said, "Let your speech be alway with grace, seasoned with salt, that ye may know how ye ought to answer every man" (Col. 4:6). Verses 12 and 13 both also are beautiful similes, extolling the virtues and good works of "a wise reprover" and "a faithful messenger." On the other hand, boasting words, with little substance to support them, according to another simile in verse 14, are "like clouds and wind without rain."

Three more striking similes are found in verses 18, 19, and 20. One who lies about his neighbor is like "a maul, and a sword, and a sharp arrow." Seeking help from an unreliable acquaintance is "like a broken tooth, and a foot out of joint." One who tries to help a person in sorrow by singing cheerful songs is like one who would take "away a garment in cold weather."

An excellent bit of advice, though it goes against one's natural inclinations, is offered in verses 21 and 22. Instead of fighting an enemy, give him food and water. These verses were cited by the apostle Paul in Romans 12:20–21. Remember also that Jesus said, "Love your enemies, bless them that curse you, do good to them that hate you, and pray for them that despitefully use you, and persecute you" (Matt. 5:44). When Solomon says, "Thou shalt heap coals of fire on his head," the reference is probably to the melting of metals by placing a heap of burning coals on them. Likewise, a hard heart can be made to melt and even burn with shame when acts of cruelty are met with acts of kindness. It seems also that carrying about a pan of hot coals on one's head was considered an act of contrition.

Verse 23 should be understood as saying, "As the north wind drives the rain, so a backbiting tongue causes an angry countenance."

Verse 24 is essentially the same as Proverbs 21:9. Solomon must have felt quite strongly about this bit of wisdom in order (perhaps inadvertently) to have included it in two of his collections! But by the doctrine of inspiration, it seems that the Lord also considered it very important as a warning to "brawling" (that is, "contentious" or "striving") women.

Verse 27 indicates that eating too many sweets was just as unwise in ancient times as it is today and was so recognized. It is compared rather vividly to the reaction generated when people seek honor for themselves. The sweets are no longer sweet, and the honor so achieved is not honor at all.

Proverbs 26

1. *As snow in summer, and as rain in harvest, so honour is not seemly for a fool.*
2. *As the bird by wandering, as the swallow by flying, so the curse causeless shall not come.*
3. *A whip for the horse, a bridle for the ass, and a rod for the fool's back.*
4. *Answer not a fool according to his folly, lest thou also be like unto him.*
5. *Answer a fool according to his folly, lest he be wise in his own conceit.*
6. *He that sendeth a message by the hand of a fool cutteth off the feet, and drinketh damage.*
7. *The legs of the lame are not equal: so is a parable in the mouth of fools.*
8. *As he that bindeth a stone in a sling, so is he that giveth honour to a fool.*

9. *As a thorn goeth up into the hand of a drunkard, so is a parable in the mouth of fools.*

10. *The great God that formed all things both rewardeth the fool, and rewardeth transgressors.*

11. *As a dog returneth to his vomit, so a fool returneth to his folly.*

12. *Seest thou a man wise in his own conceit? there is more hope of a fool than of him.*

13. *The slothful man saith, There is a lion in the way; a lion is in the streets.*

14. *As the door turneth upon his hinges, so doth the slothful upon his bed.*

15. *The slothful hideth his hand in his bosom; it grieveth him to bring it again to his mouth.*

16. *The sluggard is wiser in his own conceit than seven men that can render a reason.*

17. *He that passeth by, and meddleth with strife belonging not to him, is like one that taketh a dog by the ears.*

18. *As a mad man who casteth firebrands, arrows, and death,*

19. *So is the man that deceiveth his neighbour, and saith, Am not I in sport?*

20. *Where no wood is, there the fire goeth out: so where there is no talebearer, the strife ceaseth.*

21. *As coals are to burning coals, and wood to fire; so is a contentious man to kindle strife.*

22. *The words of a talebearer are as wounds, and they go down into the innermost parts of the belly.*

23. *Burning lips and a wicked heart are like a potsherd covered with silver dross.*

24. *He that hateth dissembleth with his lips, and layeth up deceit within him.*

25. *When he speaketh fair, believe him not: for there are seven abominations in his heart.*

26. *Whose hatred is covered by deceit, his wickedness shall be shewed before the whole congregation.*

27. *Whoso diggeth a pit shall fall therein: and he that rolleth a stone, it will return upon him.*

28. *A lying tongue hateth those that are afflicted by it; and a flattering mouth worketh ruin.*

The first 12 verses of this chapter all deal with the character and behavior of fools — that is, basically, those who give no consideration to God and His Word (Ps. 14:1–3). Even when they give a nominal assent to

His possible existence, they behave as though He has no jurisdiction over their thoughts or deeds. Verse 1 notes that, as snow is not appropriate for summer, and since rain in the season of harvest damages the crops, it is inappropriate and harmful to give honor or even respectful recognition to the words and actions of fools.

In verse 2, it is stressed that a curse pronounced without justification is as pointless as a bird flitting about with no destination, and therefore will not be fulfilled.

Verses 3 and 4 seem on the surface to be contradictory, but obviously the writer did not think so, placing them back to back in his collection. When a person is given to foolish skeptical arguments against God and His Word, it is a waste of time to argue with him. If, however, he is influencing others and becoming self-important in his self-delusion, it may be apropriate, or even necessary, to show up his folly with sound evidence.

The next several verses continue to show the irrationality of trying to deal rationally with those whom God has called fools. Verse 6 says that depending on a fool is tantamount to a self-inflicted wound. Verses 7 and 9 tell us that such people are unable or unwilling to comprehend the real message and meaning in a parable. In fact, that was the very reason why the Lord Jesus Christ taught His followers by means of parables (Mark 4:10–12, 33–34). Verse 11 says that the insistence of fools to return again and again to their foolish atheism is like dogs returning to their vomit, and then the apostle Peter, citing this proverb, applies it not only to atheists but also to religious liberals and apostates (2 Pet. 2:20–22).

It is significant that, in this diatribe against all such folly, we are reminded in verse 10 of "the great God that formed all things," who will "reward" such fools and transgressors appropriately, since it is their denial or ignoring of the Creator that makes them fools in the first place (Ps. 53). Then — lastly but significantly — verse 12 tells us that an arrogant man, "wise in his own conceit," is even more difficult to win to true trust in the God of creation and salvation than a fool.

The next four verses in the chapter — verses 13–16 — deal very picturesquely with the sin of slothfulness. Lazy people make inane excuses for not working (verse 13); they are like a door that "turneth upon his hinges" (verse 14), giving indications of activity but going nowhere; and are themselves so wise in their own conceit (verse 16) that they are ignorant of their own foolishness.

Then the remaining verses of the chapter deal scathingly with those whose careless or deceitful tongues cause so much trouble. Those who meddle in the disputes of others are as certain to be harmed themselves as "one that taketh a dog by the ears" (verse 17, referring especially to the wild dogs then so common in the Middle East). Certain harm will also come to those who think it is clever to deceive (verses 18–19).

Gossips and talebearers are strikingly rebuked in verses 20–22. The hypocrisy of such people is compared in verse 23 to a veneer of silver over a piece of broken pottery. The last five verses of the chapter (verses 24–28) have to do with those who mask the evil and hatred in their hearts with deceitful words on their lips. Sooner or later, the truth will be made known to everyone. The pit they have dug will be their own trap, and the stone they have attempted to roll upon others will crush themselves.

Proverbs 27

1.   *Boast not thyself of to morrow; for thou knowest not what a day may bring forth.*
2.   *Let another man praise thee, and not thine own mouth; a stranger, and not thine own lips.*
3.   *A stone is heavy, and the sand weighty; but a fool's wrath is heavier than them both.*
4.   *Wrath is cruel, and anger is outrageous; but who is able to stand before envy?*
5.   *Open rebuke is better than secret love.*
6.   *Faithful are the wounds of a friend; but the kisses of an enemy are deceitful.*
7.   *The full soul loatheth an honeycomb; but to the hungry soul every bitter thing is sweet.*
8.   *As a bird that wandereth from her nest, so is a man that wandereth from his place.*
9.   *Ointment and perfume rejoice the heart: so doth the sweetness of a man's friend by hearty counsel.*
10. *Thine own friend, and thy father's friend, forsake not; neither go into thy brother's house in the day of thy calamity: for better is a neighbour that is near than a brother far off.*
11. *My son, be wise, and make my heart glad, that I may answer him that reproacheth me.*
12. *A prudent man forseeth the evil, and hideth himself; but the simple pass on, and are punished.*
13. *Take his garment that is surety for a stranger, and take a pledge of him for a strange woman.*
14. *He that blesseth his friend with a loud voice rising early in the morning, it shall be counted a curse to him.*
15. *A continual dropping in a very rainy day and a contentious woman are alike.*

16. *Whosoever hideth her hideth the wind, and the ointment of his right hand, which betrayeth itself.*

17. *Iron sharpeneth iron; so a man sharpeneth the countenance of his friend.*

18. *Whoso keepeth the fig tree shall eat the fruit thereof: so he that waiteth on his master shall be honoured.*

19. *As in water face answereth to face, so the heart of man to man.*

20. *Hell and destruction are never full; so the eyes of man are never satisfied.*

21. *As the fining pot for silver, and the furnace for gold; so is a man to his praise.*

22. *Though thou shouldest bray a fool in a mortar among wheat with a pestle, yet will not his foolishness depart from him.*

23. *Be thou diligent to know the state of thy flocks, and look well to thy herds.*

24. *For riches are not for ever: and doth the crown endure to every generation?*

25. *The hay appeareth, and the tender grass sheweth itself, and herbs of the mountains are gathered.*

26. *The lambs are for thy clothing, and the goats are the price of the field.*

27. *And thou shalt have goats' milk enough for thy food, for the food of thy household, and for the maintenance for thy maidens.*

The 27th chapter of Proverbs begins with a salient warning against procrastination. "Boast not thyself of to morrow; for thou knowest not what a day may bring forth" (verse 1). A believer always should keep short accounts. The apostle James echoes this warning in the New Testament: "Go to now, ye that say, To day or to morrow we will go into such a city, and continue there a year, and buy and sell, and get gain: Whereas ye know not what shall be on the morrow" (James 4:13–14). It is vital that we be "redeeming the time, because the days are evil" (Eph. 5:16).

The most dangerous sin of procrastination, of course, is that of neglecting to come to Christ for forgiveness and salvation. "Behold, now is the accepted time; behold, now is the day of salvation" (2 Cor. 6:2). Our lives are brief, "a vapour, that appeareth for a little time, and then vanisheth away" (James 4:14). "It is soon cut off, and we fly away" (Ps. 90:10), so it is urgent that we "walk in wisdom . . . redeeming the time" (Col. 4:5).

Verse 2 stresses once again that it is counter-productive — especially for the believer who knows that all he is or has comes from God — to praise ourselves or to seek praise from others. Note also Proverbs 25:27.

The debilitating effect of envy on one's own soul is noted in verse 4. "Neither be thou envious against the workers of iniquity. For they shall soon be cut down like the grass" (Ps. 37:1–2). However, the same Hebrew word is often translated "jealous" or even "zealous" or "zeal," so this characteristic can be applied in a good sense if it is in the form of zeal for God and the truth of God. In fact, God himself said, "I the LORD thy God am a jealous God," as He gave the ten commandments for His people (Exod. 20:5).

Verse 5 would indicate that if an open rebuke is truly needed by a person, then one who truly loves that person in the sense that God loves him would lovingly administer the rebuke, rather than keeping his love secret. The "wounds of a friend" are "faithful," according to verse 6. David wrote, "Let the righteous smite me; it shall be a kindness: and let him reprove me; it shall be an excellent oil" (Ps. 141:5).

Verse 7, like Proverbs 25:16 and 27, reminds us that too much "honey" is not good and can even become loathsome. One who is truly hungry, on the other hand, will learn to appreciate even bitter things. The principle can be applied not only to food, but to life in general.

A man trying to be or do something that is not in God's will for him — that is, out of "his place" — is like "a bird that wandereth from her nest," according to verse 8. God will not allow a believer to be at rest spiritually if he is wandering away out of His will.

Verse 11 is yet another proverb addressed by Solomon first of all to "my son." It is true that whatever a son or daughter does will in some measure reflect for good or bad upon their parents, and children should never forget this.

Verse 12 is a repetition of Proverbs 22:3. A wise person will avoid evil and can sense when it is imminent. Verse 13 repeats Proverbs 20:16 and also reflects Proverbs 6:1. One who acts as surety for a stranger or immoral woman will almost certainly lose the amount or article so pledged. A "contentious woman" is again compared to continuing raindrops in verse 15 (see comment on Prov. 19:13). Hiding or controlling such a woman is like trying to hide the wind (verse 16).

As iron implements can be sharpened by other iron tools, so stimulating discussion of important topics (especially as related to the Word of God) between concerned friends can upgrade the knowledge and effectiveness of those involved. This is the assurance of verse 17.

Verse 20 speaks of "hell and destruction." In the Hebrew these words are *sheol* and *abaddon*, respectively. See comments on the same words, as found in Proverbs 15:11.

The "fining pot" (that is, "refining pot") and the "furnace" mentioned in verse 21 as used in refining silver and gold, respectively, are also mentioned in Proverbs 17:3. In the latter, their functions are compared to the Lord trying our hearts. Here, however, they are compared to how the praise of others can test the character of those receiving it.

The "mortar" and "pestle" noted in verse 22 refer to the bowls and stone rods used to crush grain into powder. However, analogous "crushing" of fools will seldom crush their foolishness out of them.

The last five verses of the chapter (verses 23–27) encourage property owners to give all due attention to their flocks and herds, in particular, for they provide both food and clothing for their households. God himself provides the grass and herbs for the animals (verse 25), and these flocks and herds, if properly managed, reproduce and even increase their numbers. Other types of riches, however, may well be very fleeting, and even kingly dynasties are subject to change (verse 24). In a very real sense, the pastoral life has been the basis of human civilization ever since the beginning.

Proverbs 28

1. *The wicked flee when no man pursueth: but the righteous are bold as a lion.*
2. *For the transgression of a land many are the princes thereof: but by a man of understanding and knowledge the state thereof shall be prolonged.*
3. *A poor man that oppresseth the poor is like a sweeping rain which leaveth no food.*
4. *They that forsake the law praise the wicked: but such as keep the law contend with them.*
5. *Evil men understand not judgment: but they that seek the LORD understand all things.*
6. *Better is the poor that walketh in his uprightness, than he that is perverse in his ways, though he be rich.*
7. *Whoso keepeth the law is a wise son: but he that is a companion of riotous men shameth his father.*
8. *He that by usury and unjust gain increaseth his substance, he shall gather it for him that will pity the poor.*
9. *He that turneth away his ear from hearing the law, even his prayer shall be abomination.*
10. *Whoso causeth the righteous to go astray in an evil way, he shall fall himself into his own pit: but the upright shall have good things in possession.*
11. *The rich man is wise in his own conceit; but the poor that hath understanding searcheth him out.*
12. *When righteous men do rejoice, there is great glory: but when the wicked rise, a man is hidden.*

13. *He that covereth his sins shall not prosper: but whoso confesseth and forsaketh them shall have mercy.*

14. *Happy is the man that feareth alway: but he that hardeneth his heart shall fall into mischief.*

15. *As a roaring lion, and a ranging bear; so is a wicked ruler over the poor people.*

16. *The prince that wanteth understanding is also a great oppressor: but he that hateth covetousness shall prolong his days.*

17. *A man that doeth violence to the blood of any person shall flee to the pit; let no man stay him.*

18. *Whoso walketh uprightly shall be saved: but he that is perverse in his ways shall fall at once.*

19. *He that tilleth his land shall have plenty of bread: but he that followeth after vain persons shall have poverty enough.*

20. *A faithful man shall abound with blessings: but he that maketh haste to be rich shall not be innocent.*

21. *To have respect of persons is not good: for for a piece of bread that man will transgress.*

22. *He that hasteth to be rich hath an evil eye, and considereth not that poverty shall come upon him.*

23. *He that rebuketh a man afterwards shall find more favour than he that flattereth with the tongue.*

24. *Whoso robbeth his father or his mother, and saith, It is no transgression; the same is the companion of a destroyer.*

25. *He that is of a proud heart stirreth up strife: but he that putteth his trust in the LORD shall be made fat.*

26. *He that trusteth in his own heart is a fool: but whoso walketh wisely, he shall be delivered.*

27. *He that giveth unto the poor shall not lack: but he that hideth his eyes shall have many a curse.*

28. *When the wicked rise, men hide themselves: but when they perish, the righteous increase.*

This chapter of Proverbs continues to provide for readers of all times and places still more of the marvelous Solomonic proverbs "which the men of Hezekiah king of Judah copied out" (Prov. 25:1) over 250 years after Solomon originally wrote them down and had them laid up somewhere in the temple. Again, although many are essentially self-explanatory and require no interpretive comments or explanations, all are words of great wisdom and deserve careful attention.

Each verse in the chapter is an individual statement, with little or no connection to adjacent verses, and many are of the "antithetic" type. For example, verse 1 contrasts the inward fears of the wicked with the stable courage of the righteous, and verse 2 contrasts the political instability of an unrighteous nation with that of a nation led by a godly ruler.

Verse 3 notes the terrible let-down for the people of a nation when some kind of political upheaval elevates a previously poor man to leadership and then, instead of helping the poor of the land, he proceeds to oppress them even worse than did his predecessors. It is like a land that has been suffering a drought but then, when the rain finally comes, it becomes a flood devastating the land more severely than the drought had done.

In verse 5 appears a gracious promise that those who seek the Lord will find true understanding in all things, in contrast to those who are proud of their reasoning powers but who do not take the Lord and His Word into their reasonings, and thus are really ignorant concerning things that matter.

Verse 6 assures us that, in God's sight, a poor man who is righteous is "better" than an unrighteous rich man. It is, in fact, interesting to note how often in the Book of Proverbs we are told that certain seemingly undesirable things are better than their more attractive counterparts. For example, "Better is little with the fear of the LORD than great treasure and trouble therewith" (Prov. 15:16). Also, "Better is a dinner of herbs where love is, than a stalled ox and hatred therewith" (Prov. 15:17).

Note also the following: "Better is a little with righteousness than great revenues without right" (Prov. 16:8). "Better is a dry morsel, and quietness therewith, than an house full of sacrifices with strife" (Prov. 17:1). "Better it is to be of a humble spirit with the lowly, than to divide the spoil with the proud" (Prov. 16:19).

Such expressions of relative values are especially significant as coming from Solomon, the richest man in the world at the time!

Prayer is a wonderful privilege and asset, but prayer actually becomes an "abomination" in God's sight, when the person praying is also deliberately flouting God's Word, according to verse 9. Note what God told Joshua when he was praying while ignoring Achan's sin: "Get thee up: wherefore liest thou thus upon thy face? Israel hath sinned, and they have also transgressed my covenant which I commanded them" (Josh. 7:10–11). Psalm 109:7 says that one's prayer can even "become sin." "If I regard iniquity in my heart," said the Psalmist, "the Lord will not hear me" (Ps. 66:18). Men must believe God's Word before they can expect him to heed and honor their words.

Verse 12 probably should be understood as saying that when wicked people come into positions of power or authority, ordinary people tend to stay to themselves as much as possible.

It is unwise and counter-productive to try to hide our sins. They cannot be hidden from God, of course, and they have a way of discovering themselves to others as well. The wise action is confession and renunciation of the sin, according to verse 13, for otherwise, we can "be sure your sin will find you out" (Num. 32:23). The New Testament, of course, concurs, and this is a primary aspect of the gospel. "If we confess our sins, he is faithful and just to forgive us our sins, and to cleanse us from all unrighteousness" (1 John 1:9). Confession means actually naming the sin as sin, of course, not simply admitting it and trying to rationalize it or justify it, perhaps even to continue it.

When verse 14 says that happiness is the companion of constant fear, the meaning obviously is that of reverential fear of God, not man.

Verse 16 speaks of a leader who is covetous of yet more power and wealth and who, ignoring the will and words of God, thereby becomes oppressive in his authority. The probability is that his power, and perhaps even his life, will shortly be cut off, either by popular uprising or divine judgment.

The "pit" mentioned in verse 17 is a word used to describe an actual dug pit, or cistern, first used in connection with the dry cistern into which Joseph was thrown by his resentful brothers (Gen. 37:20). However, it is also used occasionally to symbolize either the grave (that is, death), or even the pit of hell. The willful shedder of blood will be tormented by his guilt and cannot escape it, regardless of how fast or far he flees, unless he flees not from man but to the Lord.

There is still another pronouncement in verse 21 against those who have "respect of persons" in making decisions. See listing in comments under Proverbs 24:23. On the "evil eye," referred to in verse 22, see comments under Proverbs 23:6.

The chapter closes with verse 28, which stresses again (as in verse 12) the truth that men tend to stay away from those in authority when the latter become corrupt or despotic.

Proverbs 29

1. *He, that being often reproved hardeneth his neck, shall suddenly be destroyed, and that without remedy.*
2. *When the righteous are in authority, the people rejoice: but when the wicked beareth rule, the people mourn.*
3. *Whoso loveth wisdom rejoiceth his father: but he that keepeth company with harlots spendeth his substance.*
4. *The king by judgment establisheth the land: but he that receiveth gifts overthroweth it.*
5. *A man that flattereth his neighbour spreadeth a net for his feet.*
6. *In the transgression of an evil man there is a snare: but the righteous doth sing and rejoice.*

7. *The righteous considereth the cause of the poor: but the wicked regardeth not to know it.*

8. *Scornful men bring a city into a snare: but wise men turn away wrath.*

9. *If a wise man contendeth with a foolish man, whether he rage or laugh, there is no rest.*

10. *The bloodthirsty hate the upright: but the just seek his soul.*

11. *A fool uttereth all his mind: but a wise man keepeth it in till afterwards.*

12. *If a ruler hearken to lies, all his servants are wicked.*

13. *The poor and the deceitful man meet together: the LORD lighteneth both their eyes.*

14. *The king that faithfully judgeth the poor, his throne shall be established for ever.*

15. *The rod and reproof give wisdom: but a child left to himself bringeth his mother to shame.*

16. *When the wicked are multiplied, transgression increaseth: but the righteous shall see their fall.*

17. *Correct thy son, and he shall give thee rest; yea, he shall give delight unto thy soul.*

18. *Where there is no vision, the people perish: but he that keepeth the law, happy is he.*

19. *A servant will not be corrected by words: for though he understand he will not answer.*

20. *Seest thou a man that is hasty in his words? there is more hope of a fool than of him.*

21. *He that delicately bringeth up his servant from a child shall have him become his son at the length.*

22. *An angry man stirreth up strife, and a furious man aboundeth in transgression.*

23. *A man's pride shall bring him low: but honour shall uphold the humble in spirit.*

24. *Whoso is partner with a thief hateth his own soul: he heareth cursing, and betrayeth it not.*

25. *The fear of man bringeth a snare: but whoso putteth his trust in the LORD shall be safe.*

26. *Many seek the ruler's favour; but every man's judgment cometh from the LORD.*

27. *An unjust man is an abomination to the just: and he that is upright in the way is abomination to the wicked.*

Verse 1 of this chapter is a familiar warning against obstinacy in resisting God's will or His revealed Word. Hardening the neck was (and

is) a common idiom for stubborness, essentially used synonymously with
hardening one's heart or spirit, and with stiffening the neck. "My Spirit
shall not always strive with man," God said long ago (Gen. 6:3). Even for
believing Christians, "there is a sin unto death" (1 John 5:16).

Verse 2 could well have served as an encouragement to King Hezekiah when it was shown to him by his men who were copying out these
proverbs of his ancestor Solomon. He could have noted its application
also to King Hoshea of Israel, whose wicked reign was ending during this
same period of time in the Assyrian captivity of Israel. The same would
be true of verse 4, with its warning against kings receiving bribes.

Note also the testimony of verse 8, as we try to see it through the eyes
of King Hezekiah. The awful wrath of the Assyrians was turned back
on themselves by the wisdom of the king (as counseled by the prophet
Isaiah) in trusting God and spreading the problem before Him (see Isa.
36), rather than giving in to the scoffing threats of the Assyrian general
Rabshakeh against the city of Jerusalem.

Verse 9 speaks of the futility of arguing with a foolish man ("wise in
his own conceits," according to Prov. 26:12) about spiritual truths. It will
lead either to anger or ridicule, and no conclusion is reached.

A ruler who listens to — and therefore encourages — lying reports by
his advisers will soon find himself surrounded by liars and other scoun-
drels who want to take advantage of his duplicity to advance their own
agendas. This is apparently the message of verse 12.

When Solomon penned (or perhaps read and incorporated into his
own writings) the words of verse 14, he surely must have been reminded
of God's promise to his father David (2 Sam. 7:13) to establish his throne
forever. The promise will be fulfilled eventually and perfectly in Christ
(Luke 1:32–33).

On the use of "the rod and reproof" in child-raising (verse 15), see
also Proverbs 13:24; 22:15; 23:13–14, as well as verse 17 of this chapter.

Verse 18 is a very familiar and oft-quoted proverb. "Where there is
no vision, the people perish: but he that keepeth the law, happy is he."
Unfortunately, it is often misapplied. The word "vision" does not refer
to far-sighted imagination, as commonly expounded, but to actual divine
revelation (see 1 Sam. 3:1). Furthermore, the word here translated "perish" means "open" or "exposed." That is, when people reject or ignore
the revealed Word of God, they are open and helpless to resist the humanistic and occult doctrines of men and devils, and thus are perishing
spiritually.

On the other hand, true happiness (or blessing) is found only through
"keeping" — that is, "guarding" — God's Word, then obeying and pro-
claiming it.

Solomon has had much to say in his proverbs about the behavior and responsibilities of kings and rulers. But there are also many who are called to be servants, and these also have responsibilities before God. "Servants, obey in all things your masters according to the flesh . . . in singleness of heart, fearing God" (Col. 3:22). Masters, in turn, are exhorted to treat their servants fairly and graciously, "knowing that your Master also is in heaven: neither is there respect of persons with him" (Eph. 6:9). However, if a servant is arrogant and disobedient, refusing even to answer his master's verbal admonitions, then verse 19 implies that some kind of stronger action should be taken by the master, as set forth in the contractual terms of their relationship.

As verse 19 warns against sullen silence, verse 20 next warns against hasty verbosity. Verse 11 says that "a fool uttereth all his mind" and Proverbs 26:12 notes that a man "wise in his own conceits" is more hopeless than a fool. Such a man is in view here, self-righteous and voluble in expressing his opinions. "Be swift to hear, slow to speak" (James 1:19) is the biblical guideline.

Then verse 21 warns against being overly indulgent to servants, lest they assume the rights of sons and heirs, positions to which God has not called them.

"God resisteth the proud, and giveth grace to the humble" (1 Pet. 5:5). This is the message of verse 23 and of many other Scriptures (Isa. 66:1–2; Matt. 23:12; etc.).

A person who tacitly encourages dishonesty or cursing or other sinful acts by not rebuking them is actually on the way to participating in them himself, and thereby "hateth his own soul," as we are told in verse 24.

This and other acts of craven silence or tacit approval of wrongdoing are usually the result of "the fear of man," but this type of fear "bringeth a snare" (verse 25). The only sound answer and antidote to such fear is, of course, "trust in the LORD." As verse 26 reminds us, ultimate "judgment cometh from the LORD," not man.

6

The Inspired Wisdom
of Agur and Lemuel

Proverbs 30:1–6

1. *The words of Agur the son of Jakeh, even the prophecy: the man spake unto Ithiel, even unto Ithiel and Ucal,*
2. *Surely I am more brutish than any man, and have not the understanding of a man.*
3. *I neither learned wisdom, nor have the knowledge of the holy.*
4. *Who hath ascended up into heaven, or descended? who hath gathered the wind in his fists? who hath bound the waters in a garment? who hath established all the ends of the earth? what is his name, and what is his son's name, if thou canst tell?*
5. *Every word of God is pure: He is a shield unto them that put their trust in him.*
6. *Add thou not unto his words, lest he reprove thee, and thou be found a liar.*

The 30th chapter of Proverbs may not have been written by Solomon, but by a wise man named Agur, who is never mentioned elsewhere in the Bible. Neither is his father Jakeh referred to anywhere else. Because of this, and because of the unique style and message of the chapter, some have taken verse 1 as symbolic, possibly meaning something like "The words of the gatherer [that is, gatherer of the proverbs], the son of obedience, even the prophecy which the mighty one [the actual meaning of the Hebrew word for "man" in this verse] spake unto the one who is with God and the one who overcomes" (possible meanings of the names of Ithiel and Ucal). The word for "prophecy" is usually translated "burden," meaning an inspired utterance impressed upon the prophet by God. If anything, this is a stronger claim to divine inspiration than

173

any of Solomon's statements in other parts of the Book of Proverbs, and suggests that the material in this chapter (also in chapter 31 — see Prov. 31:1 where the same word is used) is of special significance, even more so, if possible, than the other proverbs, though all are divinely inspired.

Most expositors, however, take Agur, Jakeh, Ithiel, and Ucal to be real persons — acquaintances of Solomon himself — Agur's writing so impressed Solomon that he incorporated it in his own collection. It is, of course, the message in the chapter that is of greatest interest, rather than the precise identity of the author.

The author begins by disavowing any special "understanding" or "wisdom" or "knowledge of the holy" on his own, thereby insisting that his message is coming from God Himself (verses 2–3). Then he proceeds to pose in verse 4 one of the most profound series of questions ever uttered in the Old Testament. "Who hath ascended up into heaven, or descended?" was his first question.

This was obviously a rhetorical question, the only possible answer being God himself. Enoch (and later Elijah) had ascended into heaven without dying, but he was still there at that time.

Certain of the holy angels, however, had on occasion descended to earth, and then returned to heaven. More significantly, God himself had appeared on earth for a brief time to certain chosen individuals — to Adam (Gen. 3:8–19), Abraham (Gen. 18:1–2), Jacob (Gen. 32:30), and others. From the New Testament, we realize that such visits from God to chosen men on earth were theophanies, with Christ in a pre-incarnate state temporarily appearing in human form. "No man hath seen God at any time," we are reminded, since God dwells "in the light which no man can approach unto; whom no man hath seen, nor can see." Nevertheless, "the only begotten Son, which is in the bosom of the Father, He hath declared him" (John 1:18; 1 Tim. 6:16).

Jesus finally answered Agur's question when He told Nicodemus that "no man hath ascended up to heaven, but He that came down from heaven, even the Son of man which is in heaven" (John 3:13). Even the angelic visitations to earth from heaven are dependent on the Son. As Christ told Nathanael, "Hereafter ye shall see heaven opened, and the angels of God ascending and descending upon the Son of man" (John 1:51). Their father Jacob had long ago been given a special dream by God in which he could see that there did exist a great Ladder between heaven and earth (that Ladder was Christ!), with "the angels of God ascending and descending on it" (Gen. 28:12).

But that was only the first of Agur's great questions. "Who hath gathered the wind in His fists?" he asked. That is, who has the power to keep the winds from blowing, and then release them when and where He will, either as gentle breezes or as destructive tornadoes and hurricanes?

Naturalistic scientists may object that they can explain all that without recourse to divine miracles. They will speak of the differential heating of the atmosphere, the jet stream, the ocean currents called La Niña and Los Niños, and other such concepts. Yes, but who established the jet stream and the ocean currents and the general circulation of the atmosphere in the first place? And even yet, with all the meteorologic knowledge and instruments now available, it is impossible to predict the weather in any detail — especially the specific times and paths of monsoons and cyclones. God is still in control.

"Who hath bound the waters in a garment?" Agur asks yet another insightful question. In his day and age he was still more profoundly aware than we are today that there had been a time in the measurable past when the waters had not been bound, but had poured forth from both earth and sky to "overturn the earth" (Job 12:15). Physically and geologically speaking, there is nothing known in science that would prevent this from happening again. There is enough water in the world's oceans to blanket the earth with a global shroud of water over a mile deep, if the earth's land areas were somehow smoothed out to make it the equivalent of a simple sphere. It is conceivable that enough tectonic forces could be generated — through the earth's internal heat, or the impact of a sizeable asteroid from space, or through giant earthquakes or other possible mechanisms — to do just that.

But that will not happen, because God has promised it will not (Gen. 9:11, 15), and He keeps His promises. Through the peculiar properties of water, through the strange force of gravity, through the geophysical principle of isostasy, and perhaps other means, God has indeed bound the waters in an invisible garment which keeps them in "the place which thou hast founded for them" (Ps. 104:8), so that "they turn not again to cover the earth" (Ps. 104:9).

Next question? "Who hath established the ends of the earth?" The obvious answer to this rhetorical question, as to all the others, is God the Creator. He created the earth, not by some process of accretion from planetesimals or by some tidal pull on the sun or some other naturalistic process. "Mine hand also hath laid the foundation of the earth, and my right hand hath spanned the heavens: when I call unto them, they stand up together" (Isa. 48:13). The heavens and the earth stood up *together* (not stretched out individually over billions of years) when God spoke them into existence, as He recorded in Genesis 1:1.

But what are the *"ends"* of the earth? The popular idiomatic use of the phrase, even today, is in reference to very distant regions, and it could be so understood here. More likely, however, it refers to the land areas of the earth. The Hebrew word *eretz* is translated "land" over fourteen hundred times and "earth" only seven hundred times.

This meaning also fits the immediate context. If God has restrained the waters in definite bounds, then obviously the continental areas also have been determined. Thus, God has "established all the [boundaries of the lands]."

It is obvious that Agur knows the answer to all his rhetorical questions. The great God of creation, Elohim, the mighty one, has established the lands and seas and atmosphere of the earth, and controls them all. He even refers to the word of God in verse 5. Yet he now asks, "What is His name?"

Surely he knew God's name, revealed long before to Moses and all the patriarchs as Jehovah (or Yahweh). He even used *this* name in verse 9. There are many other names for God that had been used on various occasions in the past, one of the most common being "Lord" (Hebrew, *Adonai*).

But apparently, one key name had not yet been revealed, and Agur asked, "What is His name?" When Christ came to reveal God in His most wonderful nature, He taught us to pray with the prayer addressed to "Our Father which art in heaven, Hallowed be thy name" (Matt. 6:9).

"Father!" That is the name which Agur longed to hear. The word "father" (Hebrew *ab*) occurs more than five hundred times in the Old Testament, yet none of the writers or speakers ever address God as *ab* (or *abba*, the Aramaic equivalent). Never in the wonderful prayers of David or others in the psalms was God ever addressed as "Father."

But Christ not only called God "Father," but told us also to do so. In His prayer on the night before His crucifixion, He prayed for His disciples, saying, "Father. . . . I have manifested thy name unto the men whom thou gavest me out of the world. . . . O righteous Father. . . . I have declared unto them thy name, and will declare it." (John 17:1–26). And that name, obviously, was "Father."

On one urgent occasion, in the Garden of Gethsemane, the Lord Jesus prayed to His Father, crying, "Abba, Father" (Mark 14:36). Although no one in the Old Testament would ever address God as "Abba," Christ did. This must have been the most intimate name for His Father in the innermost councils of the Godhead.

And now, by virtue of our own adoption through Christ into God's family, even we can — when the circumstances warrant it — use the same wonderful name when praying to our heavenly Father. "And because ye are sons, God hath sent forth the Spirit of His Son into your hearts, crying, Abba, Father" (Gal. 4:6).

Perhaps this answers Agur's question concerning the then-not-yet-revealed name of the mighty Creator of all things in heaven and earth.

But Agur had still one more question — the most difficult of all. "What is His Son's name, if thou canst tell?"

How did Agur know that God had a Son? He had revealed himself over and over again as the one and only true God. "Hear, O Israel: The LORD our God is one LORD" (Deut. 6:4). "I am the LORD, and there is none else; there is no God beside me" (Isa. 45:5).

However, Agur was undoubtedly acquainted with David's psalms, and in his second psalm, there are two references to God's Son. Agur must have seen these, and this fact may have been the human reason why he was curious about the name of God's Son. In the psalm, the speaker was quoted as saying, "The LORD hath said unto me, Thou art my Son; this day have I begotten thee." Then, addressing the kings and judges of the earth, the speaker warns, "Kiss the Son, lest he be angry, and ye perish from the way, when his wrath is kindled but a little. Blessed are all they that put their trust in him" (Ps. 2:7, 12).

"But what is His name," Agur had asked, and no answer had been forthcoming. There was another somewhat cryptic reference to an eternal Son of God in 2 Samuel 7:13–14, and the parallel passage in 1 Chronicles 17:13, but these did not give his name either.

As it turns out, there now seem to be several answers to Agur's question, but the first one did not come until the time of Isaiah the prophet, with his great prophecy of the virgin birth of Christ. "Behold, a virgin shall conceive, and bear a son, and shall call his name Immanuel" (Isa. 7:14).

Immanuel — that is, the Son's name — a name that means "God with us." That is, the divine Son of God would also be Son of man, through miraculous conception and virgin birth. He would be "God with us," God, yet also man.

But that is not His only name. According to Isaiah in the same context, "For unto us a child is born, unto us a son is given: and the government shall be upon His shoulder: and His name shall be called Wonderful, Counsellor, The mighty God, The everlasting Father, The Prince of Peace" (Isaiah 9:6).

What a tremendous name — or perhaps complex of names! Yet even that is not all. Speaking of the same God/man, the prophet Jeremiah said, "This is the name whereby He shall be called, THE LORD OUR RIGHTEOUSNESS" (Jer. 23:6).

And then, when we come to the New Testament and the actual sending forth of the divine Son, there are still other names. "Thou shalt call His name Jesus," said the angel Gabriel to Mary, when she was informed that she was to be the virgin mother of the promised divine Son. To Joseph, who would become Mary's husband, he said the same thing (Luke 1:35; Matt. 1:20–21).

Finally, when He comes again to reign in power and glory there will be "on his vesture and on his thigh a name written, KING OF KINGS, AND LORD OF LORDS" (Rev. 19:16). Another of His great names in eternity is given in Revelation 19:11, where He is "called Faithful and True." We read also in Revelation 19:13 that "His name is called The Word of God."

The answer to Agur's question is thus many-fold, almost exhausting the language. God has "given Him a name which is above every name: That at the name of Jesus [that is, literally, 'the name belonging to Jesus'] every knee should bow, of things in heaven, and things in earth, and things under the earth; And that every tongue should confess that Jesus Christ is Lord, to the glory of God the Father" (Phil. 2:9–11). To the believer, of course, He is simply "the Lord Jesus Christ" (Acts 2:36; 16:31).

Then, following the profound questions of verse 4, Agur makes the even more profound statement and warning: "Every word of God is pure. . . . Add thou not unto his words, lest he reprove thee, and thou be found a liar" (verses 5–6). Note that God's *every* word is pure — not just some words. And note that it is His very *words* that are pure — not just His thoughts. This, like Paul's tremendous assertion in 2 Timothy 3:16 ("all scripture is [literally] God-breathed"), is an unequivocal claim to plenary verbal inspiration of the written words (Scriptures) of God.

All of God's words are *pure*, without error or excess. Therefore, it is wrong and dangerous to presume to change them in any way (Rev. 22:18–19). Since "Thy word is true from the beginning; and every one of thy righteous judgments endureth for ever" (Ps. 119:160), any teaching deliberately contrary to God's Word is a lie, and will draw God's severe reproof sooner or later (note Rev. 21:8). But those who put their full trust in God and His Word are safe under His impregnable shield.

Proverbs 30:7–33

7. *Two things have I required of thee; deny me them not before I die:*

8. *Remove far from me vanity and lies: give me neither poverty nor riches: feed me with food convenient for me:*

9. *Lest I be full, and deny thee, and say, Who is the LORD? or lest I be poor, and steal, and take the name of my God in vain.*

10. *Accuse not a servant unto his master, lest he curse thee, and thou be found guilty.*

11. *There is a generation that curseth their father, and doth not bless their mother.*

12. *There is a generation that are pure in their own eyes, and yet is not washed from their filthiness.*

13. *There is a generation, O how lofty are their eyes! and their eyelids are lifted up.*

14. *There is a generation, whose teeth are as swords, and their jaw teeth as knives, to devour the poor from off the earth, and the needy from among men.*

15. *The horseleach hath two daughters, crying, Give, give. There are three things that are never satisfied, yea, four things say not, It is enough:*

16. *The grave; and the barren womb; the earth that is not filled with water; and the fire that saith not, It is enough.*

17. *The eye that mocketh at his father, and despiseth to obey his mother, the ravens of the valley shall pick it out, and the young eagles shall eat it.*

18. *There be three things which are too wonderful for me, yea, four which I know not:*

19. *The way of an eagle in the air; the way of a serpent upon a rock; the way of a ship in the midst of the sea; and the way of a man with a maid.*

20. *Such is the way of an adulterous woman; she eateth, and wipeth her mouth, and saith, I have done no wickedness.*

21. *For three things the earth is disquieted, and for four which it cannot bear:*

22. *For a servant when he reigneth; and a fool when he is filled with meat;*

23. *For an odious woman when she is married; and an handmaid that is heir to her mistress.*

24. *There be four things which are little upon the earth, but they are exceeding wise:*

25. *The ants are a people not strong, yet they prepare their meat in the summer;*

26. *The conies are but a feeble folk, yet make they their houses in the rocks;*

27. *The locusts have no king, yet go they forth all of them by bands;*

28. *The spider taketh hold with her hands, and is in king's palaces.*

29. *There be three things which go well, yea, four are comely in going:*

30. *A lion which is strongest among beasts, and turneth not away for any;*

31. *A greyhound; an he goat also; and a king, against whom there is no rising up.*

32. *If thou hast done foolishly in lifting up thyself, or if thou hast thought evil, lay thine hand upon thy mouth.*

33. *Surely the churning of milk bringeth forth butter, and the wringing of the nose bringeth forth blood: so the forcing of wrath bringeth forth strife.*

Agur next makes two earnest prayers, requesting God not to burden him with either riches or poverty and also to deliver him from both vanity and lies in his lifestyle (verses 7–9). The Hebrew word for "vanity" in this passage is not the same word as that used so frequently by Solomon in Ecclesiastes. It essentially means "falsehood" or, in context, a false standard of living. Attempting to impress others with abilities or possessions we really don't have leads to deliberate lying in order to maintain appearances, and we, like Agur, should pray to be delivered from that temptation. Similarly, God has promised to supply our needs (Phil. 4:19) and we, like Paul, should learn to be content in whatever state God chooses for us (Phil. 4:11–12). God may entrust some with excessive riches or deep poverty, and He can give grace sufficient for every need, but it is unseemly for a Christian either to devote himself primarily to acquiring wealth or to be so careless and wasteful as to invite poverty for his family.

Verse 10 is obviously only a generalization, because there may be occasions when an unfaithful or wicked servant needs to be called to account. In general, however, the lot of a servant (especially that of a slave) is hard at best, and he should be treated with fairness and compassion to every extent possible, not only by his master (Col. 4:1) but also by others. The master, if he is fair, will defend his servant against false or trivial charges, causing embarrassment or even worse to the one slandering him. "Go not forth hastily to strive, lest thou know not what to do in the end thereof, when thy neighbour hath put thee to shame" (Prov. 25:8).

The next four verses (verses 11–14) throw a searchlight on four types of sinners (the term used is "generation," but these types of people are abundant in every generation). The unspeakable sin (verse 11) of cursing one's parents (and by implication, disobeying or ridiculing or dishonoring them in any way is essentially covered by the overt sin of cursing) was actually a capital crime under the law (Exod. 21:17). Even though not applicable today, this penalty does show the attitude of God to such behavior, which is almost as bad as cursing God.

Then there are the hypocrites (verse 12), the proud (verse 13), and the greedily cruel (verse 14). All are gross sinners in God's sight.

The horse leech mentioned in verse 15 is perpetually seeking blood. Its two-forked tongue is graphically portrayed as two sisters evidently both named "Give" (the word "crying" is not in the original). Like the never-satisfied leech, the grave, the barren womb, the thirsty earth, and the advancing fire (verse 16) are perpetually unsatisfied and seeking satisfaction. All of these typify all kinds of lusts in our own minds and bodies — never satisfied until we find peace and rest in Christ.

Verse 17 revisits verse 11, assuring that those who flagrantly dishonor their parents will eventually suffer severe judgment for thus flouting God's special "commandment with promise" (Eph. 6:2–3).

The author had critiqued four "generations" or classes of people (verses 11–14), then four things that would never say, "enough," or literally "wealth" — that is, "all I need" (verses 15–16). Now he lists four "things which are too wonderful for me" to understand (verses 18–19), then four things the earth cannot bear (verses 21–23), four small animals which exhibit great instinctive wisdom (verses 24–28), and finally four living creatures which are "comely in going" (verses 29–31).

The reason for the unique formula ("there are three . . . yea four") repeated several times in these listings is never specified and there seems no obvious reason except possibly as a rhetorical device for focusing special attention on the fourth item in the list.

The four unsearchable "ways" of verse 19 note that neither the eagle flying through the air nor the serpent gliding along a rock (that is, not on soft ground) nor the ship moving through the sea can be traced by footprints or spoors or anything other than the memory of the watcher. Just so, there are many different paths by which a man might woo a virgin maiden — for marriage if honorable, for seduction otherwise. The implied suggestion is for maidens to be very cautious and wise when being courted by a man. True love, as the old saying goes, if intentions are honorable, will find a way.

An adulterous woman (verse 20), on the other hand, has her own devices for concealing her "way" (as though she were wiping her mouth after a meal), all the while protesting innocence yet subtly achieving her purpose (whatever it is — money, power, blackmail, physical pleasure, etc.). Solomon described one of her "ways" in Proverbs 7:7–27.

Next, he lists four things intolerable to an earth of order and peace (verses 21–23). A man equipped by God for a servant's role, and nothing more, has occasionally risen to a position of authority, with disastrous results. As Jeremiah mourned, "Servants have ruled over us: there is none that doth deliver us out of their hand" (Lam. 5:8).

Similar disaster results when "a fool," such as Belshazzar, for example (Dan. 5:1–4), becomes dedicated to food and drink and revelry. Additional examples would be Herod (Matt. 14:6–10), Nabal (1 Sam. 25:36–38), Elah (1 Kings 16:8–10), and others.

The first two unbearable things relate to the community, the last two to the family. One of the latter is an "odious" (that is, hateful and critical) wife. The other is a handmaid that usurps the place of the wife, the most familiar Bible example being Hagar (Gen. 16:4).

The four examples of "wise" animals (verses 25–28) are ants, coneys, locusts, and spiders. All except the coneys are common to the experience and observation of practically everyone. The remarkable "instincts" of the insects, which impel them to behave with what appears to be such intelligent planning, organization, and skill, could never have been acquired by chance evolution. How can such small weak creatures as the ants find and carry loads larger than themselves, laying food up for the future? How can swarms of locusts, with no "king locust" to guide them, move in perfect order in "bands" to their determined destination? And how did spiders learn to spin such beautifully and intricately designed webs? Evolution? Don't be absurd!

As for the coneys mentioned here, these are believed to have been the "rock hyraxes" that still live among the high rocks in the region from the Dead Sea to Mount Hermon. It is also possible that the difficulty in precisely identifying the coney is because it is an animal that is now extinct. It should also be mentioned that the word translated "spider" is used only once in the Hebrew text, and is believed by some expositors to refer instead to the lizard. The identification of the ants as "a people" and the coneys as "a folk" (actually both are the same word in the Hebrew) perhaps was intended to help us appreciate them as an actual "population," established and organized by their Creator.

Then there are the four living creatures identified as "comely in going" (verses 29–31) — the lion, the greyhound, the he-goat, and the king. The words for both "greyhound" and "he-goat" are each used only once in the Hebrew text, and so are of uncertain meaning. Some expositors think the "greyhound" was really a war horse, some a fighting cock, some a leopard. The words may possibly even refer to extinct animals. The essential point of the passage, of course, is that "comeliness in going" is appropriate for a king — and, therefore, for all Christians, who have been made "a royal priesthood" (1 Pet. 2:9) and should, in our "goings," appear and behave as those that are in the family of the King of kings. We ought to "walk, even as he walked" (1 John 2:6).

Then Agur closes his special homily with appropriate final warnings (verses 32–33) against exaltation of oneself and careless denigration of others, and especially against continuing and pressing a point in an argument, thereby forcing wrath and eventually actual strife.

Proverbs 31:1–9

1. The words of king Lemuel, the prophecy that his mother taught him.
2. What, my son, and what, the son of my womb? and what, the son of my vows?
3. Give not thy strength unto women, nor thy ways to that which destroyeth kings.
4. It is not for kings, O Lemuel, it is not for kings to drink wine; nor for princes strong drink:
5. Lest they drink, and forget the law, and pervert the judgment of any of the afflicted.
6. Give strong drink unto him that is ready to perish, and wine unto those that be of heavy hearts.
7. Let him drink, and forget his poverty, and remember his misery no more.
8. Open thy mouth for the dumb in the cause of all such as are appointed to destruction.
9. Open thy mouth, judge righteously, and plead the cause of the poor and needy.

This final chapter of the Book of Proverbs is, like the previous one (chapter 30), a sort of addendum, probably not written by Solomon but surely approved by him, then later adopted by the final compilers (possibly the men of Hezekiah) as the most appropriate way to end the book.

The last 22 verses of the chapter (verses 10–31) form an acrostic poem and this section is almost certainly the most familiar part of the Book of Proverbs. As the familiar eulogy on the "virtuous woman," it has served as the text for countless Mother's Day sermons, as well as many articles and poems extolling the theme of ideal Christian womanhood.

But first we must look at the first nine verses of the chapter. This section also is remarkable, introducing one of the only two chapters of the Bible written by a woman, the other being the song of Deborah (Judg. 5).

The chapter begins (verse 1) by asserting that its words are the words of King Lemuel, but then also notes that these words were merely the "prophecy" (or inspired "burden," which is the literal meaning — see comment on Prov. 30:1) which his mother had taught him. Thus this chapter seems really to have been spoken, or written, by Lemuel's mother, then copied down by him.

But who was King Lemuel, and who was his mother? The fact is, sadly, that no one knows for sure, since his name is mentioned nowhere else in the Bible. Furthermore, neither Judah nor Israel ever had a king by this name, and it is highly unlikely that any of the pagan kings of Canaan or any other nation would ever have penned such a chapter as this. There are, in fact, no kings recorded in history anywhere in the world with such a name as Lemuel.

All of which makes it most probable that the godly king addressed in this chapter was commonly known by some other name than Lemuel, with the latter a sort of descriptive pet name applied to him by his mother.

If that is the case, then certainly the most likely person to have been given such a special name would be Solomon himself. The name Lemuel means "belonging to God," and it would have been eminently fitting for Solomon's mother, Bathsheba, to have given him this name after her traumatic experience of adultery with David, then the loss of her husband Uriah and a quick marriage to David, followed by the death of the son fathered by David (2 Sam. 11:26–27; 12:15–18).

The Bible speaks eloquently of David's confession and repentance (2 Sam. 12:13–14; Ps. 32, 51) and it mentions also that David then "comforted Bathsheba his wife, and went in unto her, and lay with her: and she bare a son, and he called his name Solomon: and the LORD loved him" (2 Sam. 12:24).

While the record does not say as much, it would seem certain that, when David "comforted" Bathsheba, he encouraged her also in confession and repentance concerning her own part in the tragic events which had led to the death of her firstborn son, just seven days after his birth. She, no doubt, would have determined and promised God that, if He would give her another son, she would raise him as best she could to honor the Lord in every way in his life.

The many references in the Book of Proverbs to his mother and his concern for her welfare would certainly indicate that she had done just that (see Prov. 1:8; 4:3; 6:20; also Song of Sol. 3:11). There are also many heartfelt expressions of concern for all godly mothers in his proverbs. Solomon surely must have had a deep love and appreciation for his own mother and what she had meant to him.

There is one more reason why it seems likely that Lemuel ("belonging to God") was really the same person as Solomon ("peaceful"). Although this is a subjective reason, it would seem that whoever was responsible for the final compilation and organization of Solomon's proverbs in book form — whether that person was Solomon himself, or Hezekiah's men, or some unknown editor — would have felt it almost mandatory that the book would end, as well as begin, with one of Solomon's writings, rather than with an addendum by some unknown author. And what would be more appropriate than to honor Solomon's mother, who had meant so much to him, by adding her own composition to his collection? Be all that as it may — and it obviously involves some degree of speculative reading between the lines — this last chapter of Proverbs is surely one of the mountain-peak chapters of Scripture.

In verse 2, the author speaks of "the son of my vows," which clearly testifies that she had made vows to God concerning her son, probably before he was even conceived. Again this sounds very much like what Bathsheba would have done, in praying for another son, after the son of her adultery died in infancy. This is similar to what Hannah had done many years before, in praying for the son who would become the great prophet Samuel (1 Sam. 1:10–11, 19–20), who later would be the one to anoint David her husband as Israel's king. It could even be the name Lemuel was first given her son because of its similarity in sound to Samuel, which seems to have meant "heard by God" or even "lent to God" (Note 1 Sam. 1:28).

Next in her song (verses 3–4), she expressed her motherly concern that he, as future king, not allow himself to yield to those moral temptations which so often overtake men of power — the seductions and availability of ambitious women and the easily acquired addiction to wine and strong drink. Her concerns, as his mother, were not so much about politics or military matters, but rather about his moral and spiritual life and influence.

Assuming that this section was, indeed, originally written for Solomon by Bathsheba, many of his own later proverbs, as we have seen, reflected these cautions. Not only was Solomon observing them himself, but he also was passing on similar warnings in even stronger terms, to his own son and to other young men. Sadly, in his later years, he seems to have rejected them himself, as we shall see in the next chapter as we study Ecclesiastes.

Nevertheless, the principles and warnings of verses 4 and 5 are still as valid as ever, not only for kings but also for all people, especially for those in positions of authority or influence. Verses 6 and 7 seem, on the other hand, not only to permit but to encourage the use of strong drink for people who are ready to die, or who are in deep poverty or misery of some kind.

In cases where someone is in serious pain and is without hope of a cure, then wine or other addictive drugs may be useful for relief of pain (see also 1 Tim. 5:23 for an instance of approved medicinal use of wine). As far as other uses are concerned, this advice is apparently given in irony to those who have drifted so far from God as to be "appointed to destruction" (verse 8) anyway. In any case, such advice could not have been intended by Lemuel or his mother (or by the Lord) to set aside such prohibitions as in Proverbs 23:31.

To the contrary, she urges Lemuel to defend and help those who have been condemned unjustly and cannot speak for themselves (verse 8), and to "judge righteously," especially in pleading the "cause of the poor and needy" (verse 9).

Proverbs 31:10–31

10. *Who can find a virtuous woman? for her price is far above rubies.*

11. *The heart of her husband doth safely trust in her, so that he shall have no need of spoil.*

12. *She will do him good and not evil all the days of her life.*

13. *She seeketh wool, and flax, and worketh willingly with her hands.*

14. *She is like the merchants' ships; she bringeth her food from afar.*

15. *She riseth also while it is yet night, and giveth meat to her household, and a portion to her maidens.*

16. *She considereth a field, and buyeth it: with the fruit of her hands she planteth a vineyard.*

17. *She girdeth her loins with strength, and strengtheneth her arms.*

18. *She perceiveth that her merchandise is good: her candle goeth not out by night.*

19. *She layeth her hands to the spindle, and her hands hold the distaff.*

20. *She stretcheth out her hand to the poor; yea, she reacheth forth her hands to the needy.*

21. *She is not afraid of the snow for her household: for all her household are clothed with scarlet.*

22. *She maketh herself coverings of tapestry; her clothing is silk and purple.*

23. *Her husband is known in the gates, when he sitteth among the elders of the land.*

24. *She maketh fine linen, and selleth it; and delivereth girdles unto the merchant.*

25. *Strength and honour are her clothing; and she shall rejoice in time to come.*

26. *She openeth her mouth with wisdom; and in her tongue is the law of kindness.*

27. *She looketh well to the ways of her household, and eateth not the bread of idleness.*

28. *Her children arise up, and call her blessed; her husband also, and he praiseth her.*

29. *Many daughters have done virtuously, but thou excellest them all.*
30. *Favour is deceitful, and beauty is vain: but a woman that feareth the* LORD, *she shall be praised.*
31. *Give her of the fruit of her hands; and let her own works praise her in the gates.*

We come now to the final section of the Book of Proverbs, the famous section on the virtuous woman. Although the text does not say so, this section was probably also written by King Lemuel's mother. If Lemuel himself wrote it, its thoughts and descriptions must have come originally from his mother, and he probably used it in his own search for such a woman to be his own wife and the mother of his children.

As discussed above, "Lemuel" was quite possibly his mother's special name for her beloved son, Solomon, which was his real name. His mother, then, would have been Bathsheba, and Naamah would be the one he chose as best fitting their ideal of the virtuous woman so beautifully described in these verses.

Whether or not these were the people really identified as Solomon, his mother, and his wife really does not affect our appreciation of the inspiring description of this remarkable woman, which has been such a blessing and inspiration to so many during the almost three thousand years since it was written. But it may help it come to life even more, as it were, if we think of it in terms of these real people that were in view at that time.

The 22 verses of this section were organized by its author, whoever he or she may have been, into the form of an acrostic poem. Each of its 22 verses begins with the corresponding letter of the Hebrew alphabet — that is, verse 10 begins with *aleph*, verse 11 with *beth*, verse 12 with *gimel*, and so on, with the 22nd and last letter of the alphabet, *tau*, beginning verse 31. The implied thought, perhaps, was that the perfections of this ideal woman would exhaust the entire language.

The poem begins with the plaintive query: "Who can find a virtuous woman?" (verse 10). If one could purchase such a woman, her purchase price would surely be "far above rubies." One can visualize Bathsheba counseling young Solomon (she would call him her beloved Lemuel) as he sets out to look for a young maiden qualified to be the wife of God's chosen king of the chosen nation.

By "virtuous" is not meant just moral purity, although this is certainly included. The adjective in question (Hebrew *chavil*) was only so rendered as "virtuous" by the translators when describing women (Ruth 3:11; Prov. 12:4). The word much more commonly means "valor," or "valiant," and was always so translated when applied to men. Thus the woman of this chapter (and the woman young Lemuel and his mother were hoping to find) would be a woman of great strength of character, courage, and energy, as well as one who was morally pure.

She would be a woman who would be faithful to her husband. He could "safely trust in her," that she would "do him good . . . all the days of her life" (verses 11–12). She would be a woman trustworthy not only in moral rectitude, but also in relation to use of money, caring for her family, and in every other way.

She would also be industrious, the kind of woman who would willingly work hard to provide for her family, shopping selectively and wisely to find the best prices for the best food for their needs, and rising early in the morning to be sure it is properly prepared. Not only in the food market and kitchen, but also in the sewing room, the virtuous woman even spins the cloth she uses to weave clothing for her household. All this and more is told us in verses 13–15 and 19–22.

Furthermore, she must be capable and willing, if needed, to purchase property and plant and work vineyards — or whatever other work might be needed to supplement her husband's income (note verses 16, 18, 24).

If, indeed, this description of a suitable wife had been originally drawn up by Bathsheba to guide Solomon in his search for a bride, as inferred above, then Naamah evidently proved a worthy candidate. She had her own flocks and vineyards, and had spent much time in the fields under the hot Arabian sun. She had even cared for her brothers' vineyards to the detriment of her own. Note in chapter 2, the discussions under Song of Solomon 1:5–6; 6:9–11; 7:12–13; 8:12; etc. Furthermore, she was morally pure (Song of Sol. 8:10; etc.), as well as beautiful and gracious.

Returning to the attributes of the virtuous woman, of which all or most were presumably characteristic of Naamah, she would be strong and healthy physically (verse 17), willing to work long hours (verses 15, 18), and kind and generous to those less fortunate (verses 20, 26).

She would need to be a credit to her husband, who would himself be esteemed as one of the "elders of the land" (verse 23). In Naamah's case, her potential husband would actually be a prince of the land, then eventually king.

Whether or not these attributes of the virtuous woman (as formulated apparently by Lemuel's mother) were actual guidelines prepared by Bathsheba for her son Solomon, as suggested above, and whether or not Naamah was chosen as Solomon's bride partially because she fit the descriptions — all of which at least seem like possible and reasonable suppositions — the fact still remains that this beautiful passage has become a classic description of the ideal wife and mother.

Such women (and there have indeed been not a few over the years) who at least approximately have fit these specifications, including this writer's own dear wife of over 60 years, as well as his six lovely Christian daughters and daughters-in-law, have, above all, each been "a woman that feareth the LORD" (verse 30). Therefore, although her present life may be filled with long hours of hard work, and perhaps troubles and heartaches of various kinds, "she shall rejoice in time to come" (verse 25), as "her children arise up, and call her blessed: her husband also, and he praiseth her" (verse 28), giving her a standing ovation as it were. Furthermore, even "her own works praise her in the gates" (verse 31), and the Lord whom she has feared and loved throughout her life as wife and mother will say one day, "Well done, thou good and faithful servant" (Matt. 25:21).

The Book of Proverbs ends — no doubt providentially — on this wonderful note. Solomon had written many warnings about the "strange woman" (Prov. 2:16; etc.), the "foolish woman" (9:13), the "brawling woman" (21:9), the "contentious woman" (21:19), the "odious woman" (30:23), the "whorish woman" (6:26), and the "evil woman" (6:24). But all of these needed warnings are pushed to the background, so to speak, as he ends the book with the description (possibly written by his own dear mother) of the strong, pure, energetic, wise, valiant, "virtuous" woman who has come to be the ideal role model for godly women in every age.

7

Solomon's Swan Song

Ecclesiastes

According to ancient legend, a dying swan was believed to sound forth a plaintive song just before dying, and so the term "swan song" came to be applied to the final work of a poet or singer or any other writer. The Book of Ecclesiastes may well have been the last of the "thousand and five" songs said to have been written by the great King Solomon (1 Kings 4:32).

It was certainly written in his old age, recording his reflections on all the mistakes of his later life, just as the Song of Solomon was perhaps the first — and evidently regarded by him as the greatest — of his many songs. This "Song of songs," as he had called it (Song of Sol. 1:1) reflected his experiences with his first and probably only true love, the beautiful Naamah, mother of his son and successor, Rehoboam.

Despite his eventual marriages to over seven hundred princesses (possibly all for politico/prestige purposes), none of these are ever so much as mentioned in Ecclesiastes. The only reference to wives at all in this book is at Ecclesiastes 9:9. "Live joyfully with the wife whom thou lovest all the days of the life of thy vanity, which He hath given thee under the sun, all the days of thy vanity: for that is thy portion in this life, and in the labour which thou takest under the sun."

No doubt he was thinking here of Naamah, realizing that she meant more (or should have, at least) to him than any or all of his seven hundred other wives. All the rest had been part of the "vanity" of life to which he refers so frequently in this final song of his, and thus he never even mentions them at all.

He did discuss in depth, however, the vanity of life and all its earthly pleasures, as we shall see shortly. By this time in life he seems to have realized that his temporary dabbling in the religions of his wives, as well as his pursuit of wealth and power, had been nothing but vanity, and had returned to his youthful trust in the one true God alone. The final challenge of his "swan song" is an exhortation to young people to "fear God and keep his commandments" (Eccles. 12:13) — the very challenge that God had given him at the beginning of his reign (1 Kings 3:14).

Even though Solomon's melancholy swan song speaks eloquently of his own failures, it still is full of profound wisdom for its future readers, and there should be no doubt that it is divinely inspired. Unanimously accepted as part of the canon of Scripture by both the ancient Jews and early Christians, it is fascinating, insightful, and profoundly moving in many, many ways.

Ecclesiastes 1:1–11

1. *The words of the Preacher, the son of David, king in Jerusalem.*
2. *Vanity of vanities, saith the Preacher, vanity of vanities; all is vanity.*
3. *What profit hath a man of all his labour which he taketh under the sun?*
4. *One generation passeth away, and another generation cometh: but the earth abideth for ever.*
5. *The sun also ariseth, and the sun goeth down, and hasteth to his place where he rose.*
6. *The wind goeth toward the south, and turneth about unto the north; it whirleth about continually, and the wind returneth again according to his circuits.*
7. *All the rivers run into the sea; yet the sea is not full; unto the place from whence the rivers come, thither they return again.*
8. *All things are full of labour; man cannot utter it: the eye is not satisfied with seeing, nor the ear filled with hearing.*
9. *The thing that hath been, it is that which shall be; and that which is done is that which shall be done: and there is no new thing under the sun.*
10. *Is there any thing whereof it may be said, See, this is new? it hath been already of old time, which was before us.*
11. *There is no remembrance of former things; neither shall there be any remembrance of things that are to come with those that shall come after.*

The Book of Ecclesiastes begins with an unambiguous statement as to its authorship. "The son of David, king in Jerusalem" (verse 1) can be no one but Solomon. However, he also calls himself "the Preacher," and this term was applied to himself by Solomon seven times — all in Ecclesiastes — and is used nowhere else in the Old Testament. In fact, the Greek Septuagint translation rendered the Hebrew term (*Kehleth*) by this very word "Ecclesiastes," a word derived from the Greek word for "church" (*ekklesia*). The idea expressed is that the "ecclesiastes" of the church should be the one who calls the assembly together for instruction and exhortation. In fact, this is actually the basic meaning of the Hebrew word, and thus it would correspond quite closely with the modern concept of the church pastor/teacher/preacher.

Solomon is thus, here in his swan song, assuming the role of a pastor guiding his flock rather than that of a general commanding an army or a king giving directions to his people. His attitude toward the world and life has obviously changed drastically in what is apparently his old age. The attitude is now clearly one of disillusionment with the world system and its humanistic values, but also one of restoration of faith and respect toward God and *His* values.

His entire premise has changed as he recognizes — and repeats — his conclusion, "Vanity of vanities . . . vanity of vanities; all is vanity" (verse 2).

The word translated "vanity" (Hebrew *hebel*) is used by Solomon in Ecclesiastes no less than 38 times — more than in all the rest of the Old Testament put together. It basically means "emptiness," something altogether transitory and unsatisfactory. That had finally become Solomon's conviction about the things of this world. And that, of course, is the teaching of the New Testament as well. "For all that is in the world, the lust of the flesh, and the lust of the eyes, and the pride of life, is not of the Father, but of the world. And the world passeth away, and the lust thereof: but he that doeth the will of God abideth for ever" (1 John 2:16–17).

Solomon raises the question in verse 3, "What profit hath a man of all his labour which he taketh under the sun?"

Lest one think that to be an overly negative attitude toward honest, productive work (after all, one of God's Ten Commandments says we are to work six days), remember that the Lord Jesus also said, "For what is man profited, if he shall gain the whole world, and lose his own soul?" (Matt. 16:26).

The key, of course, is the phrase "under the sun," which Solomon uses 29 times in Ecclesiastes (plus "under the heaven," meaning "under the sky," 3 times). His conclusion is that if a person's perspectives and motives are centered in this present life here on earth, then indeed it will all turn out to have been vanity and a completely wasted life.

The obvious conclusion, and Solomon has finally seen it, is to focus our labors *above* the sun, seeking to know and follow the will of God in all we do. "Whatsoever ye do, do it heartily as to the Lord, and not unto men" (Col. 3:23).

The next several verses stress the cyclic nature of the phenomena of earth, while earth itself "abideth for ever" (verse 4). Each generation of men tends to think of itself as the final and best product of all those before, but then it also is succeeded by yet another, which is sure that it is the best. The really abiding value of each generation, however, is this, "One generation shall praise thy works to another, and shall declare thy mighty acts" (Ps. 145:4). See also Psalm 22:31; Isaiah 38:19; Psalm 78:5–7; etc.

Note that "the earth abideth for ever." God is the Creator, not the "De-Creator." He created the earth for an eternal purpose, and though it has long been contaminated with the effects of sin (fossils of dead men and animals, for example), it will eventually be purged and renewed, and will last forever. "The earth also and the works that are therein shall be burned up." Once all the contamination has been burned out of it, however, then it will be renewed as "a new earth, wherein dwelleth righteousness" (2 Pet. 3:13).

That the earth will indeed last forever, along with the stars and the physical creation in general, is confirmed by many other Scriptures as well (Ps. 78:69; 104:5; 148:3–6; Dan. 12:3; etc.). Also see comments on Ecclesiastes 3:14.

When verse 5 speaks of the sun rising and setting each day (just as we do ourselves, even in our "scientific" age), it is not using what some have called the unscientific terminology of geocentricity, with the sun supposedly going around the earth. Rather, Solomon (like other biblical writers referring to this phenomenon) is using the completely scientific concept of relative motion in his terminology. It is scientifically pragmatic to do so, and navigators, surveyors, and practical astronomers universally adopt this approach in their calculations.

Verse 6 then indicates a remarkable understanding of the global circulation of the atmosphere. That there are definite global "circuits" of the winds of the world is a fact now known to modern meteorologists, but could not have been known to the ancients, before the development of this upper-air sounding and measuring instruments which have enabled them to track these great circuits.

The same is true of the remarkable hydrologic cycle, as outlined in verse 7. To a large extent, this water cycle is driven by the atmospheric circulation, working along with the diurnal circuit of the sun mentioned in verse 5. The hydrologic cycle is now familiar to every school child, who knows that life is made possible here on earth thereby. The sun evaporates water from the ocean, which then is carried inland by the winds, where it can condense and fall to earth and then return to the ocean whence it came — just as verse 7 says.

In fact, until the 20th century it was believed even by scientists that rain on the lands was really the result of evaporation from local lakes and rivers. Modern upper-air studies by the United States Weather Bureau, however, finally confirmed the biblical statement that terrestrial precipitation was largely from oceanic evaporation.

When Solomon says in verse 8 that "all things are full of labour," he is stating a profound scientific truth only understood in modern times. That is, not only does every product represent the result of human labor, but also the whole creation itself is the product of God's labor. In fact, it is now even possible — at least in principle — to determine the work equivalent of every individual object in the world, by determining the energy and information that would be required to construct that object. Technically speaking, work is equivalent to energy and so is information. Thus, "all things are full of information," programmed into each by their Creator and "man cannot utter it."

Verse 9 implies another great scientific principle, that of conservation of mass and energy. Nothing is now being either created or annihilated, everything is "conserved" and "there is no new thing under the sun." This fact is the most basic and best-proved law of science, finally demonstrated in the 19th century, but implied at many places in the Bible (note Gen. 2:1–3; Heb. 1:3; etc.). Matter may go through changes in state or form, and energy can be transformed from one kind of energy to another, but the totality of mass/energy (mass and energy are themselves inter-convertible under certain conditions) remains unchanged. Since everything in the physical word is either matter or energy, nothing is really new. "It hath been already of old time, which was before us" (verse 10).

While the words of Solomon can thus be applied to modern scientific discoveries, they probably were meant by him to refer to moral and social principles. The sins of the antediluvian population are the same sins so widespread today. Human nature, fallen with Adam, does not change. One would suppose that each generation would profit from the mistakes of previous generations, but somehow they forget and "there is no remembrance of former things" (verse 11), so they repeat the same old errors. Solomon himself had done this, having compromised with the pagan religions of his wives — just as professing Christians today continue to compromise with evolutionism and the many pagan religions based on it.

Ecclesiastes 1:12–18

12. *I the Preacher was king over Israel in Jerusalem.*
13. *And I gave my heart to seek and search out by wisdom concerning all things that are done under heaven: this sore travail hath God given to the sons of man to be exercised therewith.*
14. *I have seen all the works that are done under the sun; and, behold, all is vanity and vexation of spirit.*
15. *That which is crooked cannot be made straight: and that which is wanting cannot be numbered.*
16. *I communed with mine own heart, saying, Lo, I am come to great estate, and have gotten more wisdom than all they that have been before me in Jerusalem: yea, my heart had great experience of wisdom and knowledge.*
17. *And I gave my heart to know wisdom, and to know madness and folly: I perceived that this also is vexation of spirit.*
18. *For in much wisdom is much grief: and he that increaseth knowledge increaseth sorrow.*

This seven-verse wistful meditation on the futility of human wisdom begins (verse 12) with a reminder that he, "the Preacher was king over Israel in Jerusalem." His reign was eminently successful, Israel becoming perhaps the greatest kingdom in the world at that time. Furthermore, as a young man already possessed of great intelligence and knowledge, God then gave him a special gift of such depth of wisdom and knowledge that "he was wiser than all men" (1 Kings 4:31), and "there came of all people to hear the wisdom of Solomon" (1 Kings 4:34).

But then he eventually succumbed to the sin of pride of intellect, wanting to learn more and more. "I gave my heart," he says, not to seek God and His will, but "to seek and search out by wisdom concerning all things that are done under heaven" (verse 13). Research on the systems and processes of God's creation is legitimate, even commanded under God's primeval dominion mandate (Gen. 1:26–28), but not if the motivation is to explain all things without God, as our modern scientists have done. It should be, rather, to honor God and His marvelous works and to benefit mankind in ways that will cause men to give their hearts to God, not just to seek human wisdom for its own sake. As Solomon concluded from his own all-out devotion to the intellect, it can soon become "sore travail" and "vanity and vexation of spirit" (verses 13–14), unless the purpose is to glorify God and conform it to His word.

Solomon still had all his wisdom, both the intrinsic wisdom given by God and the vast knowledge accumulated by his own studies — more "than all they that have been before me in Jerusalem" (verse 16) — but it was unsatisfying, nothing but vanity. That situation is sadly and pervasively true in the intellectual world of today as well. The world is swarming with Ph.D's and publications in science, philosophy, and almost every field imaginable, but almost entirely without thought of God and His purposes for these fields. With all their learning, "that which is crooked cannot be made straight: and that which is wanting cannot be numbered" (verse 15).

In his search for more wisdom, Solomon also sought to understand the causes of madness and foolishness, but this also ended in a vexatious dead end (verse 17), for these also — more directly and flagrantly than research in physical phenomena — lead soon to "much grief" (verse 18) and utter inability to comprehend such things, as long as God is left out of the equation.

In the Book of Proverbs, Solomon had enthusiastically extolled wisdom and knowledge. Yet here in his later Book of Ecclesiastes, he says it brings trouble and grief. The difference is that in the one he is speaking of true wisdom and true knowledge, as founded on "the fear of the LORD" (Prov. 1:7–9; 9:10). In the other, he is lamenting the pseudo-wisdom and secularized knowledge of those who build on humanistic or pantheistic foundations.

In that connection, it is interesting that the name "LORD" (that is, *Jehovah*, or *Yahweh*) is used almost 90 times in Proverbs, but never in Ecclesiastes. In the latter book, the name "God" (*Elohim*) occurs some 40 times, but only about 6 times in Proverbs. *Jehovah*, of course, is the redemptive name of God, whereas *Elohim* stresses His role as Creator and judge. All men can and should recognize God as the Creator, but only those who are saved can really know Him as their personal Redeemer.

Ecclesiastes 2:1–3

1. *I said in mine heart, Go to now, I will prove thee with mirth, therefore enjoy pleasure: and, behold, this also is vanity.*
2. *I said of laughter, It is mad: and of mirth, What doeth it?*
3. *I sought in mine heart to give myself unto wine, yet acquainting mine heart with wisdom; and to lay hold on folly, till I might see what was that good for the sons of men, which they should do under the heaven all the days of their life.*

Solomon, with all his great wisdom, soon found that wisdom alone could not bring true happiness and peace of soul. So he decided to try just enjoying life, with an abundance of material possessions and the temporal pleasures they might bring. Wine, laughter, and merriment — these seem to give the party-going set pleasure, so try them and see, he decided.

But it does not take long to learn that a life of revelry is not one of genuine pleasure. "Behold, this also is vanity," Solomon soon learned (verse 1). "What doeth it?" (verse 2). There seems to be an indication here that Solomon was not really desirous of this kind of lifestyle, but rather wanted to test it out to see why others seemed to find pleasure in it, "to lay hold on folly, till I might see what was that good for the sons of men" (verse 3).

So he who had counseled so vigorously against the use of wine (Prov. 23:29–35; etc.) decided to try it anyway. Instead of pleasure, however, he simply proved his own wise counsel had been right. "Wine is a mocker . . . and whosoever is deceived thereby is not wise" (Prov. 20:1).

As far as laughter and merriment are concerned, people should remember, as Solomon soon learned, that they are very superficial and ephemeral. There is no mention in the Bible of "fun," but there is much about "joy." The modern addiction to "comedy" and amusements of various kinds was tried by Solomon long ago, and was found to be "mad" (verse 2), producing nothing of value.

There is no record of Jesus or the Apostles either laughing or inducing laughter in others by humorous preaching. Instead, Jesus said, "Woe unto you that laugh now! for ye shall mourn and weep" (Luke 6:25). And the apostle James wrote, "Let your laughter be turned to mourning" (James 4:9).

That does not mean, of course, that Christians should be gloomy and churlish. Although we never read of Jesus laughing, He was a man of great joy. He even prayed for His followers "that they might have my joy fulfilled in themselves" (John 17:13), and He told them of His earnest desire "that my joy might remain in you, and that your joy might be full" (John 15:11). But joy is not the same as fun, and is far better than mere fun. Jesus often is found weeping in Scripture, and so is Paul, and there is indeed much sorrow in the life of each true Christian. The Christian life is not fun and games. Nevertheless, we can be "as sorrowful, yet alway rejoicing" (2 Cor. 6:10), knowing that "he that goeth forth and weepeth, bearing precious seed, shall doubtless come again with rejoicing, bringing his sheaves with him" (Ps. 126:6).

Ecclesiastes 2:4–11

4. *I made me great works; I builded me houses; I planted me vine-yards:*
5. *I made me gardens and orchards, and I planted trees in them of all kind of fruits:*
6. *I made me pools of water, to water therewith the wood that bringeth forth trees:*
7. *I got me servants and maidens, and had servants born in my house; also I had great possessions of great and small cattle above all that were in Jerusalem before me:*
8. *I gathered me also silver and gold, and the peculiar treasure of*

kings and of the provinces: I gat me men singers and women singers, and the delights of the sons of men, as musical instruments, and that of all sorts.

9. *So I was great, and increased more than all that were before me in Jerusalem: also my wisdom remained with me.*

10. *And whatsoever mine eyes desired I kept not from them, I withheld not my heart from any joy; for my heart rejoiced in all my labour: and this was my portion of all my labour.*

11. *Then I looked on all the works that my hands had wrought, and on the labour that I had laboured to do: and, behold, all was vanity and vexation of spirit, and there was no profit under the sun.*

Solomon next proceeds to recount all his attempts to satisfy his heart with possessions and pleasures. As the wealthiest man of his age (he "exceeded all the kings of the earth for riches and for wisdom," according to 1 Kings 10:23), he could afford to do this. Having built the beautiful temple, he then built many other "great works." He built houses and vineyards, gardens and orchards, pools of water (verses 4–6), as well as great stables, shipyards and even whole cities (1 Kings 4:26; 10:22; 2 Chron. 8:2, 4–6; etc.).

He also acquired great flocks of cattle, more than anyone before him (verse 7). There were also singers, male and female, and all kinds of musical instruments, as well as men servants and maid servants in great numbers (verses 7–8), as well as an almost incredible storehouse of gold, silver, and treasures of many kinds (2 Chron. 9:13–20).

On top of all his vast wealth and possessions, he testified, that "my wisdom remained with me" (verse 9).

Yet even all this could not generate real happiness. "Then I looked on all the works that my hands had wrought, and on the labour that I had laboured to do: and, behold, all was vanity and vexation of spirit, and there was no profit under the sun" (verse 11).

In the meantime, the Lord Jesus Christ is preparing far up above the sun "many mansions" (John 14:2), and in His presence in that coming day will be "fulness of joy" and "pleasures for evermore" (Ps. 16:11).

Ecclesiastes 2:12–17

12. *And I turned myself to behold wisdom, and madness, and folly: for what can the man do that cometh after the king? even that which hath already been done.*

13. *Then I saw that wisdom excelleth folly, as far as light excelleth darkness.*

14. *The wise man's eyes are in his head; but the fool walketh in darkness: and I myself perceived also that one event happeneth*

> *to them all.*
> 15. *Then said I in my heart, As it happeneth to the fool, so it hap-*
>   *peneth even to me; and why was I then more wise? Then I said*
>   *in my heart, that this also is vanity.*
> 16. *For there is no remembrance of the wise more than of the fool*
>   *for ever; seeing that which now is in the days to come shall all*
>   *be forgotten. And how dieth the wise man? as the fool.*
> 17. *Therefore I hated life; because the work that is wrought under*
>   *the sun is grievous unto me: for all is vanity and vexation of*
>   *spirit.*

In reviewing his dedication to the acquisition of wisdom and knowledge, Solomon realized more than ever that "wisdom excelleth folly, as far as light excelleth darkness" (verse 13). In fact, he had made this the dominant theme in his proverbs. He had explored this comparison in greater depth than anyone before him — so much so that no one coming after him could possibly do more than "that which hath been already done" (verse 12).

And yet, in spite of this, it seemed to make little difference in life under the sun. Whether a man was exceeding wise or exceeding foolish, the Preacher had found that "one event happeneth to them all" (verse 14). He himself, with all his wisdom and wealth, would live no longer than any fool might live. "As it happeneth to the fool, so it happeneth even to me" (verse 15). In spite of the immense superiority, in so many ways, of wisdom over folly, "how dieth the wise man? as the fool" (verse 16). The same problems of life and death affect them both, and "there is no remembrance of the wise more than of the fool for ever."

The natural man may object to this, pointing out that we do remember the achievements of Plato and Aristotle and many great men for many generations. And surely great scientists such as Darwin and Einstein, and great inventors such as Thomas Edison continue to be honored and appreciated long after they are gone.

Yes, but even that is fleeting and trivial on the scales of eternity. Solomon noted that such remembrance would not be "for ever," and that is what really counts. As the old couplet put it, "Only one life — 'twill soon be past; only what's done for Christ will last." "That which now is in the days to come shall all be forgotten" (verse 16). Solomon finally had to say in his heart that even all his wise proverbs, dealing so effectively with life on the earthly level, and all his accumulated knowledge and wisdom, no matter how much better they are than foolishness — "that this also is vanity" (verse 15).

Not quite, however! Some of Solomon's wisdom has been inscribed by the Holy Spirit in the Holy Scriptures, and God's Word is forever "settled in heaven" (Ps. 119:89). Not only his wisdom, but also his failures and then his final evaluations of all these here in this remarkable Book of Ecclesiastes have apparently been ordained and recorded by God in His Word "for our admonition upon whom the ends of the world have come" (1 Cor. 10:11), and presumably for all God's saints to review and study in His inexhaustible Word in the ages to come.

Finally, Solomon concluded (unjustly) that he "hated life; because the work that is wrought under the sun is grievous unto me: for all is vanity and vexation of spirit" (verse 17). That may be true for any work that is done strictly "under the sun," but it most certainly is not true if that work is done as "unto the Lord" (Col. 3:23). Solomon eventually came to realize that also, thankfully.

That picturesque and felicitous phrase, "vexation of spirit," incidentally, occurs no less than nine times in Ecclesiastes (plus one occurrence of "vexation of his heart," in 2:22). Solomon's spirit indeed became very vexed, as would ours as well, when he finally understood that the things to which he had devoted so much of his life were mere vanity.

Ecclesiastes 2:18–26

18. *Yea, I hated all my labour which I had taken under the sun: because I should leave it unto the man that shall be after me.*
19. *And who knoweth whether he shall be a wise man or a fool? yet shall he have rule over all my labour wherein I have laboured, and wherein I have shewed myself wise under the sun. This is also vanity.*
20. *Therefore I went about to cause my heart to despair of all the labour which I took under the sun.*
21. *For there is a man whose labour is in wisdom, and in knowledge, and in equity; yet to a man that hath not laboured therein shall he leave it for his portion. This also is vanity and a great evil.*
22. *For what hath man of all his labour, and of the vexation of his heart, wherein he hath laboured under the sun?*
23. *For all his days are sorrows, and his travail grief; yea, his heart taketh not rest in the night. This is also vanity.*
24. *There is nothing better for a man, than that he should eat and drink, and that he should make his soul enjoy good in his labour. This also I saw, that it was from the hand of God.*
25. *For who can eat, or who else can hasten hereunto, more than I?*
26. *For God giveth to a man that is good in His sight wisdom, and knowledge, and joy: but to the sinner He giveth travail, to gather and to heap up, that He may give to him that is good before God. This also is vanity and vexation of spirit.*

Solomon, like many a believer before and after him, had been a very industrious man, both in the acquisition of knowledge and also in the accomplishment of many tasks. But now he was old, and knew that these earthly works could not be taken with him after death. Although he had tried to teach his son how to live (and, in fact, the first section of his collection of proverbs had been specifically directed first of all to "my son," he could begin to sense now that Rehoboam was not exhibiting the kind of wisdom he had been taught. Perhaps he had labored too much "under the sun" and had failed to teach his son the most important values "above the sun."

He actually then came to hate "all my labour which I had taken under the sun" (verse 18) because he could not tell whether "the man that shall be after me" would turn out to "be a wise man or a fool" (verse 19). As events turned out after Rehoboam became king, he had good reason to be concerned.

Many godly fathers who have spent too much time and effort on earthly matters have had similar experiences. How important it is to teach one's children not only by precept but also by example. It is good to provide for one's family, of course, but a legacy of godliness and love for God and His Word is worth far more than a legacy of physical wealth and worldly accomplishments. To have a legacy even of wisdom and equity, as well as wealth, to an undeserving heir is also "vanity and a great evil" (verses 20–21). If that occurs, then "what hath man of all his labour . . . wherein he hath laboured under the sun?" (verse 22).

Solomon, with all his wisdom and riches, had come finally to realize that this earthly life is one whose "days are sorrows," with no "rest in the night" (verse 23). We live in a world that "groaneth and travaileth in pain" under man's sin and God's curse (Rom. 8:22; Gen. 3:17–19), and even the very best that can ever be obtained under the sun is, as Moses said long before Solomon's day, "soon cut off, and we fly away" (Ps. 90:10).

And yet, by God's common grace, a man can indeed find a measure of satisfaction in a work well done, whether or not he is a believer in the true God. This is recognized by Solomon as "from the hand of God" (verse 24). Under the sun, "there is nothing better." It means far more, of course, if a man has consciously and reverently done his work as a service to the Lord, but it is good even for the unbeliever to "make his soul enjoy good in his labour." Eden's dominion mandate still applies to all men.

Solomon, despite all his melancholy meditation, still does recognize "the hand of God" (verse 24) throughout this great swan song of his. Despite his compromise with other religions and despite his inordinate seeking after worldly wisdom and wealth and pleasure, he still maintained his faith in God (note Eccles. 1:13, etc.) and recognized that all his wisdom and other blessings had really come from God. "For God giveth to a man that is good in His sight wisdom, and knowledge, and joy" (verse 26).

Man can and should, in fact, "enjoy good in his labour" (verse 24), for this is the natural viewpoint of people whose lives are centered under the sun. This would have been appropriate in the world as originally created. God did provide abundant wholesome food and drink for all His creatures, and fruitful labor was part of His "very good" creation (Gen. 1:31). All of this would indeed have been a source of great joy to all, had not sin and the curse intervened to change everything.

Ecclesiastes 3:1–8

1. *To every thing there is a season, and a time to every purpose under the heaven:*
2. *A time to be born, and a time to die; a time to plant, and a time to pluck up that which is planted;*
3. *A time to kill, and a time to heal; a time to break down, and a time to build up;*
4. *A time to weep, and a time to laugh; a time to mourn, and a time to dance;*
5. *A time to cast away stones, and a time to gather stones together; a time to embrace, and a time to refrain from embracing;*
6. *A time to get, and a time to lose; a time to keep, and a time to cast away;*
7. *A time to rend, and a time to sew; a time to keep silence, and a time to speak;*
8. *A time to love, and a time to hate; a time of war, and a time of peace.*

Having, in effect, penned his regrets and repentance of the mistakes of his later years, Solomon goes on to share many gems of wisdom and counsel resulting from these mistakes. These first eight verses of chapter 3 of Ecclesiastes constitute a remarkable litany of 14 contrasting "times," which God has set in the life of each individual. As he says in verse 1, God has a purpose and has established "a time to every purpose under the heaven." Note that these still all have to do with His seasons for things that happen "under the heaven" here on earth. Not only in heaven, but even here on earth, God "worketh all things after the counsel of his own will" (Eph. 1:11).

First of all, there is "a time to be born, and a time to die" (verse 2). None of us controls the time of our birth, but God does. There is also a time to die, and no one should hasten that time by suicide or careless living. God has a purpose for each life and has established a "season" within which we should seek to find and accomplish that purpose. Our times are in His hands (note Ps. 31:15; also Eccles. 7:17). It is of supreme importance, of course, to be ready to die when that set time arrives — first of all, by accepting Christ as our redeeming Savior, then by accomplishing His purpose for our lives here on earth. Then, of course, death will usher us into His gracious presence in heaven. As Paul said, "To me to live is Christ, and to die is gain" (Phil. 1:21).

There is also "a time to plant," not only a garden or orchard, but a work of any kind — a business, a ministry, a residence, or even a nation (Jer. 18:7), anything that is consistent with God's will — but then there will also come "a time to pluck up that which is planted" (verse 2).

And so on with all the other 24 "times" that are listed in this striking passage. There is "a time to kill, and a time to heal" (verse 3), as in a just war, for example, or the imposition of capital punishment on a murderer (Gen. 9:6). "A time to break down, and a time to build up" might be illustrated when old worn-out buildings or equipment or even old anti-biblical enmities and prejudices need to be replaced by new buildings and new relationships.

There are times for weeping and mourning but also times for laughing and dancing (verse 4) — the first over sin and its effects (e.g., suffering and death), the second when God works to bring joy out of sorrow. "When the LORD turned again the captivity of Zion, Then was our mouth filled with laughter, and our tongue with singing" (Ps. 126:1–2).

"A time to cast away stones, and a time to gather stones together." Removing stones from a plot to be used for planting and then gathering them to build a structure would be a case in point. "A time to embrace," typically might be for an expression of parental love for a child or a husband's love for his wife; and "a time to refrain from embracing" (verse 5) might be to express disapproval of wrong attitudes and actions, or to avoid embarrassing public displays of affection.

There is, for everyone, "a time to get, and a time to lose," along with "a time to keep, and a time to cast away" (verse 6). We need to learn and accept with grace the good times and the lean times here on earth. Like Paul, we then can say, "I have learned, in whatsoever state I am, therewith to be content" (Phil. 4:11). Or, as another application, we need to acquire and keep good habits and attitudes, and cast away the others.

We can easily discern both practical and spiritual applications of all these contrasting "times." One can both rend and sew garments, of course, but also friendships (verse 7), for example.

And it is obvious to all that there are times when one should keep quiet and times to speak up. Too many people, even many Christians, talk too much, often in hurtful ways. But also there are times when, because of fear or ignorance, Christians remain silent when a clear and open stand on some issue is greatly needed. "Let your speech be alway with grace, seasoned with salt, that ye may know how ye ought to answer every man" (Col. 4:6).

Finally, there is "a time to love," but also "a time to hate" (verse 8). The first needs no explication, but when and whom or what should we hate? We are even to love our enemies, Jesus said, but we are to "hate every false way" (Ps. 119:128), and to "hate vain thoughts" (Ps. 119:113). As far as hating people is concerned, David said concerning God's enemies (not his), "Do not I hate them, O LORD, that hate thee? . . . I hate them with perfect hatred" (Ps. 139:21–22). That is, he "hated" them with godly hatred — not as personal enemies but as the enemies of God who were seeking to destroy the work of God. In the time-worn phrase, we should hate the sin, but love the sinner. And especially we should learn to hate and fight the sin in our own personal lives.

Lastly, in this present life, there are times of war and times of peace. There is a time coming, however, when God "shall speak peace unto the heathen" (Zech. 9:10). At that time, "Nation shall not lift up sword against nation, neither shall they learn war any more" (Isa. 2:4).

Ecclesiastes 3:9–15

9. *What profit hath he that worketh in that wherein he laboureth?*
10. *I have seen the travail, which God hath given to the sons of men to be exercised in it.*
11. *He hath made every thing beautiful in His time: also He hath set the world in their heart, so that no man can find out the work that God maketh from the beginning to the end.*
12. *I know that there is no good in them, but for a man to rejoice, and to do good in his life.*
13. *And also that every man should eat and drink, and enjoy the good of all his labour, it is the gift of God.*
14. *I know that whatsoever God doeth, it shall be for ever: nothing can be put to it, nor any thing taken from it: and God doeth it, that men should fear before Him.*
15. *That which hath been is now: and that which is to be hath already been; and God requireth that which is past.*

In verses 9 and 10 of this section Solomon turns back to his sad complaint about the seeming futility of labor under the sun.

But then he puts even that in the context of God's perfect timing of all things. "He hath made every thing beautiful in His time" (verse 11). God's original creation was all "very good" (Gen. 1:31), so if there is anything ugly in His creation, or bad, it must be attributed ultimately to sin. God did not make it so.

Furthermore, "He hath set the world in their heart." Here the word translated "world" is much more often translated "everlasting," so that the statement really means that God has set "eternity" in every human heart. Even though we cannot now comprehend the total plan of God, each person has an innate awareness that God does exist and does have a purpose in creation. That purpose and plan has been revealed in part in the Bible, but apart from such revelation, no man could ever by scientific research or philosophical reasoning "find out the work that God maketh from the beginning to the end." Science, properly speaking, can "find out" present systems and processes, and history can search out the written records of the past, but human research can never really deal with the pre-historic past or with the unrevealed future. Only the *eternal* God can do so, but He has set the awareness of eternity and the longing for eternity in our hearts.

In verses 12 and 13 it is recognized that the ability to labor at an honorable occupation enables a person not only to enjoy the fruits of his labor himself but also to "do good in his life" to others, and that all this is not only "the hand of God" (Eccles. 2:24) but actually the gracious "gift of God."

There is another precious gift of God. "For the wages of sin is death, but the gift of God is eternal life through Jesus Christ our Lord" (Rom. 6:23).

There is a very remarkable, even scientific, truth revealed in verse 14: "Whatsoever God doeth, it shall be for ever: nothing can be put to it, nor any thing taken from it: and God doeth it, that men should fear before Him."

In addition to emphasizing the immutability of God and His works, this passage anticipates the great scientific principle of conservation (conservation of energy, mass, momentum, charge, etc.). Nothing is now being either created or annihilated. An entity may be changed in character, and even deteriorate in quality, but it must be conserved (i.e., kept constant) in quantity. All of God's "works were finished from the foundation of the world," and Christ is now "upholding all things by the word of His power" (Heb. 4:3; 1:3). The whole idea of evolution, or even of so-called "progressive creation" over the geologic ages, is falsified by this one verse (among many others in Scripture). This should be enough to cause man to believe and fear God, for there is no other legitimate way than special supernatural creation in the beginning to explain the origin and continued existence of all things. This principle of mass/energy conservation is considered by all scientists to be the most universal, best-proved law of science.

The principle is repeated in verse 15 in different words, with the added note that "God requireth that which is past." Just because a deed is past and forgotten by other men, this does not mean God has forgotten. "Every one of us shall give account of himself to God" (Rom. 14:12).

Ecclesiastes 3:16–22

16. *And moreover I saw under the sun the place of judgment, that wickedness was there; and the place of righteousness, that iniquity was there.*

17. *I said in mine heart, God shall judge the righteous and the wicked: for there is a time there for every purpose and for every work.*

18. *I said in mine heart concerning the estate of the sons of men, that God might manifest them, and that they might see that they themselves are beasts.*

19. *For that which befalleth the sons of men befalleth beasts; even one thing befalleth them: as the one dieth, so dieth the other; yea, they have all one breath; so that a man hath no preeminence above a beast: for all is vanity.*

20. *All go unto one place; all are of the dust, and all turn to dust again.*

21. *Who knoweth the spirit of man that goeth upward, and the spirit of the beast that goeth downward to the earth?*

22. *Wherefore I perceive that there is nothing better, than that a man should rejoice in his own works; for that is his portion: for who shall bring him to see what shall be after him?*

Then, having recognized that the hand of God was in all these matters, even the mundane daily activities of labor and pleasure, it follows that somewhere, sometime, there will be an accounting to God. God created us for a purpose, and so must eventually become our Judge as well as Creator.

Verses 16 and 17 indicate there is a "place of judgment" and that "God shall judge the righteous and the wicked." There is further clarification of this vital truth in the New Testament. The "wicked" (and that means essentially the unbelievers, for rejecting the sacrificial love of Christ in dying for their sins is the greatest wickedness of all) will be judged at God's great white throne and then consigned eternally to the lake of fire (Rev. 20:11-15). The "righteous" (that is, those who have been clothed with Christ's righteousness when they received His forgiveness and substitutionary death for all their sins) will be judged for rewards or loss of rewards in heaven at the judgment seat of Christ (2 Cor. 5:10).

In the time of Solomon, of course, very little had been revealed concerning the details of God's coming time of judgment. Nevertheless, Solomon certainly knew about right and wrong, and the intuitive moral consciousness in man (not to mention the behind-the-scenes fact of divine inspiration) were enough to assure him that there must be a judgment some day.

The next several verses are somewhat enigmatic, for at first they seem to suggest to men that "they themselves are beasts" (verse 18), that "they have all one breath" (verse 19), and that "all are of the dust, and all turn to dust again" (verse 20). These words, taken out of context might be thought to support evolutionism and even atheism.

In context, however, that is not the implication at all. Verse 21 makes it clear that when men and animals die, their future is altogether different. The "spirit of man...goeth upward, and the spirit of the beast...goeth downward to the earth." It is true that the bodies of men and beasts both alike return to the dust from which they were made. That was part of God's primeval curse following Adam's sin (Gen. 3:17-19). Both men and animals are made of the basic chemical elements, "the dust of the ground," and that is the ultimate end of both after death. This is part of the universal law of entropy, or disintegration.

The "spirit" is different, however, even though men and beasts both possess spirits. "Spirit," in fact, is the same Hebrew word as "breath," and the breathing apparatus in both ceases to function at death. However, the "spirit" in man also refers to that aspect of human nature which is in spiritual communication with the Holy Spirit of God, and that component of our being returns at death to the "God who gave it" (Eccles. 12:7).

In this life, therefore, apart from faith in God, "there is nothing better" for a man to do, but to labor in such a way that he can "rejoice in his own works" (verse 22).

Ecclesiastes 4:1–8

1. So I returned, and considered all the oppressions that are done under the sun: and behold the tears of such as were oppressed, and they had no comforter; and on the side of their oppressors there was power; but they had no comforter.
2. Wherefore I praised the dead which are already dead more than the living which are yet alive.
3. Yea, better is he than both they, which hath not yet been, who hath not seen the evil work that is done under the sun.
4. Again, I considered all travail, and every right work, that for this a man is envied of his neighbour. This is also vanity and vexation of spirit.
5. The fool foldeth his hands together, and eateth his own flesh.
6. Better is an handful with quietness, than both the hands full with travail and vexation of spirit.
7. Then I returned, and I saw vanity under the sun.
8. There is one alone, and there is not a second; yea, he hath neither

child nor brother: yet is there no end of all his labour; neither is his eye satisfied with riches; neither saith he, For whom do I labour, and bereave my soul of good? This is also vanity, yea, it is a sore travail.

As Solomon continued to rehearse all the evils that he had observed under the sun, he noted that one of the worst was the oppression of the weak by the powerful. His father David also had often written about this evil. In Psalm 10, for example, he wrote "The wicked in his pride doth persecute the poor. . . . LORD, thou hast heard the desire of the humble . . . To judge the fatherless and the oppressed, that the man of the earth may no more oppress" (Ps. 10:2–18). Solomon had just noted that the judges who were supposed to help those who had been wronged were themselves often guilty of perpetrating the wrongs, seeing in "the place of judgment, that wickedness was there" (Eccles. 3:16). When that situation existed, the oppressed "had no comforter" (verse 1).

Such miserable straits of those under fierce oppression have existed in every age, including our modern age, often being the lot of sincere Christians who refuse to compromise their faith. Solomon felt, as many of those suffering have felt, that death would be better than continuing to live under such circumstances, and that it even would have been better never to have been born (verses 2–3). Even godly Job came to feel thus, not only because of his physical pain but even more because of the unfeeling accusations of his "comforters." He cried out, "Why died I not from the womb? . . . then had I been at rest. . . . There the prisoners rest together: they hear not the voice of the oppressor" (Job 3:11–18). Examples are legion: one thinks of wicked Herod imprisoning and beheading John the Baptist, of the unspeakable Nero slaughtering Christians, including the great apostle Paul, of Hitler and Stalin and Mao and others in a long, long list.

And finally, of course, one thinks of the sufferings of Christ, the very Son of God. Even *He!* — "He was oppressed, and He was afflicted" (Isa. 53:7). But because He was willing to suffer, there will come a day when "He shall judge the poor of the people, he shall save the children of the needy, and shall break in pieces the oppressor" (Ps. 72:4), and tears shall be no more (Rev. 21:4).

There was also another evil under the sun that troubled Solomon. In verse 4, he could see that very often, when a man would labor diligently and accomplish "every right work," he was merely "envied of his neighbour," instead of being appreciated and followed. Even of Christ, Pilate noted that "the chief priests had delivered Him for envy" (Mark 15:10). It is especially sad when Christians become envious of the apparent success of other Christians and then seek if possible to undermine their good work by innuendo and criticism.

Solomon even considers such a carping critic to be "a fool" when he is too lazy to work as hard as the one who is successful, in effect acting like a man who "eateth his own flesh" (verse 5), too slothful to earn an honest and decent living. Then he paraphrases one of his earlier proverbs (Prov. 17:1) by noting that (assuming a man is not poor because of idleness but because of circumstances beyond his control), "better is an handful with quietness, than both the hands full with travail and vexation of spirit" (verse 6).

Still another evil that he calls "vanity under the sun" (verse 7) is the lifestyle of a man who is the opposite of the idle fool. That is, he sees a man who is alone, who "hath neither child nor brother" nor anyone else for whom to provide, yet devotes himself constantly to labor, "neither is his eye satisfied with riches" (verse 8). He is certainly not lazy; his besetting sin is greed and covetousness, as well as self-indulgence, spending his wealth on himself alone. He "layeth up treasure for himself, and is not rich towards God" (Luke 12:21). "This is also vanity; yea, it is a sore travail."

Ecclesiastes 4:9–16

9. *Two are better than one; because they have a good reward for their labour.*
10. *For if they fall, the one will lift up his fellow: but woe to him that is alone when he falleth; for he hath not another to help him up.*
11. *Again, if two lie together, then they have heat: but how can one be warm alone?*
12. *And if one prevail against him, two shall withstand him; and a threefold cord is not quickly broken.*
13. *Better is a poor and a wise child than an old and foolish king, who will no more be admonished.*
14. *For out of prison he cometh to reign; whereas also he that is born in his kingdom becometh poor.*
15. *I considered all the living which walk under the sun, with the second child that shall stand up in his stead.*
16. *There is no end of all the people, even of all that have been before them: they also that come after shall not rejoice in him. Surely this also is vanity and vexation of spirit.*

Verses 9–12 of chapter 4 deal with the merits of companionship in any individual endeavor, and in life as a whole, in contrast to the "loner" lifestyle as discussed in verse 8. As a general rule, "two are better than one" (verse 9), and this is especially true in the marriage relationship. God had said in the very beginning that "it is not good that the man should be alone; I will make him an help meet for him" (Gen. 2:18).

There are special God-called exceptions, of course, as in the case of the apostle Paul, but this is the general rule, "for if they fall, the one will lift up his fellow" (verse 10). Even Paul, though he never took a wife, arranged whenever possible to have someone (Barnabas, Silas, Timothy, etc.) to be with him as he traveled to preach the gospel. Even in his final imprisonment he was still thankful that "Luke is with me" (2 Tim. 4:11), though he also asked Timothy and Mark to come.

Verse 11 must refer especially to the companionship of husband and wife, mentioning that "if two lie together, then they have heat." When he mentioned this, he may have been thinking of his father David. Although David had many wives, including Solomon's own mother Bathsheba, when he was old, there were apparently none who were able to meet this particular need (they were all old, too!). "They covered him with clothes, but he gat no heat." Therefore his servants found young Abishag, unmarried and virginal, and brought her to lie close to the king so that "the king may get heat" (1 Kings 1:1–2). This closeness did not include sexual relations, but was only for the purpose of warmth, and Solomon understood and remembered how important this factor could be, especially to the elderly but also to husbands and wives in general.

The principle applies not only to marriage, of course, but also to fellowship in general (if the members are of one mind and spirit, of course). "A threefold cord is not quickly broken" (verse 12). Note also Christ's words: "Where two or three are gathered together in my name, there am I in the midst of them" (Matt. 18:20).

Verses 13–16 are rather cryptic and possibly sadly prophetic. Solomon knew that in some ways he himself had become "an old and foolish king" (verse 13), and that a man who had once been "a poor and wise child" would soon be coming "out of prison...to reign" (possibly referring to Jeroboam), whereas "he that is born in his kingdom becometh poor" (verse 14), possibly meaning Solomon's son Rehoboam.

When Solomon compromised his faith and witness for Jehovah, building worship centers for his pagan wives and even joined them in their worship rituals, "the LORD was angry with Solomon," and said to him, "I will surely rend the kingdom from thee, and will give it to thy servant" (1 Kings 11:9, 11).

That servant turned out to be Jeroboam who, though the son of a servant and a widow woman, "was industrious" and was placed by Solomon in a position of authority over the tribe of Ephraim (1 Kings 11:28). But when Solomon learned that God had promised Jeroboam the ten northern tribes because of Solomon's sin, he tried to kill Jeroboam, who was then forced to flee to exile in Egypt until Solomon had died.

If indeed this passage was prophetic (perhaps even so intended by Solomon), then when he said that "he that is born in his kingdom becometh poor," he would be referring to his son Rehoboam, for God had told him that Rehoboam would have the ten tribes taken from him.

Then "the second child that shall stand up in his stead" (verse 15) — that is, Jeroboam — would eventually fall into disfavor himself, for "they also that come after shall not rejoice in him" (verse 16). Jeroboam, though once a "wise child," would finally lead His people away from the true God, the end result being the captivity and exile of Israel under the Assyrians.

How much of this sad future could actually be foreseen by Solomon may be uncertain, but he did know that God had severely rebuked him when he became "an old and foolish king" in spite of all his wisdom, wealth, and worldly prestige. All indications are, at least from the tone of his writings in Ecclesiastes, that he had repented and been forgiven as far as his own soul was concerned, but the consequences of his foolishness would continue to be felt by his descendants throughout all the years to come. Therefore, "they also that come after shall not rejoice in him. Surely this also is vanity and vexation of spirit" (verse 16).

Ecclesiastes 5:1–7

1. *Keep thy foot when thou goest to the house of God, and be more ready to hear, than to give the sacrifice of fools: for they consider not that they do evil.*
2. *Be not rash with thy mouth, and let not thine heart be hasty to utter any thing before God: for God is in heaven, and thou upon earth: therefore let thy words be few.*
3. *For a dream cometh through the multitude of business; and a fool's voice is known by multitude of words.*
4. *When thou vowest a vow unto God, defer not to pay it; for He hath no pleasure in fools: pay that which thou hast vowed.*
5. *Better is it that thou shouldest not vow, than that thou shouldest vow and not pay.*
6. *Suffer not thy mouth to cause thy flesh to sin; neither say thou before the angel, that it was an error: wherefore should God be angry at thy voice, and destroy the work of thine hands?*
7. *For in the multitude of dreams and many words there are also divers vanities: but fear thou God.*

When verse 1 mentions "the house of God," Solomon was, of course, referring to the magnificent temple he had built for the people's worship, and he rightly felt that they should approach and enter it with quietness and reverence. The parallel for today would be that we also should approach the teaching of God's Word and worshiping the Lord — whether in a church house or simply in the family circle — with all due reverence and sobriety. We should come to hear and learn. To offer a sacrifice in the temple in a spirit of levity or pride or anything other than humility and repentance is called by Solomon "the sacrifice of fools" (verse 3), and God presumably would view a lighthearted attitude toward His Word and His service today in a similar derogatory way.

In verse 2, Solomon urges that our words be few and carefully chosen in our prayers to God or our conversation with others about Him. "A fool's voice is known by multitude of words" (verse 3). Also refer to such scriptures as Proverbs 17:28; Matthew 6:7; Matthew 12:36; Ephesians 5:4; 1 Thessalonians 4:11; etc.

Verses 4–7 deal with the question of making vows or promises to God. In the Old Testament economy, there were definite instructions relative to vows. Vows were not required, but once made, God expected them to be kept. "When thou shalt vow a vow unto the LORD thy God, thou shalt not slack to pay it: for the LORD thy God will surely require it of thee, and it would be sin in thee. But if thou shalt forbear to vow, it shall be no sin in thee" (Deut. 23:21–22). Note also Numbers 30:1–16; etc. In the New Testament formal vows, especially if taken in the name of the Lord, were actually discouraged by Christ (Matt. 5:33–37) and the apostle James (James 5:12). However, if a Christian does make a vow to God, he should certainly keep it (unless, of course, the vow itself was contrary to God's Word). Note the sad case of Ananias and Sapphira (Acts 5:1–10).

The words "before the angel" (verse 6) can be applied to any prophet or priest or to anyone who can speak for God (the words "angel" and "messenger" are the same in the Hebrew. One should be very slow to make a formal vow or promise to God, because it would be a serious sin against God to decide later it was a mistake. God does not play games.

Ecclesiastes 5:8–17

8. *If thou seest the oppression of the poor, and violent perverting of judgment and justice in a province, marvel not at the matter: for he that is higher than the highest regardeth; and there be higher than they.*

9. *Moreover the profit of the earth is for all: the king himself is served by the field.*

10. *He that loveth silver shall not be satisfied with silver; nor he that loveth abundance with increase: this is also vanity.*

11. *When goods increase, they are increased that eat them: and what good is there to the owners thereof, saving the beholding of them with their eyes?*

12. *The sleep of a labouring man is sweet, whether he eat little or much: but the abundance of the rich will not suffer him to sleep.*

13. *There is a sore evil which I have seen under the sun, namely,*
    riches kept for the owners thereof to their hurt.
14. *But those riches perish by evil travail: and he begetteth a son,*
    and there is nothing in his hand.
15. *As he came forth of his mother's womb, naked shall he return*
    to go as he came, and shall take nothing of his labour, which he
    may carry away in his hand.
16. *And this also is a sore evil, that in all points as he came, so shall*
    he go: and what profit hath he that hath laboured for the wind?
17. *All his days also he eateth in darkness, and he hath much sorrow*
    and wrath with his sickness.

The Preacher had been duly exercised about the existence of oppressions and injustice (Eccles. 4:1) in the world, but at the same time he realizes it is pervasive, even on occasion corrupting an entire province (verse 8). But he assures us that there is one far higher than even the governor of the province, and that He indeed is aware of these troubles and will take care of them in the proper way at the proper time.

Everyone from the king on down should realize that "the profit of the earth is for all" (verse 9), for each person necessarily depends on others. Even the king depends on the farm laborer on the field for his very food. The primeval mandate demanded that man derive his food from the ground by "the sweat of thy face" (Gen. 3:19), and so the lives of all people must ultimately rely on the fruit of the ground.

The next several verses (verses 10-17) deal with the inability of riches to satisfy. Solomon himself had intensively felt this disappointment. As the richest man in the world, with just about everything wealth can buy, he found it all to be empty vanity (verse 10; also note Eccles. 2:4–11). The more one acquires, the greater the demands on it (verse 11); the only satisfaction finally derived from riches is the mere contemplation of them, and *that* surely is vanity.

As Jesus said, "A man's life consisteth not in the abundance of the things which he possesseth" (Luke 12:15). That "abundance" will not even "suffer him to sleep" (verse 12).

"Riches kept for the owners thereof," Solomon painfully had learned, "is a sore evil which I have seen under the sun" (verse 13). Riches can be a blessing, if used for the Lord and for the benefit of others, but otherwise, "the love of money is the root of all evil" (1 Tim. 6:10). They had indeed led Solomon himself "into many foolish and hurtful lusts" (1 Tim. 6:9).

In verse 14, perhaps yet thinking of his own experience, he cited the case of a rich man who "begetteth a son," by whom "those riches perish by evil travail." He had diligently taught his son Rehoboam by precept and proverb, but not by example, as he had multiplied wealth, and wives to himself, and then compromised with pagan idols, and now he knew by divine prophecy (1 Kings 11:9–13) that most of his great kingdom would soon be wasted away by his own son. He, like his son, "came forth of his mother's womb" with nothing and "so shall he go" (verses 15 and 16). The patriarch Job, long before Solomon, and the richest man in his day, had made the same observation (Job 1:21).

Just so, the rich men of our day, or of any day, will have "laboured for the wind" if their riches have been "kept for the owners thereof to their hurt" (verses 16, 13). Their covetousness is actually a lethal sickness that at the end results in "darkness" and "much sorrow and wrath" (verse 17).

Ecclesiastes 5:18–20

18. *Behold that which I have seen: it is good and comely for one to eat and to drink, and to enjoy the good of all his labour that he taketh under the sun all the days of his life, which God giveth him: for it is his portion.*
19. *Every man also to whom God hath given riches and wealth, and hath given him power to eat thereof, and to take his portion, and to rejoice in his labour; this is the gift of God.*
20. *For he shall not much remember the days of his life; because God answereth him in the joy of his heart.*

At the same time, Solomon has also come to see that "it is good and comely for one to eat and to drink, and to enjoy the good of all his labour," if only he recognizes thankfully that it is what "God giveth him" (verse 18) as "his portion."

It is not money in itself that corrupts, but "the love of money." Furthermore, the true riches are not measured in gold and silver, but in a life of usefulness and service to God. As Paul told Timothy, "godliness with contentment is great gain" (1 Tim. 6:6). So he said, "Charge them that are rich in this world, that they be not highminded, nor trust in uncertain riches, but in the living God, who giveth us richly all things to enjoy; That they do good, that they be rich in good works, ready to distribute, willing to communicate [that is, 'share']" (1 Tim. 6:17–18).

This type of life is "the gift of God" (verse 19), a phrase which occurs only twice in the Old Testament, here and in Ecclesiastes 3:13. In both instances, the phrase has to do with God's material blessings. Its six occurrences in the New Testament, on the other hand, all refer to spiritual blessings, especially "eternal life" (John 4:14; Acts 8:20; Rom. 6:23; 1 Cor. 7:7; Eph. 2:8; 2 Tim. 1:6).

With such a life, God gives him also "the joy of his heart" (verse 20), and that will be his main remembrance of "the days of his life."

Ecclesiastes 6:1–9

1. *There is an evil which I have seen under the sun, and it is common among men:*
2. *A man to whom God hath given riches, wealth, and honour, so that he wanteth nothing for his soul of all that he desireth, yet God giveth him not power to eat thereof, but a stranger eateth it: this is vanity, and it is an evil disease.*
3. *If a man beget an hundred children, and live many years, so that the days of his years be many, and his soul be not filled with good, and also that he have no burial; I say, that an untimely birth is better than he.*
4. *For he cometh in with vanity, and departeth in darkness, and his name shall be covered with darkness.*
5. *Moreover he hath not seen the sun, nor known any thing: this hath more rest than the other.*
6. *Yea, though he live a thousand years twice told, yet hath he seen no good: do not all go to one place?*
7. *All the labour of man is for his mouth, and yet the appetite is not filled.*
8. *For what hath the wise more than the fool? what hath the poor that knoweth to walk before the living?*
9. *Better is the sight of the eyes than the wandering of the desire: this is also vanity and vexation of spirit.*

Verse 19 of the preceding chapter had noted that it was "the gift of God" when a person had obtained a position of wealth through his labor and could then rejoice in his riches and "eat thereof," by recognizing thankfully that it was indeed God's gift and should be used in ways honoring the Lord.

If, however, such a person was not thankful and not careful to honor the Lord with his wealth, then he should not be surprised to have it somehow taken away and used by others. This seems to be the thought behind verses 1 and 2. Solomon had apparently seen such a situation common among men "under the sun" and called it "an evil disease." Such developments have been all too common in every age, and have even led to violent revolutions against the wealthy classes. As James said, "Go to now, ye rich men, weep and howl for your miseries that shall come upon you. Your riches are corrupted" (James 5:1–2).

Even if such a man gets by with such a lifestyle for many years and has a large family (verse 3 — the idea of a "hundred children" may be hyperbole, but Solomon knew it would at least be possible if someone had as many wives and as much wealth as he had), and "his soul be not filled with good" (that is, with goodness in life and good works made possible by his wealth), then it would have been better for him if he had never been born. "An untimely birth," resulting in the death of the infant, is better than a life lived away from God. The stillborn infant is safe in Christ and will be with Him eternally; those who live without God will spend eternity in hell. Such a man may well even have his life end in violence as revolutionaries or thieves or others try to take over his wealth for themselves, and thus he would even "have no burial."

"For he cometh in with vanity, and departeth in darkness" (verse 4). The whole context indicates that the type of man Solomon is describing here has little concern for God and thus makes no attempt to please Him or seek forgiveness and salvation. Even if he does die in peace, it will be "in darkness," for his destiny is "the blackness of darkness for ever" (Jude 13). He has (figuratively speaking) never really "seen the sun" (verse 5) or any other of God's wonderful creation, and never really known "rest" of soul.

Even though he should manage to live "a thousand years twice told" (verse 6 — and, remember, many men in the earlier ages had lived almost a thousand years), he will have "seen no good."

Solomon raises the rhetorical question concerning such men, whether rich or poor, worldly wise or foolish, who live their lies without concern for God: "Do not all go to one place?" This present life, whether it ends early or late in life, is as nothing compared to their common destination of eternal separation from God.

As is evident from the introductory verse of this section, Solomon calls all this "an evil which I have seen under the sun" and says it is "common among men" (verse 1). Indeed, if a man lives only "under the sun," with little regard for God who is over the sun, then "all the labour of man is for his mouth" (verse 7). Whether he is wise in the eyes of the world, or a fool (verse 8), or whether poor or rich, "the appetite is not filled."

It is, indeed, sadly true, that multitudes are traveling the "broad . . . way that leadeth to destruction" (Matt. 7:13), but there is a "way, which leadeth unto life," if men would only realize it, and seek that way. Instead, however, these multitudes still today, as in Solomon's day, continue to live for this day, under the sun. To them, "better is the sight of the eyes than the wandering of the desire" (verse 9).

Interestingly, the word here translated "desire" is the Hebrew *nephesh*, most commonly translated as "soul." The word translated "wandering" is *halak*, elsewhere commonly rendered "walk" or "walking," but occasionally in such ways as "go forward." It seems that Solomon is speaking in irony here, noting that such people are concerned only with what they can see around them, considering that better than "the traveling of the soul" in seeking that which is not just under the sun. "This is also vanity and vexation of spirit."

Ecclesiastes 6:10–12

10. *That which hath been is named already, and it is known that it is man: neither may he contend with him that is mightier than he.*

11. *Seeing there be many things that increase vanity, what is man the better?*

12. *For who knoweth what is good for man in this life, all the days of his vain life which he spendeth as a shadow? for who can tell a man what shall be after him under the sun?*

These last three verses of the first half of Solomon's "words of the Preacher" (Eccles. 1:1), the Book of Ecclesiastes, seem to be a sort of summary of all he has said earlier. "That which hath been" — whether riches or pleasure or knowledge, or whatever — all are common to man and "there is no new thing under the sun" (Eccles. 1:9). None of these things are satisfying to the soul, as Solomon had learned.

If one is tempted to complain about all this, however, he should remember and acknowledge (as Job did long before — Job 9:3) that he can never really "contend with him that is mightier than he" (verse 10). "Shall the thing formed say to him that formed it, Why hast thou made me thus?" (Rom. 9:20). The answer is no, obviously, but men under the sun are always raising this question.

All of these things — riches, pleasures, etc. — seem to appeal for a time, but eventually only "increase vanity" (verse 11), or the futile emptiness of life, even more than their absence. That being experientially true, "what is man the better" when he finally achieves and tries them?

As long as he continues to live under the sun, seeking his wealth or wisdom or pleasure in man-centered activities, he will never really come to know "what is good for man in this life" (verse 12). He will spend "all the days of his vain life . . . as a shadow" of what his life could really be like if only he would live it in the will of God. "Seek ye first the kingdom of God, and his righteousness;" said the Lord Jesus, "and all these things [that is, the needed material things of life] shall be added unto you" (Matt. 6:33).

Otherwise, as God told the rich man in Christ's parable, after he had laid up great riches for himself, "Thou fool . . . whose shall those things be, which thou hast provided?" (Luke 12:20). Solomon had begun to realize that, even in his own case, much of what he had laid up for himself would soon be lost by his son. "Who can tell a man what shall be after him under the sun?"

Ecclesiastes 7:1–12

1. *A good name is better than precious ointment; and the day of death than the day of one's birth.*
2. *It is better to go to the house of mourning, than to go to the house of feasting: for that is the end of all men; and the living will lay it to his heart.*
3. *Sorrow is better than laughter: for by the sadness of the countenance the heart is made better.*
4. *The heart of the wise is in the house of mourning; but the heart of fools is in the house of mirth.*
5. *It is better to hear the rebuke of the wise, than for a man to hear the song of fools.*
6. *For as the crackling of thorns under a pot, so is the laughter of the fool: this also is vanity.*
7. *Surely oppression maketh a wise man mad; and a gift destroyeth the heart.*
8. *Better is the end of a thing than the beginning thereof: and the patient in spirit is better than the proud in spirit.*
9. *Be not hasty in thy spirit to be angry: for anger resteth in the bosom of fools.*
10. *Say not thou, What is the cause that the former days were better than these? for thou dost not enquire wisely concerning this.*
11. *Wisdom is good with an inheritance: and by it there is profit to them that see the sun.*
12. *For wisdom is a defence, and money is a defence: but the excellency of knowledge is, that wisdom giveth life to them that have it.*

The second half of Ecclesiastes opens with a series of Solomonic proverbs very similar in type to those collected in the Book of Proverbs. Why they are here instead of in the Book of Proverbs is not said. Possibly they only came to Solomon's attention or were written by him during his later years.

Verse 1 is somewhat reminiscent of Proverbs 22:1 ("A good name is rather to be chosen than great riches"). Here, "a good name is better than precious ointment." In fact, a good name is better than a great name — that is, a name that is widely known because of worldly accomplishments. But how can "the day of death" be better than "the day of one's birth"? The latter is a time of joy, the former a time of mourning. Yes, but as far as the person himself is concerned, if he has indeed earned a good name for himself throughout life (as measured by God's standards), he will be more honored and appreciated at death than at birth. Furthermore, if one's good name is acquired through living in God's will, as it should have been, then death is the entrance to a far longer and richer life than one's natural birth had procured. As the apostle Paul said, "To me to live is Christ, and to die is gain" (Phil. 1:21).

Verses 2, 3, and 4 note that sorrow and mourning are actually better than laughter and partying. At first this might seem a wrong-headed notion, but a more thoughtful assessment will confirm its profound truth. A funeral service will often cause unbelievers to rethink their skepticism or indifference concerning God and their own future, as they are made to recognize that death "is the end of all men." This may well persuade the "living" to "lay it to his heart" (verse 2) and then "the heart is made better" (verse 3). Verse 5 is an apt summary: "The heart of the wise is in the house of mourning; but the heart of fools is in the house of mirth." It is well to remember again that Jesus often wept (e.g., John 11:35), but there is no record of laughter or mirth in His demeanor. The same with Paul (e.g., Acts 20:19).

Verses 5 and 6 continue to contrast the convicting behavior of "the wise" with "the song of the fool" and "the laughter of fools." Note also "the rebuke" of the apostle Paul concerning "foolish talking" and "jesting" (Eph. 5:4) and of the apostle Peter against "revellings" and "banquetings" (1 Pet. 4:3).

Verse 7 is difficult to understand, since the Hebrew for "mad" is *halah*, usually translated "praise." Thus the thought may well be that "oppression" imposed upon a truly wise man will not discourage him but rather cause him to praise the Lord. As David's musician Asaph had written, "Surely the wrath of man shall praise thee" (Ps. 76:10). Accepting a bribe, on the other hand, "destroyeth the heart."

Impatience, pride, and anger are also rebuked again in verses 8 and 9, as utterly inappropriate for one of God's people. So is the one who prefers the "former days" (verse 10) to the time in which God has called him to serve. The virtues of true wisdom, on the other hand, are extolled in verse 11 and 12, as Solomon had often done, in other contexts, in his Book of Proverbs.

Ecclesiastes 7:13–29

13. *Consider the work of God: for who can make that straight, which He hath made crooked?*

14. *In the day of prosperity be joyful, but in the day of adversity consider: God also hath set the one over against the other, to the end that man should find nothing after him.*

15. *All things have I seen in the days of my vanity: there is a just man that perisheth in his righteousness, and there is a wicked*

man that prolongeth his life in his wickedness.

16. *Be not righteous over much; neither make thyself over wise: why shouldest thou destroy thyself?*

17. *Be not over much wicked, neither be thou foolish: why shouldest thou die before thy time?*

18. *It is good that thou shouldest take hold of this; yea, also from this withdraw not thine hand: for he that feareth God shall come forth of them all.*

19. *Wisdom strengtheneth the wise more than ten mighty men which are in the city.*

20. *For there is not a just man upon earth, that doeth good, and sinneth not.*

21. *Also take no heed unto all words that are spoken; lest thou hear thy servant curse thee:*

22. *For oftentimes also thine own heart knoweth that thou thyself likewise hast cursed others.*

23. *All this have I proved by wisdom: I said, I will be wise; but it was far from me.*

24. *That which is far off, and exceeding deep, who can find it out?*

25. *I applied mine heart to know and to search, and to seek out wisdom, and the reason of things, and to know the wickedness of folly, even of foolishness and madness:*

26. *And I find more bitter than death the woman, whose heart is snares and nets, and her hands as bands: whoso pleaseth God shall escape from her; but the sinner shall be taken by her.*

27. *Behold, this have I found, saith the preacher, counting one by one, to find out the account:*

28. *Which yet my soul seeketh, but I find not: one man among a thousand have I found; but a woman among all those have I not found.*

29. *Lo, this only have I found, that God hath made man upright; but they have sought out many inventions.*

The remainder of chapter 7 consists not of individual proverbs, but rather a series of brief homilies on certain key themes. The first (verses 13–14) stresses God's sovereignty, noting that no one can change a work of God, nor can man predict the future.

Then verses 15–20 deal with the contrast between righteousness and wickedness, and with the fact that this life alone does not balance things in compensation for this contrast.

Note especially verse 20, which concludes that "there is not a just man upon earth, that doeth good, and sinneth not." Solomon thus would have to recognize that no one could deserve salvation, in this life or in a future life, because God had said "Cursed be he that confirmeth not all the words of this law to do them" (Deut. 27:26).

When he says, however, "Be not righteous over much: neither make thyself over wise" (verse 16), he is not warning against true righteousness, but against self-righteousness or ostentatiousness in one's goodness. Neither is he warning against true wisdom, but against self-pride in one's intellectual achievements. He also warns against being "over much wicked" (verse 17), for this could well lead to premature death, "before thy time." God has apparently appointed an optimum life span for each person (Eccles. 3:2), but it can be shortened by insistent flouting of God's law.

As he recognized, however, no one is sinless. Only Jesus lived a sinless life (Rom. 3:23; James 2:10). Salvation from sin, therefore, can come only by receiving Him (or, in Old Testament times, through trusting His future work as typified by the sacrificial offerings they brought to God) by faith as our sin-bearing substitute before a holy God (Rom. 6:23).

Solomon had sought diligently to understand all these matters, but as He said (a thousand years before Christ made it all clear), "That which is far off, and exceeding deep, who can find it out?" (verse 24). Solomon, with all his great wisdom, tried diligently to understand these mysteries, "but it was far from me," he said (verse 23).

"This only have I found," he finally concluded, "that God hath made man upright, but they have sought out many inventions." God made man in his own image (Gen. 1:27). The fact that now there is not a righteous man on earth is due entirely to the fact that all men, beginning with Adam, have deliberately disobeyed God and gone their own way, seeking many devices (e.g., evolutionism, pantheism, humanism, occultism) to escape from God.

Ecclesiastes 8:1–8

1. *Who is as the wise man? and who knoweth the interpretation of a thing? a man's wisdom maketh his face to shine, and the boldness of his face shall be changed.*
2. *I counsel thee to keep the king's commandment, and that in regard of the oath of God.*
3. *Be not hasty to go out of his sight: stand not in an evil thing; for he doeth whatsoever pleaseth him.*
4. *Where the word of a king is, there is power: and who may say unto him, What doest thou?*
5. *Whoso keepeth the commandment shall feel no evil thing: and a wise man's heart discerneth both time and judgment.*
6. *Because to every purpose there is time and judgment, therefore*

> *the misery of man is great upon him.*
> 7. *For he knoweth not that which shall be: for who can tell him*
>   *when it shall be?*
> 8. *There is no man that hath power over the spirit to retain the*
>   *spirit; neither hath he power in the day of death: and there is*
>   *no discharge in that war; neither shall wickedness deliver those*
>   *that are given to it.*

Solomon, with all his innate wisdom, as given him by God, plus all his acquired wisdom, developed by his own studies and experience, had also determined to search out the meaning of wisdom itself (especially in comparison with folly), and to learn "the reason of things" (Eccles. 7:25). Apparently he had sought out in the process any wise men and wise women he could find, but he could find no such women and only one in every thousand men (Eccles. 7:28). And (parenthetically) in his search, he had encountered many clever women seeking to entrap men and it embittered him (Eccles. 7:26) toward women in general (though certainly not toward his own mother and other truly "virtuous women" such as his beloved Naamah. Although he had at one time "loved" his seven hundred wives and three hundred concubines (or at least loved the prestige such a large harem seemed to bring him), they had led him to compromise his own commitment to the Lord, and he had apparently become bitter toward them because of it and because of God's judgment on him and his son as a result of that compromise. He never so much as mentioned any of them in this last book (or song) of his.

Now he raises the question, "Who is as the wise man? and who knoweth the interpretation of a thing?" (verse 1). It is one thing to possess wisdom, but another to know how to apply it in understanding a problem and communicating its solution. That kind of wisdom comes only from God's revealed truth, and one who truly possesses and uses it will have a "boldness of his face" when it "maketh his face to shine" with his love and knowledge of God.

One aspect of a wise man's behavior is that he must "keep the king's commandment" (verse 2), not because of any intrinsic perfections in any earthly king (certainly not in Solomon, as Solomon himself surely realized), but because of "the oath of God." "The powers that be are ordained of God" (Rom. 13:1; note also 1 Pet. 2:13). Solomon in particular had been chosen by God before he was born to succeed David on the throne of Israel. Therefore, "where the word of a king is, there is power" (verse 4) — not only the military and police power which he can use, but the power of God who called him to be king. One must only "resist the power" when it becomes obvious that the king's commands contradict those of God, who is the highest King.

As Solomon said of any absolute monarch such as himself, "Who may say unto him, What doest thou?" It is interesting that this same testimony was given concerning God himself, many centuries later, by another absolute monarch, Nebuchadnezzar of Babylon. That great king was finally impelled to say, "All the inhabitants of the earth are reputed as nothing: and he doeth according to his will in the army of heaven, and among the inhabitants of the earth: and none can stay his hand, or say unto him, What doest thou?" (Dan. 4:35).

Reflecting the earlier revelation given by God to Solomon, stressing that God has a time for everything (Eccles. 3:1-8), Solomon reminds us that every purpose of God has a "time and judgment" scheduled by Him and that "a wise man's heart discerneth both time and judgment" (verses 5–6). God warns that those who keep His commandments "shall feel no evil thing," but otherwise "the misery of man is great." Even though God has a time for every purpose, we ourselves cannot know "that which shall be" or "when it shall be," so our responsibility is to "be instant in season, out of season" (2 Tim. 4:2), familiar with the Scriptures, and constantly sensitive to the leading of the Spirit of God.

"No man . . . hath power over the spirit to retain the spirit" (verse 8). A man's spirit has been given him by God, and its continued presence in the body is beyond man's power to assure. Only Jesus in His humanity was able arbitrarily to dismiss His spirit when He was ready; no man could have taken it from Him until then (Luke 23:46; John 10:17–18).

Furthermore, "there is no discharge in that war." That is, in our struggle to preserve life as long as possible, we can never escape the certainty of death. "It is appointed unto men once to die" (Heb. 9:27). Neither righteousness nor wickedness can "deliver those that are given to it." The one exception, of course, will be those few believers who are still living on earth at the time of Christ's second coming (1 Thess. 4:16–17).

Ecclesiastes 8:9–14

9. *All this have I seen, and applied my heart unto every work that is done under the sun: there is a time wherein one man ruleth over another to his own hurt.*

10. *And so I saw the wicked buried, who had come and gone from the place of the holy, and they were forgotten in the city where they had so done: this is also vanity.*

11. *Because sentence against an evil work is not executed speedily, therefore the heart of the sons of men is fully set in them to do evil.*

12. *Though a sinner do evil an hundred times, and his days be prolonged, yet surely I know that it shall be well with them that fear God, which fear before Him:*

13. *But it shall not be well with the wicked, neither shall he prolong his days, which are as a shadow; because he feareth not before God.*

14. *There is a vanity which is done upon the earth; that there be just men, unto whom it happeneth according to the work of the wicked; again, there be wicked men, to whom it happeneth according to the work of the righteous: I said that this also is vanity.*

Solomon again reminds us that he had "applied my heart unto every work that is done under the sun" (verse 9), diligently and sincerely trying to understand all that God had done in creating all things and how He was dealing in all ways with His creatures. He had learned much also about man's dealing with man, concluding that everything under the sun was mere vanity.

He had seen the death and burial of many powerful men, including many who once had access to the holiness of God but had abandoned that opportunity, and then were soon forgotten, even in the realm where they had reigned or been powerful in some important way (verse 10).

God's judgmental wrath eventually is visited upon such men, but other men take little note and thus continue in the same broad way of destruction. "Because sentence against an evil work is not executed speedily, therefore the heart of the sons of men is fully set in them to do evil" (verse 11). The apparent prosperity of the wicked has long been both a stumbling block to faith and an encouragement to evildoers. Yet Solomon knew that the sentence would indeed be fully executed eventually, and that "it shall be well with them that fear God" (verse 12), and that "it shall not be well with the wicked." Even though the days on earth of individual wicked men may be prolonged, yet they are only "as a shadow" in light of eternity without God (verse 13).

Thus, it may often seem that "what is done upon the earth" (verse 14) is inequitable in terms of God's recompense for the respective deeds of the right-eous and the wicked, but such thoughts are only "*vanity*." The true measure and understanding will not be found just on earth.

Ecclesiastes 8:15–17

15. *Then I commended mirth, because a man hath no better thing under the sun, than to eat, and to drink, and to be merry: for that shall abide with of his labour the days of his life, which God giveth him under the sun.*

16. *When I applied mine heart to know wisdom, and to see the business that is done upon the earth: (for also there is that neither day nor night seeth sleep with his eyes:)*

17. *Then I beheld all the work of God, that a man cannot find out the*

work that is done under the sun: because though a man labour
to seek it out, yet he shall not find it; yea further, though a wise
man think to know it, yet shall he not be able to find it.

As Solomon had noted before, he had once tried mirth and pleasure, wine and laughter as a means of enjoying life, but had found all these also to be vanity. Nevertheless, if one is determined to live only "under the sun," there is nothing better (at least for many) than "to eat, and to drink, and to be merry" (verse 15), considering that to be the fruit of "his labour the days of his life." As Paul the Apostle said concerning the sufferings he was enduring for preaching the gospel, "What advantageth it me, if the dead rise not? let us eat and drink; for to morrow we die" (1 Cor. 15:32). If we are not the products of God's creative purpose and Christ's work of redemption — if this life is all there is — then, indeed, a life of pleasure is the best we can get.

But, of course, that is *not* all there is! Solomon knew there was much more, because he still had saving faith in God, though he had sadly compromised that faith with his pagan wives. But not much had been revealed in Solomon's day concerning all the great events that were in the mind of God for the future.

And what God had not revealed, Solomon had learned could not be discerned by human wisdom, no matter how extensive his knowledge or insightful his understanding. "When I applied mine heart to know wisdom, and to see the business that is done upon the earth . . . Then I beheld all the work of God, that a man cannot find out the work that is done under the sun: because though a man labour to seek it out, yet he shall not find it; yea further; though a wise man think to know it, yet shall he not be able to find it" (verses 16–17).

Ecclesiastes 9:1–10

1. *For all this I considered in my heart even to declare all this, that the righteous, and the wise, and their works, are in the hand of God: no man knoweth either love or hatred by all that is before them.*
2. *All things come alike to all: there is one event to the righteous, and to the wicked; to the good and to the clean, and to the unclean; to him that sacrificeth, and to him that sacrificeth not: as is the good, so is the sinner; and he that sweareth, as he that feareth an oath.*
3. *This is an evil among all things that are done under the sun, that there is one event unto all: yea, also the heart of the sons of men is full of evil, and madness is in their heart while they live, and after that they go to the dead.*

4.   *For to him that is joined to all the living there is hope: for a living dog is better than a dead lion.*

5.   *For the living know that they shall die: but the dead know not any thing, neither have they any more a reward; for the memory of them is forgotten.*

6.   *Also their love, and their hatred, and their envy, is now perished; neither have they any more a portion for ever in any thing that is done under the sun.*

7.   *Go thy way, eat thy bread with joy, and drink thy wine with a merry heart; for God now accepteth thy works.*

8.   *Let thy garments be always white; and let thy head lack no ointment.*

9.   *Live joyfully with the wife whom thou lovest all the days of the life of thy vanity, which He hath given thee under the sun, all the days of thy vanity: for that is thy portion in this life, and in thy labour which thou takest under the sun.*

10. *Whatsoever thy hand findeth to do, do it with thy might; for there is no work, nor device, nor knowledge, nor wisdom, in the grave, whither thou goest.*

As just expressed, Solomon was intensely aware that he could never, even with his great wisdom, really understand the mind of God and His future plans for mankind, either as a whole or individually. He could see that "all things come alike to all" (verse 2) as far as the circumstances of this life are concerned. As Jesus later confirmed, "He maketh His sun to rise on the evil and on the good, and sendeth rain on the just and on the unjust" (Matt. 5:45). On the human level of looking at things, it would seem that "this is an evil among all things that are done under the sun" (verse 3).

Yet in spite of appearances, Solomon still had faith that "the righteous, and the wise, and their works, are in the hand of God" (verse 1). That being so, and God being a just and loving God, he (and all believers in the God of creation) can have confidence, with father Abraham, that "the Judge of all the earth" will certainly "do right" (Gen. 18:25). They are safe "in the hand of God" and, as Jesus said, "No man is able to pluck them out of my Father's hand" (John 10:29).

As far as this life is concerned, one should use every opportunity he can for good, knowing that death will inevitably come and he will have no further opportunity. It is in this sense, of course, that "a living dog is better than a dead lion" (verse 4) and the dead have not "any more a reward" (verse 5), nor "any more a portion for ever in any thing that is done under the sun" (verse 6). This does not mean that there is no future life or consciousness after death, but only that nothing more can be done to earn heavenly rewards. Even the greatest men are soon forgotten after they die; thus it is important to make one's brief life span as productive for God as possible (not just for human approval, of course, but all as "unto the Lord" — Col. 3:23). As long as there is life, "there is hope" (verse 4).

If, therefore, we do have "a lively hope . . . anchored . . . within the veil" (Heb. 6:19), we can, as Solomon urges, "eat thy bread with joy, and drink thy wine with a merry heart" (verse 7). God grants His people temporal blessings as well as heavenly, and joys as well as sorrow and burdens, and we can be thankful for them and seek to use these also "to the glory of God" (1 Cor. 10:31).

Surely one of the greatest blessings of our lives on earth is that of a godly marriage, especially when husband and wife are united while young and then live together happily all their lives, sharing the good times and hard times together, and all "in the Lord."

Solomon had such a wife, the beautiful and loving Naamah, as discussed in chapter 2 of this book, and as chronicled so elegantly in Solomon's "Song of Songs." She was the mother of Rehoboam, who succeeded Solomon on the throne, and was frequently referred to in the Book of Proverbs, though not by name, as the mother of "my son," to whom Solomon addressed much of his counsel in that book.

Solomon took many additional wives in his later years, but it is doubtful whether they were for reasons other than politics and prestige (since no children are ever mentioned, except Rehoboam and two sisters). Whether Naamah was still living during these later years is never mentioned. If so, one would suppose that she did not approve of these foreign wives, but there was nothing she could do to prevent it. Solomon himself no doubt came to regret it deeply, especially after God rebuked him for supporting these wives in their worship of false gods.

It is significant that, here at least, Solomon counsels young men to "live joyfully with the wife whom thou lovest all the days of the life of thy vanity, which he hath given thee under the sun . . . for that is thy portion in this life" (verse 9). There seems no doubt here that he really did love Naamah deeply all his life, regardless of the nature of his "love" for all his pagan wives. Whether he really lived "joyfully" with her is another question, but if not, he surely wished he had, and strongly advised other men to do so.

That word "joyfully," incidentally, occurs only this once in the Old Testament. In combination with "love," it seems to have the connotation of keeping one's marriage "alive and happy," not allowing it to become ordinary and routine. Solomon had also counseled "my son" to "rejoice with the wife of thy youth" (Prov. 5:18), and to be "ravished always with her love." One would like to think — and hope — that this had always been the case with his marriage to Naamah, the wife of *his* youth, and that his references to marriage here and in Proverbs were based on his own happy experience. Perhaps, in the absence of any statement in Scripture to the contrary, we can assume that this was so.

Verse 10 is also excellent advice, paralleling Colossians 3:23, to which we have referred more than once. "Whatsoever thy hand findeth to do, do it with thy might." God does not expect us to do more than we are able, but He does expect us to do it right and as unto Him.

Ecclesiastes 9:11–18

11. *I returned, and saw under the sun, that the race is not to the swift, nor the battle to the strong, neither yet bread to the wise, nor yet riches to men of understanding, nor yet favour to men of skill; but time and chance happeneth to them all.*

12. *For man also knoweth not his time: as the fishes that are taken in an evil net, and as the birds that are caught in the snare; so are the sons of men snared in an evil time, when it falleth suddenly upon them.*

13. *This wisdom have I seen also under the sun, and it seemed great unto me:*

14. *There was a little city, and few men within it; and there came a great king against it, and besieged it, and built great bulwarks against it:*

15. *Now there was found in it a poor wise man, and he by his wisdom delivered the city; yet no man remembered that same poor man.*

16. *Then said I, Wisdom is better than strength: nevertheless the poor man's wisdom is despised, and his words are not heard.*

17. *The words of wise men are heard in quiet more than the cry of him that ruleth among fools.*

18. *Wisdom is better than weapons of war: but one sinner destroyeth much good.*

"Time and chance happeneth to them all" (verse 11). This sounds almost like the rationale of the philosophy of naturalistic evolutionism. The false religion of materialism, centered around the Darwinian supposition of random changes preserved by natural selection operating over vast aeons of time, is claimed by evolutionists to account for all the animals and plants and people of the world.

The fact is, however, that it does not. Random changes can never produce complex, functioning, living creatures, no matter how many billions of years are postulated for it. Only creation by an intelligent and powerful Creator can do this.

But the idea does manage to gain followers because of the humanistic notion that time and chance, rather than God, seem to affect many human activities. "The race is not [always] to the swift, nor the battle [always] to the strong" (verse 11), because unexpected situations develop that affect the activities and their outcomes. The rationalist may attribute this all to chance, but the believer may well believe that God has intervened in answer to prayer. Solomon is presenting this truth in a typical humanistic context because he is evaluating such events as those reasoning "under the sun" would see them.

But he has already noted that God establishes and controls the timing of events in each individual life (Eccles. 3:1–8) and also that He has established a time for judgment (Eccles. 8:6), with good and bad coming respectively for the godly and ungodly (Eccles. 8:12–13).

Even though God knows a man's time, the man himself "knoweth not his time" and so may be suddenly caught unprepared "in an evil time" (verse 12).

Solomon then inserted a sort of parable to the effect that a poor wise man was able to save a city by his wise counsel from capture and destruction by a much superior army and its king (verses 14–15). A somewhat similar event had actually occurred during his own father's reign, except that the one who saved her city against Joab's army was a wise woman (2 Sam. 20:13–22).

The sad aftermath of the event, however, was that the "poor man's wisdom is despised, and his words are not heard" (verse 16). Solomon would have considered such a development to have been still another example of the vanity of life under the sun.

In spite of this worldly lack of appreciation for such wisdom, still it is generally true that "the words of wise men are heard in quiet" (verse 17). Certainly "wisdom is better than weapons of war" (verse 18), but it is still true that "one sinner" can undermine "much good" (verse 18). One good example is Jeroboam, who won over the ten northern tribes of Solomon's kingdom (1 Kings 22:52) from Solomon's son, and soon led his whole nation into idolatry.

Ecclesiastes 10:1–7

1. *Dead flies cause the ointment of the apothecary to send forth a stinking savour: so doth a little folly him that is in reputation for wisdom and honour.*

2. *A wise man's heart is at his right hand; but a fool's heart at his left.*

3. *Yea also, when he that is a fool walketh by the way, his wisdom faileth him, and he saith to every one that he is a fool.*

4. *If the spirit of the ruler rise up against thee, leave not thy place; for yielding pacifieth great offences.*

5. *There is an evil which I have seen under the sun, as an error
    which proceedeth from the ruler:*
6. *Folly is set in great dignity, and the rich sit in low place.*
7. *I have seen servants upon horses, and princes walking as servants
    upon the earth.*

Solomon, in this tenth chapter of Ecclesiastes, again records a number
of one-or-two-verse proverbs, similar to those in his Book of Proverbs.
He first (verse 1) uses the figure of dead flies trapped in the perfumer's
ointment to illustrate how a little folly can destroy the reputation of a good
man. It is often true that a seemingly minor sin by an otherwise honorable, wise, godly leader can lead to serious consequences. We remember
the case of Noah relaxing with wine after surviving the great flood, and
Moses smiting the rock after leading the Israelites for many years in the
desert (Gen. 9:20–27; Num. 20:7–12), for example. We need to "be sober,
be vigilant; because your adversary, the devil, as a roaring lion, walketh
about, seeking whom he may devour" (1 Pet. 5:8).

The second proverb (verse 2) draws on the fact that the right hand
is usually stronger and more dexterous than the left. Thus a wiser man
is strong and true of heart, contrasting with the faint heart of a fool.
There are many references to the strong and righteous right hand of
the Lord (Ps. 44:3; 45:4; 48:10; Isa. 48:13; etc.). Verse 3 speaks of a man
who professes to be wise, but in the end "his wisdom faileth him, and he
saith to every one that he is a fool." Such are the men Paul speaks of in
Romans 1:22 who, "professing themselves to be wise, they became fools."
The foolishness of such professedly intellectual men, who abound today
in our halls of learning, becomes evident when they abandon God for
evolution, changing "the glory of the uncorruptible God into an image
made like to corruptible man, and to birds, and fourfooted beasts, and
creeping things" (Rom. 1:23).

In verse 4, the word translated "yielding" is so translated nowhere else,
being more commonly rendered "remedy" or "healing." It is translated
"wholesome" in Proverbs 15:4 ("a wholesome tongue is a tree of life").
Similarly, "offenses" is usually translated "sins," and "pacifieth" means
"let alone," and is usually so rendered. Thus, this particular bit of advice
seems to be telling any person who has committed an offense against the
ruler (and Solomon no doubt would often have encountered such offend-
ing citizens) that he would be best served not by either cowardly retreat
from his position or by angry words against the ruler, but by a calm and
reasonable defense and explanation of his action.

Verses 5, 6, and 7 point out another type of situation which Solomon
found to be an evil under the sun, and for which the ruler is commonly
responsible. "Folly is set in great dignity" whereas men who ought to be

"princes" somehow are seen "walking as servants upon the earth." As king, he had undoubtedly made some mistakes of this sort (one thinks of Jeroboam, for example, who had been a servant's son and later, after Solomon promoted him to a position of authority, rebelled against Solomon (1 Kings 11:26). Note also Proverbs 19:10; 26:1; 28:12, 28; 30:21–22. This type of evil becomes especially harmful when unworthy compromisers ascend to positions of high authority in the church or church schools, and then lead many others into error. "Seekest thou great things for thyself? seek them not" (Jer. 45:5). Let God do the promoting!

Ecclesiastes 10:8–14

8. *He that diggeth a pit shall fall into it; and whoso breaketh an hedge, a serpent shall bite him.*
9. *Whoso removeth stones shall be hurt therewith; and he that cleaveth wood shall be endangered thereby.*
10. *If the iron be blunt, and he do not whet the edge, then must he put to more strength: but wisdom is profitable to direct.*
11. *Surely the serpent will bite without enchantment; and a babbler is no better.*
12. *The words of a wise man's mouth are gracious; but the lips of a fool will swallow up himself.*
13. *The beginning of the words of his mouth is foolishness: and the end of his talk is mischievous madness.*
14. *A fool also is full of words: a man cannot tell what shall be; and what shall be after him, who can tell him?*

Verses 8 and 9 give four pithy illustrations as to how those who plan evil may have it come back to hurt them more than those for whom it was intended. The classic example would be Haman of Persia, who ended up hanging on the gallows which he had constructed for his enemy Mordecai (Esther 5:14; 7:10). Note also Psalm 7:16; 94:23.

A blunt axe will not chop wood, and surely the woodsman will have enough wisdom to sharpen the axe rather than simply to chop harder (verse 10). This homely illustration evidently is intended to show the foolishness of teachers who attempt the important work of teaching the Scriptures when they have neglected first to sharpen their own knowledge thereof. "Study to shew thyself approved unto God, a workman that needeth not to be ashamed, rightly dividing [literally 'cutting straight'] the word of truth" (2 Tim. 2:15).

Then the next four verses (verses 11–14) return to a subject often decried by Solomon — as well as throughout Scripture as a whole — the careless use of the tongue. Just as a venomous snake will bite unless a snake charmer controls it, so "a babbler is no better" (verse 11). His careless stream of talk can be as deadly as a serpent's bite. As James says, "The tongue can no man tame; it is an unruly evil, full of deadly poison" (James 3:8).

A man who is truly wise, however, will allow God the Holy Spirit to tame his tongue, and "the words of a wise man's mouth are gracious" (verse 12). Christians are exhorted to "let your speech be alway with grace, seasoned with salt, that ye may know how ye ought to answer every man" (Col. 4:6). Of the Lord Jesus, it was prophesied that "grace is poured into thy lips" (Ps. 45:2), so that even his enemies had to testify that "never man spake like this man" (John 7:46).

Since Christ is "made unto us wisdom" (1 Cor. 1:30), He can enable us to speak with wisdom, rather than babble, if we ask Him (James 1:5) and seek to follow His example (1 Pet. 2:21).

It is sobering to us as Christians to realize that we are said to be acting like fools if we are "full of words" (verse 14). Remember that Jesus said that "every idle word that men shall speak, they shall give account thereof in the day of judgment" (Matt. 12:36). Remember also that even these words of warning were among the "gracious words, which proceeded out of his mouth" (Luke 4:22).

Ecclesiastes 10:15–20

15. *The labour of the foolish wearieth every one of them, because he knoweth not how to go to the city.*
16. *Woe to thee, O land, when thy king is a child, and thy princes eat in the morning!*
17. *Blessed art thou, O land, when thy king is the son of nobles, and thy princes eat in due season, for strength, and not for drunkenness!*
18. *By much slothfulness the building decayeth; and through idleness of the hands the house droppeth through.*
19. *A feast is made for laughter, and wine maketh merry: but money answereth all things.*
20. *Curse not the king, no not in thy thought: and curse not the rich in thy bedchamber: for a bird of the air shall carry the voice, and that which hath wings shall tell the matter.*

The foolish man, though full of self-promoting words, doesn't even know how "to go to the city" (verse 15). This probably was a kind of proverbial expression in Solomon's day. And if the fool cannot even find the town, how can he expect to find God? "Profane and vain babbling, and oppositions of science falsely so called" (1 Tim. 6:20) will certainly not do it! Neither will "vain repetitions" of religious clichés by those who "think that they shall be heard for their much speaking" (Matt. 6:7).

There are even fools in the ranks of royalty, including childish kings and "princes" who "eat in the morning" (verse 16). When the leaders of a nation spend time and energy at all-night feasting and revelry, the nation itself is in great peril. One thinks of the emperor Xerxes of Persia (the same as Ahasuerus in Esther 1:15) who hosted an extended feast lasting many days for all his nobles and princes. When it was all done, he went forth with his great fleet of ships, planning to invade and conquer Greece, only to suffer (according to history) bitter defeats at Thermophylae and Salamis, and finally had to return home in shame.

On the other hand, God blesses a nation whose king is truly of the nobility and whose leaders eat only "in due season, for strength, and not for drunkenness" (verse 17). That character trait marked the honored founding fathers of our own nation. They may not have been among the officially noble families of Europe, but they were truly God's noblemen. Rather than feasting and drinking, they suffered almost incredible hardships in bringing our nation to freedom, and our "land" has been "blessed" as a result. As we more and more turn to "idleness," however (sports, amusements, alcohol, immorality, etc.), the "building" which is our nation is in increasing danger of decay and failure (verse 18).

Money, properly used (verse 19), is better than feasting and drinking. It not only can provide food and drink, but "all things." Finally, as Solomon had spoken of the responsibilities of kings and nobles, he now also addresses their subjects, warning them not to speak — or even think — evil of their rulers (verse 20). They had been ordained of God (Rom. 13:1). The old saying, "A little bird told me," probably had its origin in this verse. And, of course, the warning is relevant not only to the danger of "speak[ing] evil of dignities" (2 Pet. 2:10), but far more to blasphemy in word or thought against our King of kings.

Ecclesiastes 11:1–6

1. *Cast thy bread upon the waters: for thou shalt find it after many days.*
2. *Give a portion to seven, and also to eight; for thou knowest not what evil shall be upon the earth.*
3. *If the clouds be full of rain, they empty themselves upon the earth: and if the tree fall toward the south, or toward the north, in the place where the tree falleth, there it shall be.*
4. *He that observeth the wind shall not sow; and he that regardeth the clouds shall not reap.*
5. *As thou knowest not what is the way of the spirit, nor how the bones do grow in the womb of her that is with child: even so thou knowest not the works of God who maketh all.*

> 6. *In the morning sow thy seed, and in the evening withhold not thine hand: for thou knowest not whether shall prosper, either this or that, or whether they both shall be alike good.*

In the last two chapters of Ecclesiastes, Solomon is bringing together all the observations and complaints of the previous chapters into final words of advice to the young, based on his many years of study and leadership, wisdom and folly, and coming from his uniquely qualified perspective. It is interesting that he begins with an admonition to "cast thy bread upon the waters: for thou shalt find it after many days" (verse 1).

Why would one cast bread on the waters, when it would seem that the waters would just carry it away to the sea, with nothing accomplished? One interpretation is that the "bread" (or the grain from which the bread would be made) was a prominent item of sea-going commerce. Investment in selling and shipping this "bread corn" to other nations would eventually bring much profit to the growers.

More in keeping with the context, however, is the practice of casting the grain, not into the river, but on the flood-plain waters in the annual river overflow, such as in the Nile River valley. When the flood waters subsided, then the grain would settle into the rich soils of the flood plain, and eventually yield an abundant harvest. The waters could also be understood as water-laden marsh soils. The Hebrew word for "bread" can be understood as "bread corn" when the context warrants. It is so translated in Isaiah 28:28, for example, and could well be so translated here in this verse.

In any case, the spiritual application obviously intended by Solomon is for generous seed-sowing, far and wide, with the seed understood either as actual grain or as spiritual seed, living and witnessing for the true God. It will not produce actual wheat, in the literal sense, or spiritual fruit in the broader sense, for many days, but the harvest will come in due time. The metaphor may also refer in part to God's original command to mankind to "be fruitful, and multiply" (Gen. 1:28).

In the famous parable of the sower (Matt. 13:3–8), the farmer sowed in all kinds of soil, only some of which would eventually be fruitful. Jesus then explained that "the seed is the word of God" (Luke 8:11), and that the fruit would be redeemed lives. Isaiah the prophet said, under divine inspiration, "Blessed are ye that sow beside all waters" (Isa. 32:20).

Assuming the primary intent of the Holy Spirit, who led Solomon to pen these words, is that we should be spreading God's Word everywhere, it is clear that while it is more productive to sow the seed in prepared ground, it should not be sown *only* there. Cast it everywhere you can, says Solomon, and you will surely find it later — though sometimes *much* later.

We are also to be generous with our time and resources, as God enables.

We are to give to "seven" (symbolic of completeness) and even more than that ("eight"), according to verse 2. "As we have therefore opportunity, let us do good unto all men, especially unto them who are of the household of faith" (Gal. 6:10). And we need not worry that such generosity will result in our own impoverishment. "Now he that ministereth seed to the sower both minister bread for your food, and multiply your seed sown, and increase the fruits of your righteousness; Being enriched in every thing to all bountifulness, which causeth through us thanksgiving to God" (2 Cor. 9:10–11).

Verse 3 suggests that the remaining time for seed-sowing and Christian service to others may be short, so we should be "redeeming the time" (Col. 4:5). Whatever the nature of the rain that falls — whether nourishment for the seed, or destruction from the flooding, or both — is not under our control. Our business is to sow the seed. When a tree dies and falls, that's where it is; similarly, when we are cut off, we can no longer sow or reap; therefore, do it now!

This exhortation is stressed further in verse 4. "He that observeth the wind shall not sow." One can always find excuses not to follow God's leading now, and therefore to put it off, as did Felix, unto a more "convenient season" (Acts 24:25), which never seems to arrive. The same applies to reaping.

The utter incompleteness of our understanding of God's ways, apart from His revelations in Scripture, is illustrated by our ignorance even of such a common occurrence as the conception, growth and birth of a child (verse 5). We are "fearfully and wonderfully made" (Ps. 139:14) and we still understand only a small part of "how the bones do grow in the womb of her that is with child." Beyond that, apart from the Bible, we know absolutely nothing of "the way of the spirit," and how it is imparted by God to the embryo, or how it leaves and where it goes at death. Despite the tremendous growth of scientific knowledge, we still do not understand "the works of God who maketh all." "As the heavens are higher than the earth," says the Lord, "so are my ways higher than your ways, and my thoughts than your thoughts" (Isa. 55:9).

It is presumptuous for scientists or philosophers to ignore or reject the ways and thoughts and revelation of God, when they are still so ignorant of His thoughts and ways, and still refuse to believe what He has revealed in Scripture concerning them.

We who *do* believe His word need simply to obey it and proclaim it the best we can. In particular, He says to be about the business of seed-sowing, morning and evening (verse 6).

This is the same message as in verse 1. Spiritual seed should be sown not only far and wide but also both morning and evening. Then it is "God that giveth the increase" (1 Cor. 3:7). "And let us not be weary in well doing: for in due season we shall reap, if we faint not" (Gal. 6:9). We can have faith that some "shall prosper, either this or that," and maybe "they both shall be alike good" (verse 6).

Ecclesiastes 11:7–10

7. *Truly the light is sweet, and a pleasant thing it is for the eyes to behold the sun:*

8. *But if a man live many years, and rejoice in them all; yet let him remember the days of darkness; for they shall be many. All that cometh is vanity.*

9. *Rejoice, O young man, in thy youth; and let thy heart cheer thee in the days of thy youth, and walk in the ways of thine heart, and in the sight of thine eyes: but know thou, that for all these things God will bring thee into judgment.*

10. *Therefore remove sorrow from thy heart, and put away evil from thy flesh: for childhood and youth are vanity.*

Continuing his counsel to young men, the Preacher stresses still further the inevitability of the imminent ending of life. Even if a person has enjoyed a good life under the sun all the days of his life, the dark days are coming and they shall be many more than the days of light, if he has not prepared for the coming judgment. "The light is sweet" (verse 7), but "the days of darkness" that are coming "shall be many" (verse 8), and he shall learn that all these future days, like his life under the sun, will be vanity, and a time of everlasting regret for all those "to whom the mist of darkness is reserved for ever" (2 Pet. 2:17).

Now Solomon speaks directly and personally to each young man, saying that he can indeed "rejoice, O young man, in thy youth, and let thy heart cheer thee in the days of thy youth" (verse 9). However, this exhortation may well have been spoken in irony, especially if that young man is ignoring the fact that "for all these things God will bring thee into judgment," and proceeds to sow his youthful wild oats, so to speak, without regard to the laws of God.

When one finally reaches old age, as Solomon now had done, he may well find himself recalling wistfully the days of his youth. All too often, there are sorrowful regrets for wasted opportunities and careless living, so he must now urge young people not to make the same mistakes he did. Unfortunately, too many young people (not all, thankfully) tend to listen more to their peers than to their elders. As the old cliché puts it, we are "too soon old, and too late smart." So the cycle continues, generation after generation. But a judgment day is coming, and the misdeeds of youth will be judged along with all the rest, unless repentance and faith in the saving work of Christ have brought forgiveness and salvation.

"Childhood and youth are vanity," just like every other aspect of life if it is lived only under the sun (verse 10). Therefore, as Paul later would write to young Timothy, "Let no man despise thy youth; but be thou an example of the believers, in word, in conversation, in charity, in spirit, in faith, in purity" (1 Tim. 4:12). "Flee also youthful lusts: but follow righteousness, faith, charity, peace, with them that call on the Lord out of a pure heart" (2 Tim. 2:22). It is natural and proper for young people to enjoy their youthful years, but they should do so in ways pleasing to God, knowing that "for all things God will bring thee into judgment" (verse 9).

Ecclesiastes 12:1–8

1. *Remember now thy Creator in the days of thy youth, while the evil days come not, nor the years draw nigh, when thou shalt say, I have no pleasure in them;*
2. *While the sun, or the light, or the moon, or the stars, be not darkened, nor the clouds return after the rain:*
3. *In the day when the keepers of the house shall tremble, and the strong men shall bow themselves, and the grinders cease because they are few, and those that look out of the windows be darkened,*
4. *And the doors shall be shut in the streets, when the sound of the grinding is low, and he shall rise up at the voice of the bird, and all the daughters of musick shall be brought low;*
5. *Also when they shall be afraid of that which is high, and fears shall be in the way, and the almond tree should flourish, and the grasshopper shall be a burden, and desire shall fail: because man goeth to his long home, and the mourners go about the streets:*
6. *Or ever the silver cord be loosed, or the golden bowl be broken, or the pitcher be broken at the fountain, or the wheel broken at the cistern.*
7. *Then shall the dust return to the earth as it was: and the spirit shall return unto God who gave it.*
8. *Vanity of vanities, saith the preacher; all is vanity.*

In many ways, this last chapter of Ecclesiastes is the greatest — or at least the climactic — chapter of this remarkable book. It directly continues the previous chapter, being addressed especially to young people, but it also begins a marvelous excursus on old age and dying which is uniquely picturesque and a true masterpiece of literature.

"Remember now thy Creator in the days of thy youth" (verse 1). Solomon has just reminded any youthful readers that "God will bring thee into judgment" (Eccles. 11:9) for any youthful indiscretions and misdeeds, so now he urges them to remember that the God who will judge them is not only the far-off Creator of heaven and earth but also "thy Creator!" He has formed each "spirit of man within him" (Zech. 12:1), just as with the first man, when He "breathed into his nostrils the breath of life; and man became a living soul" (Gen. 2:7).

As our Creator, He has made each of us for a specific purpose here on earth, with "a time to be born, and a time to die" (Eccles. 3:2). To accomplish that purpose, we must first have our sins judged and forgiven by that same Creator, who became our redeeming Savior and suffered and died in our stead. He then defeated death and now offers salvation to all of us who will accept Him by faith as our Creator/Savior. Then we must seek to know and follow His will through study of His inspired Word, through prayer and through guidance by the now-indwelling Spirit of God.

By far the best time to accomplish that purpose is to begin in the strength and idealism of youth, and then continue all through life — not waiting until late in life when most of our assigned years have already passed and much of our strength is gone as well.

Remember thy Creator! First of all, we have to believe there *is* a Creator who made us, not some naturalistic process of evolution. Satan, in his long war against God, all through the ages has been seeking to persuade men, through various forms of the evolutionary idea, that God (if He exists at all) is so far away and acted so long ago that He is not concerned with our puny little world and its inhabitants. In the present age, this great enemy has gained almost complete control over the minds of youth through the schools, teaching them that they are the products of an impersonal evolutionary process just like all the other animals, and thus they can live their lives without concern about some mythological past creation and hypothetical future judgment.

But this is all wrong, lethally wrong! Evolution is a completely false and deadly notion, contrary to all true science and history, and certainly contrary to the inspired Word of God. God is not long ago and far away, but is "not far from every one of us: For in him we live, and move, and have our being" (Acts 17:27–28). How urgent it is for young men and women (and certainly for older people as well, if they have wasted their youth) to remember their Creator and accept Him now as Savior and Lord and coming King.

Because the "evil days" will come, and "the years draw nigh, when thou shalt say, I have no pleasure in them." The days will come when the sun and moon and stars will seem to be covered with clouds, and even after a sky-clearing rain, the clouds will quickly return to darken the heavens again (verse 2).

In verses 3–7, Solomon then paints a dark picture of the coming old-age period for every person who survives that long. The imagery is uniquely beautiful in a literary sense, but the picture is very sad, especially for those who come to that period of life without God and only a misspent life to remember.

"In the day when the keepers of the house shall tremble, and the strong men shall bow themselves" (verse 3). The "house" is the aging body, and the shaking "keepers of the house" are the trembling hands and arms. The "strong men" that have acted as the supporting foundation of the house all these years are the legs and thighs which now are beginning to buckle and fail.

Some or all of the teeth have been lost, so that chewing one's food has become difficult — "the grinders cease because they are few." Furthermore, the eyes have become weak and almost blind, so that "those that look out of the windows be darkened," like those of Isaac when he mistook Jacob for Esau (Gen. 27:1, 23).

That is not all. "The doors" — that is, the means by which the occupant of the house can enter the outside world and interact with neighbors and visitors — "shall be shut in the streets" (verse 4), so that it is difficult or impossible to communicate with others. Both the difficulty of speaking and that of walking have rendered him essentially a "shut-in."

"The sound of the grinding is low." One can no longer hear well, so that even loud noises like the grinding of millstones are difficult to distinguish. "The daughters of musick shall be brought low." Just as the young girls of the family have grown and left home, so one's ability to enjoy music (the vocal chords, ears, and emotions) have so deteriorated that his ability to sing or enjoy the music of others is very low. Furthermore, he has difficulty sleeping, so that he wakes very early, "at the voice of the bird" — not to go out to his work, but simply to sit and complain about his inaction.

"They shall be afraid of that which is high" (verse 5). No longer can they climb stairs or hills, and there is greater fear of falling even on low surfaces. "Fears shall be in the way," fear of stumbling or bumping into obstacles, or even of being defenseless against robbers or mockers.

"The almond tree shall flourish, and the grasshopper shall be a burden." The white blossoms of the almond tree are here compared to the white hair of the aged. The elderly are easily irritated, especially by insects, and even the chirping of the grasshopper becomes a burden: "Desire shall fail." This description probably refers not only to sexual desire, but also to pleasures of any kind. Interest in life itself fails, although the non-believer usually wants to cling to it as long as possible, fearing what may lie ahead after death.

The Christian, on the other hand, normally desires to live as long as he feels he can be useful to his family and to Christ here on earth, but he does not fear death. He knows, from God's promises in His Word, that to be "absent from the body" is to be "present with the Lord" (2 Cor. 5:8).

In both cases, however, the termination of this present life for all — saved and unsaved alike — is physical death. "Man goeth to his long home, and the mourners go about the streets." Since God is the Creator (not the "un-Creator"), every person will exist in a "long home" somewhere. For Christians, Christ has prepared "mansions" (John 14:2 — literally, "dwelling-places"), where they can abide forever in His presence. Those who have rejected Christ, however, will dwell in "the blackness of darkness for ever" (Jude 13). Although the friends and relatives of the deceased Christian will mourn for a while, they will not sorrow as those "others which have no hope" (1 Thess. 4:13).

Verse 6 describes the actual event of physical death in terms of four metaphors. When the cord containing strands of silver breaks loose, then the golden bowl suspended from it falls and breaks. Similarly, the pitcher used to carry water from the fountain and the wheel whose turning draws the bucket up from the well may break. The silver cord, the golden bowl, the wooden wheel, the clay pitcher — all function well for a while, like the human body, but all eventually wear out and break, and the body dies. It is possible that the cord represents the spinal chord, the golden bowl the human skull and brain, the wheel and the pitcher the two ventricles of the heart. This analogy may be too imaginative, but the imagery, whatever it is, speaks clearly of physical death. At that point "shall the dust return to the earth as it was: and the spirit shall return unto God who gave it" (verse 7).

This has been the case for every man and woman since the first man and woman brought sin (and therefore death) into the world. At that time, God pronounced the great curse on His originally "very good" creation (Gen. 1:31): "Cursed is the ground for thy sake . . . for out of it wast thou taken: for dust thou art, and unto dust shalt thou return" (Gen. 3:17–19).

Although the body returns to the dust, the spirit does not disintegrate. The spirits of those who die unsaved will continue to exist, but must eventually be banished at God's last judgment to "everlasting destruction from the presence of the Lord, and from the glory of his power" (2 Thess. 1:9). This is not annihilation but destruction. As Jesus warned, "Fear him which is able to destroy both soul and body in hell" (Matt. 10:28). This destruction is eternal punishment, the essence of which is permanent separation from the God whom the unsaved man or woman refused to have as their Savior.

The spirits of the saved, however, will not only return to God, but will remain with God, forever. Thus, for them, old age and death need not be the gloomy experience described by Solomon in these verses. It is true that the present body deteriorates and dies, but it is also a time of joyous anticipation of the future glorious body, like that of Christ, which He will give them when He returns to earth as He promised (Phil. 3:20–21). In the meantime, between the time of death and resurrection, the spirit is "absent from the body, and . . . present with the Lord" (2 Cor. 5:8).

God had not revealed all these glorious New Testament truths as yet to Solomon, of course, and he was largely forced to limit his counseling to life "under the sun." And that life, he had found, despite all his wisdom and riches and power, was essentially vanity. "Vanity of vanities, saith the preacher: all is vanity" (verse 8).

Nevertheless, he knew there was something more to come. He knew there was the Creator, and that the Creator had a purpose in creation, for He had created each human spirit. Unlike that of the beast, man's spirit returned "upward" at death, to the God who gave it (Eccles. 3:21; 12:7). Furthermore, he knew there was a judgment to come (Eccles. 11:9; 12:14). Surely he knew also the promise of the coming Seed of the woman (Gen. 3:15), as well as the promises of other ancient prophets who could foresee the coming of a Savior (Enoch, Balaam). He probably had access to the Book of Job, who had written of a living Redeemer who would stand on the earth in the latter days (Job 19:25). And he surely knew the many prophetic intimations in the psalms of his father David (Ps. 2, 16, 22, 72, etc.). Thus, he could gladly conclude his book of earth's vanities under the sun with a more hopeful outlook for the future.

Ecclesiastes 12:9–14

9. And moreover, because the preacher was wise, he still taught the people knowledge; yea, he gave good heed, and sought out, and set in order many proverbs.

10. The preacher sought to find out acceptable words: and that which was written was upright, even words of truth.

11. The words of the wise are as goads, and as nails fastened by the masters of assemblies, which are given from one shepherd.

12. And further, by these, my son, be admonished: of making many books there is no end; and much study is a weariness of the flesh.

13. Let us hear the conclusion of the whole matter: Fear God, and keep His commandments: for this is the whole duty of man.

14. For God shall bring every work into judgment, with every secret thing, whether it be good, or whether it be evil.

These last six verses of Ecclesiastes form a sort of epilogue to the entire book and, for that matter, to the life and career of Solomon — with all of his writings — as a whole. Still calling himself simply the Preacher, he assured his readers that, despite all his failures and disillusionments, he "still taught the people knowledge" (verse 9), and that he was still able to "set in order many proverbs." Presumably, some of these were actually incorporated here in his Book of Ecclesiastes (e.g., Eccles. 10). He had already testified that he still had the great wisdom for which he was noted (Eccles. 2:9); here again he said he "was wise." Furthermore, he was still diligently studying and learning — "he gave good heed" to all the relevant data and thus was still able to teach knowledge.

His diligence included careful study to select just the right words with which to convey his knowledge and wisdom to others, "to find out acceptable words" (verse 10), above all taking care to know that they were really "words of truth" and not just his own possibly wrong opinions. Here is the only instance where Solomon mentioned the word "truth" in Ecclesiastes, but it is significant that he places it near the end, in order to assure us that all his words in this book had been true words. There was no distortion or deception anywhere. He had written truth only and this means to us that he is — perhaps unknowingly — assuring us that what he had finally written down was actually from God himself, destined to be incorporated in the "Scripture of truth" (Dan. 10:21).

Once these "words of the wise" (verse 11) are understood by the Preacher to be indeed words of truth, given to him by God, then he must seek to drive them home to his hearers and readers so clearly and firmly that they will be understood and applied correctly in their lives. He uses two shepherd's tools as a metaphor to illustrate how this is done. One tool is that of goads, such as would constrain an animal to stay on the right path. These are analogous to those inspired words of truth which are "profitable . . . for reproof, for correction, for instruction in righteousness" (2 Tim. 3:16), to keep Christians on the path that leads to heaven. The second tool consists of "masters of assemblies" and the "nails" fastened by them. These probably represent the biblical writers who penned the original autographs of the Scriptures and those later scribes who identified them as truly God-inspired and then fixed them in the developing canon of Scripture.

Literally speaking, these "masters of assemblies" under the "one shepherd" may have been the various under-shepherds of the extensive flocks of the great king, corralled and assembled in various sheepfolds. The one chief Shepherd, of course, in the New Testament analogy becomes the Lord Jesus Christ, "that great shepherd of the sheep" (Heb. 13:20) who, through these "words of the wise," now inscripturated in the Bible, "calleth His own sheep by name . . . and goeth before them, and the sheep follow him: for they know his voice: (John 10:3–4).

Then Solomon makes a remarkable observation. "Of the making of many books there is no end; and much study is a weariness of the flesh" (verse 12). It is amazing that such a statement could be made three thousand years ago! What would Solomon think today, if he could see all the millions of books and journals and papers pouring forth from the printing presses of the world in this 21st century after Christ? Plus all the "information" now streaming from the millions of web sites on the worldwide internet? Talk about "weariness of the flesh." No one today can possibly hope to read even all the books and articles being published just in his own field. And, of course, most books are really not worth reading at all.

But there is one Book that all should read. Although even reading that Book can become physically tiring because of our weak flesh, it never wearies the soul! "My soul melteth for heaviness: strengthen thou me according to thy word." "This is my comfort in my affliction: for thy word hath quickened me" (Psalm 119:28, 50). "They that wait upon the LORD shall renew their strength; they shall mount up with wings as eagles; they shall run, and not be weary; and they shall walk, and not faint" (Isa. 40:31).

But can it be literally true that of the making of books there will be no end? All the present world-mountain of books will, of course, one day be destroyed when "the earth also and the works that are therein shall be burned up" (2 Pet. 3:10).

Don't forget, however, that there are endless ages yet to come, and all the redeemed will be serving the Lord in various capacities during the ages. There are already many books in heaven. "For ever, O LORD, thy word is settled in heaven" (Ps. 119:89). Furthermore, "a book of remembrance was written before him for them that feared the LORD, and that thought upon his name" (Mal. 3:16). Over the ages, this book of remembrance must now have grown into many volumes.

But also there are innumerable record books, presumably one for each person who has ever lived, and these will be brought forth at the judgment throne one day. John, in his great vision of that day, wrote about it. "And I saw the dead, small and great, stand before God; and the books were opened . . . and the dead were judged out of those things which were written in the books, according to their works" (Rev. 20:12). Since no one can be saved by his works, all these will be sent away from God forever. But those whose names have not been blotted out of God's "book of life," who have been saved "by grace . . . through faith . . . not of works" (Eph. 2:8–9) will be given the joy and privilege of continuing to serve the Lord in heaven as they have on earth (Rev. 22:3).

And it is probable they will also be writing books! God's original dominion mandate "to have dominion . . . over all the earth" and to "subdue it" (Gen. 1:26–28) implied the development of science, technology, and education to accomplish such a commission, and that commandment has never been withdrawn. It seems likely that the commandment will be enlarged to include the whole creation in the ages to come, so that God's servants will have eternal time to explore and understand and develop an infinite universe. We will never run out of challenging, interesting work to do for our Lord! It is at least reasonable to assume that the results of all this work will be recorded in books for others to enjoy as well. There will be plenty of time to read and study and learn in that day, and "much study" will no longer be "a weariness of the flesh," for we can no longer grow old and tired in that glorious day to come.

So it may well be literally true that "of the making of many books, there is no end." There is still one other cache of books to mention. After writing his gospel, the apostle John said, "There are also many other things which Jesus did, the which, if they should be written every one, I suppose that even the world itself could not contain the books that should be written. Amen" (John 21:25).

This seeming exaggeration is also literally true, because John's gospel contains only some of those things that Jesus began to do and teach (Acts 1:1). But after He ascended back to heaven, He continued His works and teaching in the "acts of the apostles," through His Holy Spirit who was sent by Him to indwell and teach and guide them. The Holy Spirit is continuing that ministry even today. Thus the books that could be written about Christ could well include biographies of every one of His followers down through the centuries. Perhaps these also will be recorded in heaven when "every one of us shall give account of himself to God" as we "stand before the judgment seat of Christ" (Rom. 14:10, 12).

Solomon then finally brings his extensive writings to a close, summarizing all his counsel and all the results of his many and varied experiences into what he calls "the conclusion of the whole matter" (verse 13). His conclusion is very simple. "Fear God, and keep his commandments: for this is the whole duty of man." Just two things — fearing God and keeping His commandments — are said to constitute the whole of man (the word "duty" has been inferred by the translators but was not in the original Hebrew text). Man was created in God's image and, except for sin, would still be like Him in character. That image has been marred by sin and the curse, but can be "renewed in knowledge after the image of him that created him" (Col. 3:10) when we receive Him by faith as our Savior and Lord.

Then, once we have been "born again" by thus receiving Christ by faith, these two attributes do, indeed, characterize redeemed men and women, as they seek in everything to do His will and honor Him. This is the fifth time in Ecclesiastes that Solomon mentioned the fear of God (Eccles. 3:14; 5:7; 8:12; 8:13; 12:13). However, he had referred to the "fear of the LORD" no less than 16 times in his Book of Proverbs (as noted before, he commonly spoke of God as *Jehovah* in Proverbs, but only as *Elohim* in Ecclesiastes).

First of all, he had stressed that "the fear of the LORD is the beginning of knowledge" (Prov. 1:7), but then also that "the fear of the LORD is to hate evil," "the fear of the LORD is the beginning of wisdom," "the fear of the LORD is strong confidence," "the fear of the LORD is a fountain of life," and so on (Prov. 8:13; 9:10; 14:26; 14:27; etc.). Thus, fearing God means much more than just fearing to break His laws.

But then also Solomon says we who are whole in Him ought to keep His commandments — not out of fear, but out of love and thanksgiving. Solomon, no doubt, was recalling with deep regret that this had been the burden of his own commission from God when he became king. At that time, God had said to him, "If thou wilt walk in my ways, to keep my statutes and my commandments, as thy father David did walk, then I will lengthen thy days" (1 Kings 3:14).

Instead of lengthening his days beyond the biblical norm of 70 or 80 years (Ps. 90:10), however, Solomon died after reigning just 40 years (2 Chron. 9:30) after ascending the throne when he was very young. For he had not kept God's command not to go after other "gods." The Lord had clearly charged him not to serve the false gods of his many wives, but he was persuaded to do so anyway, and "the LORD was angry with Solomon, because his heart was turned from the LORD God of Israel . . . And had commanded him concerning this thing, that he should not go after other gods: but he kept not that which the LORD commanded" (1 Kings 11:9–10).

This partial apostasy happened "when Solomon was old" (1 Kings 11:4), when he should have known better, especially after all the blessings of wisdom, riches, and fame that God had given him when he was younger.

Now, sadder and wiser, he had written in some depth about trying to find happiness and contentment in all sorts of worldly pursuits, only to find it was all "vanity and vexation of spirit." He realized, too late, that he should have centered *all* his life, not just his younger years, in fearing God and keeping His commandments. The best he could do now was to counsel others to do that.

And what are His commandments? In Old Testament times, provision had been made in the prescribed sacrificial offerings to find forgiveness and restoration when one had sinned against the laws of God. David, his father, had done that when he had broken God's command against adultery — ironically with the woman who later would become Solomon's mother. Presumably, by the time Solomon wrote Ecclesiastes, he also had sought forgiveness and restoration for *his* sins. But sins have consequences, even when they have been paid for, and it was too late for Solomon not to lose much of his great kingdom when his son became king. It is rather sad to see Solomon at this late date addressing his exhortation once more (as he often had in the first section of Proverbs, before his own seduction away from serving God alone) to "my son" (verse 12), urging *him* to keep God's commands in spite of his father's failure.

From our New Testament perspective, what does it mean to "keep His commandments"? John answers, "For this is the love of God, that we keep His commandments: and His commandments are not grievous" (1 John 5:3).

But what are His commandments? First of all, "This is His commandment, That we should believe on the name of his Son Jesus Christ, and love one another, as he gave us commandment" (1 John 3:23).

As far as the detailed "laws" of God are concerned, once we believe on Christ and receive His forgiveness and begin to share His love for others, then His commands are not a burden, but a delight, because our desire is now simply to please Him. We can pray with the Psalmist, "Make me to go in the path of thy commandments; for therein do I delight" (Ps. 119:35).

A final word from Solomon. We must not forget that "God shall bring every work into judgment, with every secret thing, whether it will be good, or whether it be evil" (verse 14).

God knows all about each of us, including every *secret* thing, even our thoughts. All who are genuine believing Christians will never be judged by our works as to whether we spend eternity in heaven or hell, as will the unsaved (Rev. 20:11–15). However, even *we* — assuming we are genuine Christians, saved eternally through Christ — "must all appear before the judgment seat of Christ; that every one may receive the things done in his body, according to that he hath done, whether it be good or bad" (2 Cor. 5:10).

There even our secret sins and evil thoughts will be revealed for all to see. "For there is nothing covered, that shall not be revealed: neither hid, that shall not be known" (Luke 12:2).

That is, unless it is no longer there! "If we walk in the light, as he is in the light . . . the blood of Jesus Christ his Son cleanseth us from all sin" (1 John 1:7). "Their sins and iniquities will I remember no more" (Heb. 10:17). Because Christ died for all our sins, future as well as past, we have His promise that "if we confess our sins, he is faithful and just to forgive us our sins, and to cleanse us from all unrighteousness" (1 John 1:9). Each sin must be recognized and identified in prayer before God in repentance and faith (that is implied in "confessing our sins"); then God forgives and forgets.

All that remains then at Christ's judgment seat is the giving of rewards. "Every man's work shall be made manifest: for the day shall declare it, because it shall be revealed by fire; and the fire shall try every man's work of what sort it is. If any man's work abide which he hath built thereupon, he shall receive a reward. If any man's work shall be burned, he shall suffer loss: but he himself shall be saved; yet so as by fire" (1 Cor. 3:13–15).

This brings us to the end of our study of the life and writings of King Solomon. We have tried to trace his career from his youthful love and marriage to the beautiful young Naamah, then his unique gift of wisdom as he ruled God's chosen nation of Israel at the height of its worldly power, followed by his tragic semi-apostasy as he tried to please his multitude of pagan princess-wives acquired through his later politically arranged marriages, and finally the regrets of his old age as he realized the futility of all efforts to find happiness "under the sun."

Solomon probably wrote many books on many subjects, but only three have survived — Song of Solomon, Proverbs, and Ecclesiastes — written, respectively, in his early, middle, and latter years. They have survived because they were divinely inspired by the Holy Spirit, for the edification of God's elect in all the centuries following Solomon. Each of the three is unique, not only in comparison to each other but also with reference to all the other books of the Bible. Like all Scripture, they are not only God-breathed, but also profitable for our learning and our growth in the Lord (2 Tim. 3:16).

They leave us, however, with many unanswered questions — about Naamah's later life, about Solomon's in-depth understanding of the future life and God's prophetic plan, about the seven hundred wives and three hundred concubines, about the identities of Lemuel and Agur, and many other matters we have tried to understand by reading between the lines.

At the very end of his last book, Solomon mentioned the future time of judgment. He will be there, and so shall we, so perhaps we can ask him these questions after that. In the meantime, he was (and presumably still is) a man of remarkable wisdom, and we still can learn much from his three unique books.

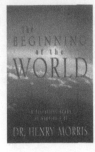

The Beginning of the World

Dr. Henry Morris gives a thorough explanation of the first 11 chapters of Genesis, the most contested chapters in the Bible. He shares his scientific insight and understanding in a format that can also be used for Bible studies.

Science and Faith • 184 pages • Paperback • 10.99
978-0-89051-162-6

The Bible Has the Answer

Dr. Henry M. Morris & Martin E. Clark
How do we know the Bible is true? How will we spend eternity? Here is a complete resource to these and other tough questions facing every individual today.
Apologetics • 394 pages • Paperback • $16.99
978-0-89051-018-6

Biblical Basis for Modern Science

Here is the most detailed analysis of all aspects of creation/evolution in one volume for the layperson. Includes illustrations, charts, tables, and appendixes and contains expositions of 12 major scientific disciplines, with all important Bible passages dealing with each.

Science & Faith • 475 pages • Paperback • $19.99
978-0-89051-369-9

Biblical Creationism

This unique book discusses every passage in the Bible that deals with creation or the Flood. Dr. Morris shows that creation is taught not only in Genesis, but also throughout the whole Bible. Easy to understand and invaluable for all serious Bible students.

Science & Faith • 280 pages • Paperback • $14.99
978-0-89051-293-7

Christian Education for the Real World

Dr. Henry Morris has developed a thoroughly biblical approach to education in the world today, based on over 50 years of experience in teaching and educational administration.

Education • 296 pages • Paperback • $10.99
978-0-89051-160-2

Creation and the Second Coming

In this book, renowned creation scientist and theologian Dr. Henry Morris goes back to the beginning to unveil the details and events of our future. He begins the prophetic countdown at creation and reveals many fresh insights into Scripture.

Theology • 194 pages • Paperback • $10.99
978-0-89051-163-3

Available at **MASTERBOOKS.COM**
— *Where Faith Grows!* —

Days to Remember

This devotional, the final book from a great champion of the faith, gives fascinating background to Judeo-Christian holidays. Learn the purpose and context of Christmas, Easter, and other holidays.
Inspiration / Motivation / Devotional • 224 pages • Paperback • $12.99
978-0-89051-472-6

Defending the Faith

Dr. Henry Morris shows Christians the danger in compromising with a philosophy like evolution, so contrary to the love of God. This insightful work offers a fresh look at Satan's age-old war against God and the harmful effects it has had on society.
Apologetics • 224 pages • Paperback • $12.99
978-0-89051-324-8

For Time and Forever

Another classic from the "father of the modern creationism movement," this book explores the fallible, atheistic view of the universe, contrasted with the divine plan God set in motion. • 224 pages • Paperback • $12.99
Christian Living / Practical Life / Science, Faith, Evolution
978-0-89051-427-6

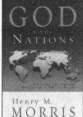

God and the Nations

A very interesting topic: how does God view individual nations, and what is His plan for each nation? Dr. Morris examines the history of nations in light of biblical history, and looks at the future of the nations in biblical prophecy. • 176 pages • Paperback • $10.99
Science & Faith / Prophecy
978-0-89051-389-7

The God Who Is Real

The perfect evangelistic tool, this quick-read helps Christians with some of the philosophical objections seekers have when confronted with the gospel. Morris contrasts other faiths with the true path to serenity, and does so by unabashedly pointing to the God of special creation.
Apologetics • 126 pages • Paperback • $9.99
978-0-89051-299-9

The Long War Against God

This wonderful work thoroughly documents the fact that the idea of evolution did not originate with Darwin. Evolutionism is basic in ancient and modern ethnic religions and in all forms of pantheism. Modern evolutionism is simply the continuation of Satan's long war against God.
Theology • 344 pages • Paperback • $16.99
978-0-89051-291-3

Available at **MASTERBOOKS.COM**
—— *Where Faith Grows!* ——

Many Infallible Proofs

Dr. Henry M. Morris & Henry M. Morris III
Widely used as a textbook, many consider this to be the most useful book available on the whole scope of Christian evidences and practical apologetics. *Christianity Today* calls it a "very valuable handbook in defense of biblical inerrancy."
Science & Faith • 400 pages • Paperback • $15.99
978-0-89051-005-6

The Modern Creation Trilogy

Dr. Henry M. Morris & John D. Morris
Produced by father and son, Drs. Henry and John Morris, this is the definitive work on the study of origins from a creationist perspective. This three-volume set looks at the creation/evolution issue from three main aspects: Scripture, science, and society. A masterpiece. • Includes CD-ROM
• Free Study Guide at www.masterbooks.net

Volume 1 - Scripture & Creation • 232 pages
Volume 2 - Science & Creation • 343 pages
Volume 3 - Society & Creation • 208 pages

Science & Faith
Gift-boxed set • Paperback • $34.99
978-0-89051-216-6

Men of Science, Men of God

The *Baptist Bulletin* says, ". . . Should be required reading for teachers and students." Here are 101 mini-biographies of great Bible-believing scientists of the past, many of whom were the "founding fathers" of modern science.
Education 8-HS • 107 pages • Paperback • $8.99
978-0-89051-080-3

Miracles

Do miracles still occur today as they did in the Bible? Can we believe in miracles? Dr. Henry Morris covers all the bases in a fascinating study of these phenomena, looking at miracles from both a scientific and a scriptural viewpoint.
Apologetics • 128 pages • Paperback • $9.99
978-0-89051-413-9

The Remarkable Journey of Jonah

Did Jonah really exist? Was he really swallowed by a whale? Contained in this book are some rich insights into the biblical account of Jonah from one of the world's foremost Bible commentators.
Commentary • 144 pages • Paperback • $9.99
978-0-89051-407-8

Available at MASTERBOOKS.COM
— Where Faith Grows! —

The Remarkable Record of Job

With its extensive treatment of behemoth and leviathan, the Book of Job is a revelation of God and His creation. Dr. Henry Morris presents it here as an amazing scientific record that provides clues to the great flood of Noah and the dinosaurs.

Commentary • 146 pages • Paperback • $9.99
978-0-89051-292-0

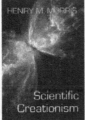

Scientific Creationism

This book is an excellent reference handbook for students and teachers with answers on important creationist viewpoints of history and science, easily understood by readers with non-scientific backgrounds.

Science & Faith • 284 pages • Paperback• $13.99
978-0-89051-003-2

What Is Creation Science?

Dr. Henry M. Morris & Gary Parker
This is the best introduction available to the science of creation. Perfect for pastors, parents, and instructors as well as the science student, great evidence is shown for design in both physical and biological sciences.
Science & Faith • 336 pages • Paperback • $12.99
978-0-89051-081-0

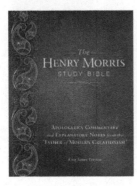

The Henry Morris Study Bible

This Bible is truly one of a kind. No other resource offers the comprehensive analysis of biblical creation and authority of Scripture as this one presents.
Bible • 2200 pages of text
Casebound • $39.99 • 978-0-89051-657-7
Black - Genuine Leather, Boxed • $94.99 • 978-0-89051-658-4
Brown - Soft Leather Look • $69.99 • 978-0-89051-694-2